RANTS, RAVES AND REFLECTIONS

OF AN
AMERICAN HISTORIAN

Ginny — I thought
you might like a few
essays in this.

Bob

Word Association Publishers
205 Fifth Avenue
Tarentum, Pennsylvania 15084
www.wordassociation.com
1.800.827.7903

ISBN: 978-1-63385-262-4

Library of Congress Control Number: 2018908017

RANTS, RAVES AND REFLECTIONS
OF AN
AMERICAN HISTORIAN

Robert MacDougall

WORD ASSOCIATION PUBLISHERS
www.wordassociation.com
1.800.827.7903

*For Diane, Becky, Ben, Dave, and Ashley who tolerate
my obscure historical references,
and for Eli, Aaron and Noah who will.*

CONTENTS

COLLECTION III: STATUES AND MONUMENTS

COLLECTION IV: LITTLE KNOWN CONSEQUENTIAL PEOPLE

COLLECTION V: WHAT THEY COULDA, SHOULDA SAID

COLLECTION VI: HISTORY AND PRESIDENT TRUMP

INTRODUCTION

I love American History. Because I love it, I try to put myself in the middle of the many stories that make up the great saga of our country. For example, I imagine I'm standing in the front row as Lincoln delivers his address at Gettysburg. The man next to me is smoking a fragrant cigar; the woman on my other side is dressed totally in black, very likely the mother of one of the soldiers buried in the cemetery. The November air is chilly as Lincoln rises slowly, takes off his hat and prepares to speak . . .

I like to imagine I'm experiencing history by digging into my own past and remembering how I felt during certain occasions in my lifetime when larger-than-life people were on the stage making history happen right before my eyes. Or, I try to imagine what I might have felt or done if I had lived through the many decades that came just before me – decades I heard about from my parents and grandparents. In my previous book, I made a point of noting that there have been only *three* eighty-year lifetimes since the Declaration of Independence was signed. A person born at the time of the Civil War (1860) would have lived to see World War II (1940)! Any person who gets to be eighty has seen a lot of history!

One of the assignments I gave to my high school students was to write a paper and create a visual presentation called "History and Me." I asked students to describe an historic event that *they* had been part of – such as immigrating to the United States – or that their parents or grandparents had told them about – such as serving in the army during the Vietnam War. The point of the assignment was to help students see not only their own connections to history, but also the fact that history is made up of millions of personal stories just like their own — and those of their ancestors — and those of their classmates.

During the past year, I have been fortunate enough to have had the time to let my mind wander over all the many events in American History and to write about various topics that have amused me or caught my attention in some way. Sometimes I have written about my own recollections of historic events that occurred within my lifetime. Other times, I have set down my thoughts about a famous person, perhaps in reaction to a controversy over a monument or statue. For a while, I became preoccupied with the contributions of people who are completely unknown but who had a major impact on American history, and I spent time researching and writing their stories. Finally, I have often thought and written about American History as it relates to the man who currently occupies the White House and, for better or worse, is having a huge impact on American life.

I averaged a little over one essay per week, so what I have compiled here are sixty essays on American History that I wrote in a very whimsical way, taking up topics as they occurred to me because of a personal interest or the events currently in the news. For this book I have placed the essays into six "collections" organized by theme and, within each collection I have ordered the essays chronologically according to their topics.

Since I began teaching in 1966 my mission has been to help people get excited about American History and profit from it by seeing it as a fascinating story populated by people who are interesting because they are so much like us. I hope people can see that history is more engaging than a fictional story because the "characters" *actually lived* – right here, not in a galaxy far, far away — and what they did *actually happened*! In the essays that follow, I have tried to humanize history, to introduce you to the people who made it and to tell some of their stories in new ways.

Note to the reader: When it seems as if the same story appears in two different essays, you haven't lost your mind, and neither have I. It is simply that some stories illustrate more than one concept or idea.

HISTORY AND ME

Events, People and Ideas
in American Life That Have Affected
Me Personally

THE SCOTTISH CONNECTION

ONE WOULD THINK THAT WITH A NAME LIKE
ROBERT MACDOUGALL I WOULD PRACTICALLY
BLEED PLAID. FOR TWENTY-SIX YEARS, NOT SO
MUCH. THEN I GOT MARRIED.

Our family's Scottish ancestry never meant much to my father. In fact, in 1923 when he was in the first grade and the teacher asked the students to reveal their national background, my father — Malcolm Alexander MacDougall, Jr. — announced that he was German. He was actually ashamed of being Scottish and, five years after World War I, when we were just starting to call "liberty cabbage" sauerkraut again, he preferred to tell people he was German rather than admit he was Scottish. The teacher must have choked back a laugh. Dad's concern for not being identified as Scottish continued right through his adult years. When he was a cost-cutting manager at General Electric Company, he bridled when his office staff called him "frugal MacDougall, the demon Scot with the red pencil."

It wasn't until I married Diane Johnston that I began to appreciate my Scottish heritage. Her father was born in Scotland and came to the United States with his mother when he was five years old. They made the trip across the Atlantic in 1916 when the Germans were briefly adhering to their post-Lusitania promise not to torpedo passenger ships. Thomas John Johnston, Jr. was very proud of his Scottish heritage and would often tell his children — and, later, me — about his origins in the town of Rothsay on the Isle of Bute, not far from Glasgow. When I finally got around to investigating my own family background I discovered that the MacDougall clan had its origins in the Argyle district near Glasgow and, in the thirteenth century, invaded Rothsay and took over the castle. If Diane's dad knew about that he never made an issue of that old grievance.

Thus, Diane and I – and our family — are very, very Scottish and our families even come from the same region of Scotland. When we finally had the time and the means to visit Scotland in 1998, we went to Glasgow and to Rothsay and immediately fell in love with the beauty of the region and the people who live there. Our sense of kinship was palpable, and we have returned four times since. This summer we rented a house on Loch Katrine, twenty-five miles north of Glasgow, and had the whole family there for two weeks. One day we took the group to Oban, site of one of the prominent MacDougall castles named Dunollie. There is only one tower of rocks left from Dunollie, but the commanding view of Oban harbor is magnificent. Standing there we could picture the MacDougall warriors, their kilts fastened with the clan broach that bears the inscription "to conquer or die," looking across the waters prepared to defend the castle to the death. We had our children and grandchildren with us and we hope they will know and appreciate their Scottish heritage.

As I have finally connected with my Scottish roots I have developed a deep appreciation for the major contribution the Scottish people have made to the development of the United States, and indeed the entire world. I have been aided in this by my visits to Scotland and reading Sir Walter Scott's *Rob Roy*, which takes place in the Trossachs, exactly where we were this summer. Then there is a very enjoyable book with a hyperbolic title: *How the Scots Invented the Modern World; The True Story of How Western Europe's Poorest Country Created Our World and Everything In It*, by Arthur Herman. Although Herman certainly exaggerates the Scottish contribution to the world – his title implies that he does – he makes a very good case for saying that without the Scots America today would be a very different place! Allow me to make the case.

One of the most prominent and consequential immigrant groups to come into North America in the two hundred years after 1620 were the Scots. They came for the same reason many other groups made the arduous journey – economic hard times, the failure of crops, and political and religious persecution. After the failed uprisings against the Hanoverian dynasty in 1715 and 1746, Scots emigrated to North America in droves. The defeat of the clans at the Battle of Culloden in 1746 and the persecution of the clans by the British army that followed that battle (banning of the tartans, arrests and executions for treason, etc.) created a Scottish diaspora that brought two hundred thousand Scottish immigrants to North America by 1770. Along with the highlanders (which included the MacDougalls) and the lowlanders from Glasgow and Edinburgh, came many Ulster Scots from Northern Ireland, people who came to be referred to as "Scotch-Irish."

These new settlers brought a distinctive culture and personality to the new world. Some stayed in the coastal cities such as Philadelphia and became merchants or tradesmen, but many others made their way inland to settle in the Appalachian valleys: the Shenandoah Valley of Virginia and the Piedmont region of North Carolina. By 1760, according to Herman, "North Carolina was practically a 'little Scotland: a 'mac-ocracy.'" These new settlers were a rough group, independent-minded and prone to violence to defend their families, their land, and their beliefs. Their descendants included Andrew Jackson who, before he became President, killed two men in duels and led armies against the Native-Americans and the British with a fierce vengeance. Later, there was James K. Polk who, as President, provoked war with the Mexicans and annexed half their country. The group also included Patrick Henry who became famous for simply stating emphatically what all Scotch-Irish people believed: "Give me liberty or give me death!" And finally, less honorable, was John C. Calhoun who, as Senator from South Carolina, justified slavery as a "positive good" and was ready to split the country in half to preserve the "peculiar institution."

When they settled in North America, the Scotsmen brought with them many of the traditions of their culture. The "Virginia Reel" and its cousin, "square dancing", along with the jaunty music that goes with them, came straight from the highlands.

The Scots were the first to distill whiskey (or "whisky" as they spell it) in the new world. This does not surprise anyone who has spent more than a few hours in Glasgow where there is free whisky available in the Carlton George Hotel and where Prince Phillip once asked a driving instructor how he got his Scottish students sober long enough to take the road test!

The Scottish settlers also gave us the term "redneck" which means, "Presbyterian," not the actual color of the neck of a poor farmer who spends hours in the sun. And then there was Captain William Lynch who ruled his largely Scottish county in North Carolina with an iron fist and ordered liberal doses of corporal punishment. The term "lynching" derives from this man's methods and, of course, its racist component for which he was also responsible.

Clearly, while my Scottish ancestors bequeathed much in the way of courage and loyalty – and brutal honesty! – what they brought to this country was not all good!

During the period of the American Revolution the Scots and Scotch-Irish played major roles on both sides of the struggle. In the cities of the east many Scotsmen were loyal to the British crown. They were "Tories," and when the British army evacuated Boston many Tories went with them to Nova Scotia: "New Scotland." If I had lived in Boston in 1776, I must say I probably would have been one of those who went with the British. As a Scot I guess I feel some strange affinity for the "Loyalists" who went to Canada. I cannot explain it any other way.

Other Scottish urban rebels included Henry Knox, a Boston book dealer who served heroically as Washington's first lieutenant and later became Secretary of War under Washington, and Alexander Hamilton of New York, the illegitimate son of a Scottish West Indies merchant, who served as an aide to the general and later became Secretary of the Treasury.

Then, there was Alexander McDougall (no relation), a New York merchant and seaman. He became a friend of Hamilton's and was regarded as one of the most able of the military leaders. After the war he became a member of the New York State Assembly and a leader of the Bank of New York. Had he lived he might well have played a role in the writing of a new constitution for the United States, but he died in 1786 just when the inadequacies of the Article of Confederation were becoming evident.

Finally, the roster of those Scottish military leaders who played major roles in winning the Revolutionary War would likely be headed by John Paul Jones. His principal claim to fame rests on his victory as commander of the warship *Bonhomme Richard* over the British warship *Serapis*, a feat which later contributed to his being named the founder of the American navy.

The intellectual foundation for the American Revolution was, of course, spelled out by Thomas Jefferson in the Declaration of Independence. While not a Scotsman himself, Jefferson absorbed much of his political thinking from Scottish intellectuals such as David Hume, an Edinburgh philosopher, and John Witherspoon, a Scottish immigrant who was one of the first presidents of Princeton College. Some of the very words used by those Scotsmen – "unalienable rights," "self-evident truths" – appear in Jefferson's great declaration. That doesn't make Jefferson a plagiarist. He spelled out these Scottish concepts in clear, memorable and forceful language, and therein lies the greatness of his contribution to the revolutionary cause. At the Continental Congress, after Jefferson's declaration was adopted, one third of the men who signed it were Scottish.

The very same year that Jefferson laid the intellectual groundwork for the new American nation, a Scotsman in Edinburgh produced one of the most significant books of all time and laid the foundation for the economic system of the fledgling country. Adam Smith's *Wealth of Nations* spelled out the basic tenants of capitalism – the virtues of free enterprise and open markets. It could be argued that in 1776 Scottish thinking laid the foundation for the United States as we know it or, at least as we would like it to be – a land of freedom, free enterprise, and democracy.

A little known yet major contributor to the American political system was James Wilson. Born in St. Andrews, Scotland, and educated at the Universities of St. Andrews, Glasgow, and Edinburgh, he was as Scottish as a person can be. He came to America in 1766 and almost immediately began writing about the injustices of British taxation without representation. He was a signer of the Declaration of Independence, but his most important role in establishing the new government of the United States was his service at the Constitutional Convention. Along with James Madison (who, while not a Scot, was heavily influenced by Witherspoon at Princeton) Wilson wrote all the words of the United States Constitution, words that have been analyzed and parsed by scholars, lawyers and judges for 230 years. I have always marveled at the clarity and economy of expression of the U.S. Constitution and for that we owe a great debt to the Scotsman, James Wilson.

Once the United States was founded, the next step in creating the modern world was the industrial revolution, and for this we owe a debt to Scottish intellect and energy. James Watt, a Glasgow mechanical engineer, made huge improvements to the steam engine. His work in the early 1780s made steamships possible, which eventually made Glasgow a center for steamship manufacture. His steam engines provided the power for a wide variety of factories such as textile and lumber mills, and, of course, for steam locomotives which made the enormous railroad industry possible.

The speed of communication was enhanced by the work of two Scotsmen – Samuel Morse and Alexander Graham Bell. Morse's invention of the telegraph in the 1830s made communication across the country instantaneous, albeit a little cumbersome. Forty years later Bell made long distance communication much better with his invention of the telephone which enabled transmission of actual voice messages across great distances. Imagine our society today without the telephone!

Undoubtedly the man who contributed the most to the industrial revolution was the Scotsman Andrew Carnegie. Born into poverty, the son of a weaver in Dunfermline, Scotland, Carnegie emigrated to the United States when he was twelve, took menial jobs, saved money to invest, eventually got into steel manufacturing and built the greatest empire of steel mills in the world. When he sold his company to J.P. Morgan in 1900 the price was $400 million. United States Steel was the largest corporation in the world and the producer of ninety percent of the nation's steel. In 1900, the United States was the largest producer of steel in the world, a fact that played a major role in our ability to defeat the aggressive dictatorships in two world wars. Carnegie went on to donate almost his entire fortune to libraries, colleges, and other worthy civic enterprises across the country.

There are many other famous Scotsmen in our nation's history and, of course, millions of ordinary Scots who have, in various ways, enriched our lives. Unlike my father, I have become a Scottish nationalist who supports everything Scottish, including bagpipes and haggis. When I hear a joke such as: "The limbo was invented by a Scotsman trying to get into a pay toilet," I can laugh with everyone else, but then feel obliged to say that Scottish people are not cheap, they have just been a poor nation and they have learned to make the most of what they have. They are hardworking, honest and brave people. I hope I have shown here a little of what they have contributed to this country, but their contribution as solid citizens is probably the most important thing and that cannot be described in heroic terms.

By the way – if you want to go to Scotland and you only have one day to experience that wonderful country, do this: fly to Glasgow, stay at the Carlton George Hotel, and enjoy a dram or two of the *free whisky* available in your room. Then take the "clockwork orange" subway to Kelvin Grove, walk around the park and enjoy the gardens (take a raincoat; it will probably shower) and go to a nearby restaurant/pub called Stravaigin and order a McEwan's Ale and a dinner of "haggis, meeps, and tatties (haggis with mashed potatoes and mashed turnip). Be sure to say "aye" when they ask if you want whisky sauce poured all over it. Then, after taking the clockwork orange back to the center of the city, take a train from Queen Station (right next door to the Carlton George) to Edinburgh (45 minutes). In Edinburgh walk the "Royal Mile" up to the castle, tour the castle and savor the views, then go down to the corner of Prince's park by the Sir Walter Scott memorial and listen to the bagpiper. After that, you'll be ready for another dinner so go to "Dirty Dick's at 159 Rose Street. This is an old (1859), quirky pub that has everything in the world hanging from the walls and ceiling – old musical instruments, golf clubs, hub caps, license plates, beer mugs, etc. It's always crowded, but worth the hassle. Some locals say "Dirty Dick's" has the best Scottish food in Edinburgh, so order *their* haggis, meeps and tatties covered with whisky sauce and see how it compares with the haggis dinner you had at Stravaigin a few hours before in Glasgow. Then take the train back to Glasgow (they run every 30 minutes), walk out of Queen Station, turn right and go right into the Carlton George Hotel. Have a wee dram of the free whisky (not spelled *whiskey*, mind ye!), fall into bed beneath the tartan tapestries and get a good night's sleep before flying out the next morning.

If you have *two* days to enjoy Scotland, take a train from Glasgow north to Inverness and enjoy the scenery of the highlands as you travel. The lochs, the long valleys studded with heather, and the craggy peaks of the mountains provide one breath-taking vista after another! In Inverness enjoy a Belhaven Ale at one of the pubs and sample *their* haggis, meeps and tatties with whisky sauce. After becoming sufficiently mellow, take a tour out to the nearby Culloden battlefield and experience the site of the final crushing of the "rising" of bonny Prince Charlie's Jacobites. The battle was horrific, and it had enormous consequences. One doesn't "tour" the site at Culloden, one experiences it. You'll know what I mean if you do it.

After an afternoon in Inverness, take a train back to Glasgow. If you're there in the summer, ye needn't worry about it getting dark on ye. In June it stays light in Inverness until eleven P.M. and the sun appears again at 3:30 A.M.

You *could* rent a car in Glasgow and drive up to Inverness, but you'd regret it. The roads in Scotland are not for the faint of heart. Through the highlands the roads are narrow, winding, hilly, and treacherous. If you don't know what a "blind summit" is, you'll find out if you drive a car through the highlands. Sometimes it appears there is no possible way that you, going up the *left* side of the road, are going to miss a head-on collision with the huge lorry coming right at you in the middle of the road. The truck's side-view mirror looks like it will hit you right in the face. Clearly, I have survived all such encounters, but I would much rather sit in a train and be served haggis, meeps and tatties covered with whisky sauce while I watch the beautiful mountains and glens glide by.

Final word: do not ask what is *in* the haggis. It is enough to know that Scotland has always been a poor country abundantly rich in natural beauty but poor in material wealth. Its people cannot afford to waste a single part of a slaughtered lamb. Just eat the haggis and enjoy!

MALCOLM AND MILDRED

EVENTUALLY WORLD WAR II CAUGHT UP WITH
ALMOST EVERYONE, AND EVERYONE HAD A
UNIQUE STORY.

My parents went together like peas and carrots as Forrest Gump would say. They started "dating" in the first grade, went together all through school, and got married in 1940 when they were both twenty-two. Their names were Mildred and Malcolm — "Mil" and "Mal" – and they were so much alike that people said the only difference between them was a vowel.

On December 7, 1941, Mil and Mal were enjoying a Sunday afternoon Christmas party at a friend's house in Quincy, Massachusetts. As the "twenty somethings" sipped eggnog and decorated the Christmas tree, a late arrival to the party burst into the house and announced that he had just heard on his car radio that the Japanese had attacked the U.S. naval base at Pearl Harbor in Hawaii. Suddenly all merriment ceased as the couples, most of them married, gathered around the big radio cabinet and tried to tune in a news broadcast. They all knew that many of the men would soon be in uniform and be off fighting in a war against Japan, and probably Germany and Italy as well. The women would be left alone, some of them with new babies.

World War II had been raging for two years and now it had finally come to the United States. For those young people who were going to have to do the fighting it was a scary time. In the heat of the moment, some young men rushed to enlist. Others, such as my father, waited to be called.

It took two years for the draft to catch up to Dad. For a while his job at General Electric, a company that was providing parts for naval aircraft, made him "essential to the war effort." Finally, in October of 1943, the letter from "Uncle Sam" arrived and Malcolm Alexander MacDougall, Jr. was off to join the United States Navy. After basic training in Norfolk, Virginia, he came home on a short leave to see his new baby son, born on January 17, 1944. The boy's name was Robert ("Bobby"). There was time for only a brief reunion with Mil and a day with Bobby, and then it was off for a long cross-country train ride to San Francisco. There he boarded a troop ship for the endless voyage to New Guinea where the American general, Douglas MacArthur, had driven the Japanese out, and had occupied the island.

Years later Dad would say that the sail to New Guinea was the worst part of the war for him. There were thousands of men crammed into a converted Italian ocean liner. Everyone slept in hammocks that were hung three high in the hold of the ship. Because the ship was crossing the equator, the quarters for the men were stifling, sweaty and smelly. With little to do but lie there for six weeks, he listened to some of the younger homesick guys sobbing and amused himself by watching the sweat stain on the canvas under the guy above him grow larger and larger.

New Guinea was hot and humid all the time. It was difficult for a New Englander to get used to the constant sweat and the insects the size of birds. During his first year on the bug-infested island, he saw many snakes and naked natives, but no combat. Almost all his time was spent unloading ships as the supplies necessary for MacArthur's "island hopping" campaign built up. The closest he came to getting killed was when a five-gallon drum of paint fell from a cargo net sixty feet above and crashed onto the dock just a few feet from where he stood. The barrel burst, and Dad got showered with white paint but was otherwise unhurt. What an inglorious way to become a casualty that would have been!

Finally, in May of 1945 Dad was shipped to the Philippines. All the letters he sent to Mom were censored by the military and all references to his location and where he was going next were "redacted" with scissors. The Navy did this in case a mail plane was shot down and the Japanese might learn troop movements from the mail. To keep his letters intact and still get the messages through, Dad and Mom had developed a code: the first letter of each sentence would spell out where he was. Thus: "**P**lease excuse my late letter. **H**ow is little Bobbie doing? **I**s he growing like a weed? **L**ately it has rained a lot here" . . . **PHIL**. With the code Mom knew he was in the Philippines and was going to be part of the force that would invade Japan in the fall of 1945!

Because of the ferocity with which Japan had fought to hold all the islands approaching their home territory ("Kamikaze" planes, etc.) everyone assumed the casualties in a U.S. invasion of the Japanese home islands would be very high. Naturally, Mom and Dad were very nervous.

The two years Dad was away were the most difficult of my mother's life. There was the constant worry and the boredom and the ration coupons she needed to buy basic food items for her and me. She had no car because gasoline was strictly rationed, so she calmed her nerves by walking miles around Quincy pushing me in a baby carriage. She wore out a set of buggy wheels doing that and couldn't replace them because rubber was rationed. It was almost worse for her not knowing what was happening than it was for Dad who knew exactly what was happening.

What was happening for him in July and early August of 1945 was uncertainty. He packed his gear into a huge duffel bag to be ready to board a ship bound for the base from which the invasion of Japan would be launched. Then he gradually unpacked as he needed his stuff and the orders to ship out did not come. He knew something was "up".

In August, President Truman ordered an atomic bomb — a fearsome weapon none of the men in Dad's unit had ever heard of – dropped on Hiroshima, Japan. Three days later, another fell on Nagasaki. On August fourteenth Japan surrendered. An invasion would not be needed! For the rest of his life Dad was a vehement defender of Truman's controversial decision to use the bomb. It actually saved lives, he would say, because an invasion would have been horrifically bloody on both sides. Dad's unit always said they hoped to see "the Golden Gate in '48" – the Golden Gate Bridge in San Francisco in 1948. Instead, because of the bomb, they were "home alive in '45!"

Dad was mustered out of the Navy and he gratefully returned to civilian life on December 7, 1945. He died on December 7, 2000. Mom died on February 17, 2010.

MISS STONE IN 1955

SHE WAS A VERY "OLD SCHOOL" TEACHER. THAT'S
NOT A BAD THING.

In the mid-1950s the George Washington School in Melrose, Massachusetts, had not changed much since it opened in 1898. Neither, so it seemed, had some of the teachers such as Miss Georgia Stone who had been there, we all thought, from the day the school first opened its doors.

It was September, 1954. "Aw, she's at least eighty," my friend Tony Miller jeered as we walked to the first day of school. My stomach churned at the thought of the ordeal that awaited me. I had been assigned to the fifth-grade class of the oldest and most feared teacher in the school. Tony was lucky enough to have a new teacher, Miss Murphy, for fifth grade. Having her for a teacher *had* to be better than getting stuck with Miss Stone!

When the bell rang we scrambled up the granite stairs and through the big, green front doors. Every year the smell of the varnished wooden railings, my stiff, new "Boy Scout" shoes, my itchy long pants and the knot in my stomach blended together into first-day-of-school anxiety. This year, as I climbed the stairs to the second floor, the discomforts, especially the stomach knots, were worse than ever.

Before I could collect myself, there in her classroom doorway loomed Miss Stone herself. In her flower-print dress she appeared massive and forbidding. Beneath her snowy hair all set in tight little waves her face seemed frozen into a permanent scowl.

Then, as I arrived at the door, she broke into a smile and extended her hand. "How do you do?" she asked in a musical voice. "I'm Miss Stone and I'll be your teacher this year." As I shook her hand I noticed that one of her front teeth was silver. (Fortunately, the "Home Alone" movie had not yet been made.) I started to walk into the room, but she held onto my hand and pulled me back in front of her. "Well," she demanded, "aren't you going to introduce *yourself*?" I stammered out my name and she smiled and said, "Nice to meet you, Robert. Please take any seat you like."

The desks were heavy, wooden ones set in straight rows facing the teacher's desk. They had always been bolted to the floor but now, in a reckless flirtation with disorder, they were free to move about. I found one safely in the middle of the room. Around me several other poor lambs were already in their seats awaiting execution. Minutes earlier we had all been shouting and running around on the playground and enjoying the last minutes of summer vacation. Now, enclosed once again in a stuffy classroom we sat, timid, apprehensive, waiting.

Finally satisfied we were all there, Miss Stone came in and stood before us. As she began to talk I studied her dark blue, flower print dress with three-quarter-length sleeves lined at the bottoms with lace. On one of them, tucked under the lace, was Miss Stone's hanky. I marveled that such a powerful and fearsome woman could own such a dainty hanky.

"This fifth-grade year is very important," she was saying. During it you will pass the half-way point on your way to high school." I didn't think that was a very threatening thing to say to us. It even implied that we would pass the fifth grade and be able to go to high school! "I expect you to work hard and to always do your very best," she proclaimed. "Now, would you please pick up the pencil that is on your desk and we will begin our first writing lesson."

I had expected a tirade. I had expected her to pick up a student and shake him, or perhaps use a ruler on someone. Instead, she had us writing within five minutes of the first bell. No shaking or swatting was needed. I knew that we were going to work, Miss Stone was going to be in charge, and, because she knew probably everything, we were going to learn.

When I walked home for lunch that day with Tony I didn't want to admit that my morning had not been a terrible ordeal. I made vague references to horrors and implied that I would rather not talk about it. He was smug because Miss Murphy was young and looked like Marilyn Monroe.

Miss Stone quickly established classroom procedure that emphasized orderliness, courtesy and discipline. The firmness of her will kept the desks in straight rows as well as any bolts ever had. Each student was assigned a task and was expected to do it well without being told. My job was to fill the inkwells at the corners of all the desks. Every Monday and Thursday morning I would go into the closet, get the large bottle of ink off the shelf and screw the spout onto it. Then I would go from desk to desk carefully putting the spout into each well, tipping the bottle up and bringing it back down when the first tiny bubbles appeared in the opening. On the closet floor I noticed a large black stain where, clearly, some pitiable creature had once spilled half the bottle.

"Your signature is part of yourself," Miss Stone always reminded us as we dipped our pens in the inkwells and scratched our names on our papers. "Take pride in how you write your name and do it well. The way it looks says a great deal about the kind of person you are." My signature looked like an orangutan's and was disastrous to my self-image. Miss Stone's finger would rap on the desk as she insisted I do better. Her insistence was not carping; it was simply a firm statement of confidence that a little work would produce better results. Her refusal to accept a slip-shod performance made me realize that she cared about my writing, and I began to care, too.

Miss Stone demanded that we use words correctly. "'Kids' are baby goats," she'd say, "You people are not kids, you are 'children.'" "Horses sweat," she told me when I complained about how hot it was, "human beings *perspire!*" While we worked at our seats we saw her at her desk correcting papers, peering at every word through her bifocals. Once I submitted a paragraph on the Revolutionary War in which I opined that the British generals were "lousy." In large, red letters she wrote, "Lousy means 'full of lice' and is not correct here, unless you know something I don't about the cleanliness of British generals!"

I could not have explained it then, but I found it reassuring to know that Miss Stone was establishing firm standards of performance and conduct. We students could not always reach those standards – which was why so many of us feared her – but we always knew what the goals were. Miss Stone was like a mooring firmly planted in bedrock beneath turbulent waters.

Besides her stated goals, Miss Stone – like all teachers whether they are aware of it or not – had an unspoken agenda, a catalog of qualities she instilled in us by the way she conducted the class and by the example she set. She developed in us feelings of pride, dignity, self-confidence, and a strong sense of what was right.

She helped us gain poise when she had each of us stand before the class at least once a week to answer questions or give a report. One day, as I was standing before those thirty critical faces (no group I have stood before since has seemed so threatening!), several classmates began disagreeing with me. I don't remember what the topic was; I only remember being confronted. I argued back, but I was about ready to give up rather than create a scene when Miss Stone said from her desk at the rear of the room, "Stick to your guns, Robert!" I was surprised by her support. She made me picture myself defending a fortress and blazing away at the attacking enemy. Since that day, when I find myself holding an unpopular opinion, I get the same feeling of confidence I had that day in the fifth grade and I hear Miss Stone saying, "Stick to your guns, Robert!"

Miss Stone stuck to *her* guns. She was at her post every day; no "mental health days" for her! Once, during the winter, it snowed all day on a Sunday, and on Monday it was still snowing. Though I was sure no one would be at school (they didn't officially cancel schools in Melrose), I thought it would be a challenge to get there, so I waded through snow over my knees and finally arrived at the big, green front door. It was unlocked. I went upstairs and down the strangely quiet hall to our room. There, working at her desk, was Miss Stone! She smiled. "It's nice to see you, Robert. You're the only one who came today, but I'm glad you're here."

"It sure is blowing around out there!" I said as I hung my dripping coat in the coatroom. I noticed she was wearing heavy, black boots that hung open below her long dress in a confusion of rubber and buckles. "Oh, it's the worst storm we've had in a long time," she agreed. "I was planning on putting up a bulletin board on Washington and Lincoln. You can help me."

I followed her into the closet and stood looking at the inkbottle and the stain on the floor while she, hunched over, fumbled through the ancient boxes and occasionally handed me pictures and alphabet letters. Then we spent the rest of the morning arranging and stapling a collage that depicted the lives of the two presidents. I felt good about the way we discussed matters like two adults.

"Why don't we put things more at angles to each other instead of straight up and down," I suggested. She stepped back to look at the board and weigh the merits of my suggestion. Her white hair looked bedraggled and a wet curl hung over her cheek. "That's good," she pronounced, and walked with clinking buckles to the board to move some of the pictures.

Finally, we stood back to admire our work. "I think it looks pretty nice," she said, her smile revealing her silver tooth. "Thank you for helping me with it, Robert."

It was noon and Miss Stone said we might as well go home for the day. We went out the front door together; she said good-bye and trudged off through the wind that whipped stinging bits of snow around her legs. She lived by herself on Grove Street, not far from the school. I lived in the other direction, so I ran off toward my house thinking of finding my friends and going "coasting." A young boy always looks ahead to the next bit of fun and never stops to savor a moment. Yet, many years later, I still remember that snowy winter morning with Miss Stone.

When spring came, Miss Stone took us on a bus tour of Boston's historic sites. She told us we were going to be in a large city and we should dress well in order to make a good impression. Even though it was hot, the girls wore starched dresses, patent leather shoes and white ankle socks. The boys wore white shirts and ties. We were uncomfortable and squirmy as we sat in the pews of the Old North Church. The rector beamed at us with approval and said we were a fine-looking group of young people. "Big deal," I thought as I ran my finger around the inside of my sweaty (perspirey?) collar. I looked at Miss Stone and noticed that she, too, was dressed for the occasion; she was wearing a hat and white gloves. As I looked back at the smiling rector, I realized that he felt good because we considered him and his beautiful church important enough to dress up for. I never forgot that scene, even when the hippies of the 1960s ridiculed the very idea of decorum.

On the last day of school that year Miss Stone walked downstairs to the front door with us and shook each of our hands as we went out into the sunshine. When it was my turn she said, "It was very nice having you in class, Robert. Good luck to you."

I wanted to say something nice to her, but nothing came. There were other kids around, so I only said, "Good-bye." As I walked down the steps I began talking with the other boys about getting up a baseball game on the common that afternoon. She most likely thought I went off into the summer and quickly forgot about her.

Shortly afterward, I moved with my family away from New England. But, rather than forget Miss Stone, I increasingly appreciated what she had done for me. Other teachers were more cheerful and more fun, but no one made me see what I could achieve through hard work, and no one affected my values as she had.

In 1972, after returning to Massachusetts, I went to the Washington School. I thought it might still be possible to see Miss Stone since my idea of what constitutes old age had changed considerably since the fifth grade. The building looked pretty much the same, although reading nooks had been installed along the corridors and the old coatrooms were now "activity centers" filled with educational games and "manipulatives." Students seemed to be outside their classrooms and doing their own things more. Most of the teachers were young, some of them were men, and all of them wore pants. There was no sign of Miss Stone.

On the second floor I stood and looked through the doorway of Miss Stone's room. The desks were arranged in clusters around the floor. The young teacher was seated with one group, talking with the children, while the others were engaged in their own activities. As if they sensed my presence at once, they all stopped what they were doing and stared at the stranger. I was tempted to walk in and look at the room more closely. Was the ink stain still on the closet floor? But, I was an intruder, a visitor from another era. (Today, I'd be arrested!) The room belonged to them now and I hoped that, in their own way, they were learning as much as I had. I turned and walked down the corridor to the stairs.

As I passed the other classrooms full of activity I realized the traditional world of Miss Stone, for better or worse, had vanished. So, it appeared, had Miss Stone. No one in the office, not even the elderly custodian, had any recollection of her.

No one in the school administration offices could help me, either. One secretary did remember having Miss Stone in the 1930s. We agreed that because she was firm and made us work hard, she had made a profound impression on us. She remembered Miss Stone as a little woman, while I thought of her as large and commanding. Perhaps, over the years, I transferred her personality into her physical presence.

Reluctantly I went to Melrose City Hall to check the death records. The woman in the clerk's office showed me an orange card stating that Miss Georgia Stone died on November 30, 1962, at the age of 69. She was listed as a retired schoolteacher.

All that was left was a card in the town clerk's files. I felt like I had been hit in the chest with a rock. I wanted to thank her, to tell her what I'd been doing – I was a teacher! – and how I had benefitted from her work. Had anyone ever thanked her? Surely some grown up smiling person had walked into her room as she worked at her desk and said, "Hi, Miss Stone! Remember me?"

But I had never said anything. For seventeen years I had been thankful that Miss Stone had been one of my teachers, but I had never told her. She seemed so indestructible. How could it be possible that she died?

As I stepped out onto the sunbaked sidewalk it occurred to me. Miss Stone in 1972 was more than a room in an old school building or an orange card in a file. She had not died. She was alive in me and in hundreds of her former students. The skills and values she had taught us were here long after she was gone. The *good* that we do lives after us. That is one more lesson I learned from Miss Stone.

FAVORITE YEARS / HIDEOUS YEARS

IN HISTORY, AND IN LIFE,
PERSPECTIVE MEANS A LOT.

Sometimes when I'm in a half-sleep I revisit some of the best years I have lived. I like replaying them – sort of like I enjoy re-reading a beloved book or watching a favorite movie for the fifth time. Yet, an important aspect of these semi-dreams is that, as a historian, I am acutely aware that those same years that are my favorites were years from hell for many people. And I am not only talking about starving people in faraway places; I'm talking about people right here in the United States who, in some cases were living right in my own neighborhood or in the neighborhood next door.

Let me give you a sample of some of the wonderful years I have recently revisited in my somnolent moments and reveal the dichotomy between what I experienced and what others in the United States and in places around the world endured in those very same years.

1955:

For me, the word "halcyon" was invented to describe 1955. I was eleven, I was living in a comfortable, middle class home in Melrose, Massachusetts, a charming suburb of Boston, and every single day was sunny. . . or snowy in the winter, which I loved. I walked to school every morning with my friend, Tony Miller – except when we were fighting – and after school we played baseball in his back yard. It was the first year I tried out for Little League and was actually chosen for a team. (In the 50s, if you stunk, you didn't make a team. You'd be told, "Practice some more, kid, and try again next year.") The Red Sox were terrible – again. They were perennially terrible in the 50s, but there was always Ted Williams. We would turn on the radio at 1:00 to listen to the Sox game and come back to it every twenty minutes or so when it was likely Williams would have another at bat. In between Ted's at bats I would hit small stones into the woods behind our house. A small granite cliff was fifty feet away and every zinger I hit over it was a dramatic homer that won the game in the bottom of the ninth . . . for the Red Sox, of course.

Our family bought a new car that year – a 1955 turquois and cream Chevrolet with white sidewall tires. I loved it, and I loved riding in it up to Lake Rescue in Vermont where we rented a cottage for a week that summer. Life was great for me, a white, middle class kid . . . er, boy . . . in 1955.

BUT: What if you were a black boy in America that year? What if your name was Emmett Till and you went that summer to visit your uncle and play with your cousins in a town called Money, Mississippi?

One day Emmett told his cousins that he had a girlfriend back in Chicago and they dared him to speak to the white lady who ran the candy store they were standing in front of. Emmett went into the store, bought some candy, and said something – no one later could agree on just what – to Carolyn Bryant, the woman behind the counter. He didn't know it, but he had just broken a major rule in southern race relations in 1955; he had talked "fresh" to a white woman.

Two nights later Carolyn Bryant's husband, Roy, and his brother-in-law, J.W. Milam, showed up at the cabin where Emmett was staying with his uncle. They dragged him out and took him away in their truck. A few days later Emmett's mutilated body was fished out of the Tallahatchie River. His face was beaten to the point that it was unrecognizable and there was a cotton gin fan tied around his neck to hold his body under water.

Bryant and Milam were charged with murder but, in the trial *a month later*, a jury of twelve white men did "their duty," as the defense attorney put it, and found the two men "not guilty." A few months after that, free from prosecution under the "double jeopardy clause" of the Fifth Amendment, Bryant and Milam told a national magazine that they did, indeed, murder Emmett Till – to protect the honor of Bryant's wife and the security of white women everywhere.

In 2017, over sixty years later, Carolyn Bryant, now very old, finally told the truth. Emmett Till never said anything "fresh" to her. I cannot imagine how that woman has been able to live with herself for all that time!

So, at the very moment I was getting into our new turquois car to go up to the lake in Vermont, Emmett Till was being murdered by two angry white men because he talked to a white woman. And, of course, Till was not the only victim of racial hatred that summer. If you were black in 1955 it was not a halcyon year of little League games, trips to the lake and new cars. It was very different.

1971:

My wife and I were newly married and deeply in love. We took a road trip across the country and then moved from Michigan to Massachusetts fulfilling my ambition to move back to Boston as soon as I could. We took an upstairs flat apartment in Winchester, Massachusetts, and settled in to be teachers. Life was perfect.

BUT: Tony Miller, my old friend from Melrose of whom I had lost track after we moved away in 1956, was a navy pilot in Vietnam. On a flight back to his aircraft carrier in January, 1971, he had to ditch his plane into the Gulf of Tonkin. He was never found.

For most of my friends and me, the draft had passed us by and the war was winding down. But for Tony and thousands of other soldiers the war was still on and they were still determined to win it. Nineteen seventy-one was the year I got to return to Massachusetts with my new wife. For Tony, it was the year he gave his life for his country.

1975:

In April I ran the Boston Marathon. It was a sunny, cool day with a light breeze from the west – perfect conditions. I fairly flew into Boston from Hopkinton, beating my goal time by four minutes. I was thrilled! That same spring my wife and I bought our house – a small Cape Cod in Andover – and we spent a happy summer painting, carpeting and landscaping. We were living the middle class American dream.

BUT: The people in Saigon, South Vietnam that spring – both Vietnamese and Americans – were living a horror. In April the communists were moving toward Saigon and the South Vietnamese army was melting before them. As I was running the marathon, I could hear radios in the crowd telling about the communist advances and I even wondered if Saigon would fall before I finished the race. On April 30th North Vietnamese troops rumbled into the city in Soviet-made tanks and the last, desperate defenders of the city were killed, or captured or had crammed themselves into tiny boats to make their perilous way into the South China Sea.

That year my wife and I were enjoying all the good things life in middle class America had to offer. The Americans in Saigon were taking the last desperate flights by helicopter out of Saigon and leaving South Vietnamese friends on the rooftops. Many of the people all over South Vietnam were being shot or dragged off to prison camps as the communists clamped their oppressive rule on the country.

1987:

In the summer our family hosted an exchange student from Japan for two weeks. Her name was Satoko, and she was a delight. Then, we took a trip out to Michigan to visit old friends and went on to Seattle to visit relatives. Our children were young (eight and four) — just old enough to look after themselves but young enough to get excited about small things. We went white-water rafting on the Skagit River, climbed a mountain, and took several ferry rides across beautiful Puget Sound. It was a great summer to have a young family in America.

BUT: If you were living in Eastern Europe with a young family that year your options for any kind of fun were very limited. Your job probably paid very low wages and travel under the rigid restrictions of the communist regime was always an ordeal. If you lived in communist East Germany and had family in West Germany you could not travel to see them because of the tight border controls and, in Berlin, the massive wall that separated the two halves of the city.

On June 12th President Reagan gave a speech in front of the Berlin Wall in which he demanded: "Mr. Gorbachev, tear down this wall!" I snickered at the simplistic demand and never dreamed that in three years the wall actually would come down.

In 1987 while my family and I were living in comfort, hosting an exchange student, traveling across the country and visiting relatives as we chose, the people in Eastern Europe were merely surviving under oppressive regimes. Better days for them were ahead, but they had no way to know that in 1987.

These years, 1955, 1971, 1975 and 1987 are just the most recent ones I have thought about. I could pick any one of the years since 1944 and the theme of all of them would be: I have had it very good compared to most people around the world and millions of people in this country. One of the major reasons I love history is that it helps me put my own life in perspective. For the most part I have been very happy because I can see how truly blessed my family and I have been.

MY FRIENDS FREDDY AND TONY

"THE CHILD IS THE FATHER OF THE MAN"

Wordsworth

In the early 1950s, when I was a young boy growing up in Melrose, Massachusetts, I had two close friends. One was Carlton "Tony" Miller, a wiry, red-haired, tough little guy who picked his nose a lot and loved to fight. He had a particularly annoying habit of dragging the snot from his nose to his mouth and eating it. The other was Frederick "Freddy" Martone, a dark, sturdy boy who was very proud of his Italian heritage. Tony went to public school with me; Freddy went to St. Mary's, which sounded like a very scary place where nuns in full habit wacked you with a ruler if you misbehaved.

Tony was truly pugnacious. One winter morning as we walked to school (The George Washington School) he showed me his new mittens that were made of faux leather and looked like boxing gloves. That similarity was not lost on Tony and he kept shadow boxing all the way to school. As I watched him jab into the air I knew it would not be long before he would want to box a real person, probably me. Sure enough, when we got to the schoolyard, he turned a simple disagreement into a cause for war. He said that on a hot day it was the hottest at 4 P.M., but I stood firm for 2, and so that meant we had to fight! The next thing I knew he was swinging those gloves at me like he was Rocky Marciano. A teacher intervened and we both ended up sitting in the principal's office with bloody noses.

Not long after that fight Tony was out of school for a month. While climbing the big tree in his back yard he fell fifteen feet to the ground and broke his collarbone and his jaw. When he finally returned to school his face was still bruised and his arm was in a sling.

Meanwhile, Freddy was going to parochial school and was only available to play on weekends since his mother kept him inside doing homework on school days. One Saturday we went to see the World War II movie "To Hell and Back" and on the walk home we got to talking about Italy where some of the battles in the film took place. Soon he launched into his usual speech about how Italians are the greatest people on earth, how almost all the great music and art was produced by Italians, and Rome was the most beautiful city ever built. I had nothing much to say about my Scottish heritage. At the time, as I've indicated elsewhere, I knew nothing about Sir Walter Scott, Robert Burns, or Edinburgh. The movie "Brave Heart" was forty years in the future. Besides, even if I had known about William Wallace, how could a guy who hacked Scotland's enemies to death with a broadsword be favorably compared with the artists who painted the Sistine Chapel and the Mona Lisa?

I was friends with Tony and Freddie for five years. Then, in May of 1956, my family moved from Melrose to Buffalo, New

York, and it wasn't until 1971 that I returned with my wife to Massachusetts. I had totally lost track of Tony and Freddy. But, when the age of Google arrived, I looked them up to see what had happened to them. The results were astounding but, in a way, predictable.

During the Vietnam War Tony enlisted in the Naval Air Corps. He was recognized by his fellow "flyboys" as a daring and courageous pilot. On January 6, 1971, he missed his landing on an aircraft carrier and was forced to ditch into the Gulf of Tonkin. He didn't make it and his body was never found. The boy who loved to fight and take risky climbs up tall trees became the man who volunteered for duty in Vietnam and fell from the skies to his place on the Memorial Wall.

Freddy's extra homework paid off. He went to Holy Cross and became a lawyer. He entered the judiciary and became a justice on the supreme court of Arizona. Then, in 2001, he was appointed by President George W. Bush to be a justice on the United States District Court in Arizona. During his time on the bench he was widely acclaimed for his judicial expertise and well-written conservative opinions. As an Italian, he was Arizona's Antonin Scalia.

As they grew up, my old friends changed a great deal. But, in some important respects, they did not change at all.

1967, THE YEAR EVERYTHING CHANGED

SOMETIMES YOU JUST KNOW THINGS WILL NEVER BE THE SAME AGAIN!

1967 was *fifty* years ago! Good grief . . . half a century! Those of us who were adults that year remember it through a hazy mist . . . or, perhaps, through a cloud of marijuana smoke. I remember that year well for many reasons, many of them not very good, but before I get into 1967 and its significance, a little background is necessary.

In August of 1966 I received a notice from the United States Department of Defense to report to Fort Wayne in Detroit for a draft physical. That September, after being temporarily deferred from military duty for physical reasons (a hernia), I started my high school teaching career teaching American History at Southfield High School in Southfield, Michigan. Southfield High had a large Jewish population and not a single African-American student.

In October I read in the *Detroit News* that the Red Sox, whom I still supported even though we had moved away from Boston ten years earlier, had finished in the cellar of the American League. Average attendance at a Red Sox game was 8,000 dispirited "fans." I was not surprised. The Sox had been awful for all of the fifteen years I had rooted for them.

Little did I know that these facts about the world that swirled around me at that time were setting the stage for the events of 1967 that were going to change the world – and my personal life – in dramatic ways.

As 1967 began my biggest concern was the mail that arrived every day. In the pile of bills and random fliers that dropped through the slot onto the floor I feared there would be that letter from "Uncle Sam" that so many young men my age (or younger) were dreading. How long would a simple hernia hold up against the army's crying need for soldiers as our troop commitment to the Vietnam War escalated to over 400,000? Along with many of my peers, I was growing increasingly skeptical of how successful the United States could be at propping up a government that was no good, except it wasn't communist? We were killing more of the communists than they were of us, but there were no front lines, no signs of progress, no sign of the enemy retreating as there had been in World War II or Korea. To measure our success all we had to go on were "body counts," and there were reports that the counts of Vietcong killed were actually very inflated. One American officer who was interviewed on the CBS Evening News was asked how we could win in Vietnam when the French had killed thousands of Vietcong and still lost. He took a long drag on his cigarette and emitted a steady stream of smoke as he shook his head and answered, " . . . they didn't kill *enough* 'cong.'" Ugh!

When you are in your twenties, single, and still trying to figure out your life – still trying to avoid the feeling that life is just something that happens to you – world events seem like annoying intrusions. Vietnam, Vietnam – every night on the news – Vietnam. Soldiers on TV moving warily through thick jungle, whole villages burning, peasant farmers not really caring which side is moving in, just wanting to be at peace. What were we to think of a war like that? There was a growing peace movement on college campuses. What was *I* to think? Was I a "hawk" or a "dove?" Was escalation – more bombing and more troops – the answer? Or, should we cut our losses and get out? I was a hawk in 1966; I thought we needed to contain communism and we needed to do whatever it took to keep the communists from winning in Vietnam. But now, as George Kennan, the State Department operative who had invented the concept of "containment," came out against the war, I was starting to question whether Vietnam was the place to draw the line, at least in the way we were trying to draw it — building up "body counts."

Of course, there was much more than that damnable war going on. Racial tensions were reaching fever pitch. As the year progressed we were all afraid of another long, hot summer of race riots. The 1964 Civil Rights Act did not seemed to have settled anything. The poverty lines and the racial hatreds were still in place. We were asking ourselves which cities would follow Newark and Los Angeles and go up in flames this year?

The leafy suburb I lived in and the fast-growing town I taught high school in seemed like the eye of a hurricane. Surely one of the storms – the draft, race riots, or something else – would hit me and all happy thoughts of a teaching career, love, marriage, and children would be blown away. Life for me as a single, draft-eligible twenty-three-year-old seemed very unsettled.

For relief there was always radio and the latest music. In June, the long anticipated new album by The Beatles appeared. For me it was, at first, a disappointing shock. It was so different and, well, weird. The cover showed the lads wearing crazy-looking silk, old-timey band uniforms surrounded by dozens of pictures of famous people. It was called *Sgt. Pepper's Lonely Hearts Club Band* and it seemed as if the Beatles were losing their identity. They certainly were changing their musical style. Many of the songs had psychedelic overtones, some featured sitar playing, and hardly a song on the entire album was one you could dance to. I hated it, yet I shouldn't have been too surprised because their previous album, *Revolver*, had introduced some of the same elements.

And yet – everyone I knew was talking about how great it was – so I played it for myself a few more times and, as it played, I read the words to each song that were printed on the jacket (I love it when they do that!). Gradually, even though I didn't want the Beatles to take me on a drug-induced trip (*Lucy in the Sky With Diamonds*), or amuse me with crazy images (*For the benefit of Mr. Kite*) or bring me down with a maudlin story (*She's Leaving Home*), their songs began to intrigue me and soon I couldn't get the melodies out of my head. I was hooked. I gradually became convinced that, far from being a flop, it was the greatest album ever recorded. It didn't take a mystic to predict that the innovations in *Sgt. Pepper* – the sound mixing, the experimentation with a variety of instruments and styles – would forever change the way music was produced. It did just that, and the fiftieth anniversary of its release in June of 2017 saw even more sales of it and the release of an enhanced version that even millennials are scooping up.

The same week that the *Sergeant Pepper* album came out, war broke out in the Middle East and the many Jewish students at Southfield High School, led by the seniors, many of whom I had in class, were deeply shaken. The war pitted Israel against five Arab states that surround that little country on all sides: Egypt,

Lebanon, Syria, Jordan, and Saudi Arabia. Adding to Israel's mix of enemies were the Palestinian Arabs who had fled to Gaza and the West Bank of the Jordan River when the Jewish state of Israel was created by the U.N. in 1948. It seemed Israel's chances were slim, that it would need all the help it could get, and many of Southfield's seniors made plans to go to Israel right after graduation and enlist in the Israeli army.

Within a few days, the students at Southfield High could stop worrying. The Israeli air force wiped out every warplane Egypt had; Israeli intelligence knew the exact location of the planes on the ground and a swift strike during the first hours of the war eliminated Egypt's hopes of controlling the skies. Then, Israeli forces, using swift-moving American-made tanks, drove the Egyptians out of Gaza and the Sinai Peninsula. Within a few days Israeli forces controlled the Suez Canal. Meanwhile, the Israeli Army captured the strategic Golan Heights from Syria and drove the Jordanians out of the West Bank, including Jerusalem. For the first time since 70 AD when the Romans ruled, Israel controlled all of Palestine.

They called it the "Six Day War" because in six days the forces of Israel's enemies were in ruins and it was all over. Naturally, Israel's great victory caused great rejoicing at Southfield High. Israel now controlled territory that gave it additional security on all its borders and the Arabs were deeply humiliated.

However, as is always the case when a country humiliates its enemies, there were reasons for caution. In their despair the Arabs thirsted for revenge. Foremost among those in despair were the Palestinian Arabs who lived in the West Bank and Gaza, both of which were now Israeli-occupied. For many Arabs, the way forward lay in greater devotion to Islam. In the Arab defeats of 1967 lay the seeds of a much more militant and violent form of Islam, a movement that was going to grow and emerge in many different incarnations: the Muslim Brotherhood in Egypt, Hezbollah in Lebanon, Hamas in Gaza, Al Qaeda in Afghanistan, and ISIS in Syria and Iraq. The terrorist attacks, starting with the airplane hijackings of the 1970s and moving on to the gruesome suicide bombings of the 21st century, all had their genesis in the "Six Day War" of 1967.

In the summer of 1967 I went back to the job I had held for six years – athletic director at a camp on the shores of Lake Ontario. In my isolation at camp I only heard the major news from the east and the west. From the east came good news. My beloved Boston Red Sox were suddenly the "it" team in baseball when they ran off a ten-game winning streak and vaulted into first place in the American League. There were three other teams hot on their heels — Tigers, White Sox and Twins – but, still, to have the Red Sox in contention for the first time in eighteen years was a thrill. People in Boston were starting to fill Fenway Park and I wished I could be there. One day I saw a *Sports Illustrated* lying on the table in camp headquarters. Inside was an article on Carl Yazstremski. The picture showed *the man* taking an aggressive lead off first base and the headline read: "Yaz: Boston's Razmattazz." The story told of Yazstremski's key role in the rebirth of baseball in Boston and it was fun to read at a time when there wasn't much fun to be had.

The news that summer from the west – back home in Detroit – was not about the Tigers who were also contending in the American League. It was about something much more serious and gruesome. On the night of July 23rd one of the worst race riots in American history began when Detroit police began arresting patrons in an all-night bar (a "blind pig") on Twelfth Street in the inner city. They conducted the arrests in very brutal fashion, with much kicking of "black ass." That night and the next day people swarmed into the streets looting stores, burning buildings, and fighting policemen and firefighters who were trying to restore order. By the end of the second day the situation had escalated so much – whole blocks on fire, stores looted, dead bodies in the streets – that military force was needed. Jerome Cavanaugh, the Democratic mayor, was reluctant to turn to Governor George Romney, a Republican, to send in the National Guard. Romney, in turn, was slow to turn to the President, Lyndon Johnson, for federal troops because Romney planned to run against Johnson for the presidency in 1968. But, the violence became so severe that all political considerations had to be set aside and Johnson ordered the 101st Airborne Division – the same division Eisenhower had ordered into Little Rock ten years earlier – to move into Detroit with troops and tanks and put the city under martial law.

It took almost a week for the army to bring some level of calm to the streets. By then, entire city blocks were smoldering ruins, 41 people were dead, hundreds more were wounded, and the hate talk was well under way. When I came home from camp to my comfortable suburb a few weeks later I was appalled by the devastation in the downtown area and by the talk I was hearing all around me. One neighbor told me he had several rifles and pistols stashed under his bed and he was ready to do battle with the N—-s if they ever came out our way.

I had always naively thought racial tensions were a southern thing, but old-timers in Detroit told me there had been a race riot during the war (1943) that was almost as bad. A few years later, when we moved to Boston, I saw more racial hatred during the school busing controversies. The Detroit riots showed me – showed the entire country, really – that racism in the United States is a virulent force, *north and south*. Now, fifty years after that terrible riot we are still experiencing the racial divide that was revealed so clearly in 1967.

Ironically, one of the long-term consequences of the Detroit race riot was a steady migration of upwardly mobile African-American families out of the inner cities to the closest suburbs. In 1969, the first black student at Southfield High arrived. His name was Derrick Glass. I still remember him because he was a flamboyant personality who reveled in his status as the only black student. In the next several years, after I moved to Boston, many more black families moved into Southfield and today the school's student population is predominantly African-American.

As the summer of 1967 moved along, we began hearing about what was happening out in San Francisco. It was being called the "Summer of Love." Young people in their late teens and twenties spent their days hanging out in the Haight-Ashbury district playing music, smoking weed, and talking about peace, love and freedom. A song that became popular described it: "If you're going to San Francisco, be sure to wear some flowers in your hair; if you're going to San Francisco, you're going to find some gentle people there." We were witnessing the birth of the "counter-culture," a movement that embraced all the things the older generation hated: sloppy dress, drugs, loose sex, psychedelic music, antipathy toward work, disdain for rules and laws, and a visceral hatred for all things military, middle class and materialistic. For many years there had been a disconnect between the buttoned-down conservative "organization men" on one side and the bohemians or, later, the "beatniks" on the other. But the folks in the "summer of love" launched a new movement – the "hippies." They were going to bring rebellion against the establishment to a higher level and fuel events such as the Chicago riots at the Democratic Convention in 1968, the Woodstock concert in 1969, and the Kent State riots in 1970. In the process they ignited a conservative backlash that has swept Republican presidents into power in nine out of the last fourteen presidential elections.

When the fall of 1967 finally arrived with crisper temperatures and colorful trees, most of us were feeling a little beat up. Race riots and a frustrating war will do that to you. But, there was still good music. Besides the Beatles and the other Brit groups such as the Rolling Stones and the Dave Clark Five, there were light-hearted American groups such as the Turtles and the Monkees. There was a huge hit in the summer of '67 by a new singer named Bobbie Gentry called "Ode to Billy Joe" that had everyone wondering what Billy Joe and his girlfriend threw off the Tallahatchie Bridge.

There were funny TV shows, as well, such as "Laugh-In" and the campy "Batman." Almost everyone had a color TV by now and the television industry was starting to try to break new ground and become a more creative art form.

But still, every night there were the escalating troop commitments and the latest battles and atrocities in Vietnam, all brought right into our living rooms in full color. Racial tensions remained high. The hopes of the early sixties embodied in songs such as "We Shall Overcome" and in the young president, John F. Kennedy, all seemed to be as dead and gone as he was. Perhaps, thought some, JFK's younger brother, Bobby, could pick up the torch and lead us out of the wilderness of war and racism. Little did we know what lay ahead for him and for us.

But, as James Earl Jones says in the movie "Field of Dreams," "Always there was baseball." On October first, the last day of the season, with four teams still in contention – within a game of each other – the Red Sox won their final game and the other teams lost and won in the right algorithm, and Boston had its first American League pennant since 1946. It was the most exciting conclusion to a pennant race ever. The Sox became America's dream team; they had gone from last in '66 to first in '67. For a brief moment, at least, those of us who loved the Red Sox could put thoughts of war, race riots, and violent death aside and enjoy the moment. It almost didn't matter if the Red Sox won the World Series. After all, what team that year could beat the Cardinals who had Bob Gibson, he of the 100-mph fastball? Gibson won games 1,4 and 7 to give the Cards the series. But, it was fine. From that season on, Fenway Park, with its fabled green wall was the baseball Mecca of America.

One other song that was very popular in 1967 was the theme song for the "flower children." The Beatles' "All You Need Is Love" came out in July and it laid out a simple truth that the whole country – indeed the whole world – could take to heart. For me, it was an unattainable dream. In the midst of everything that was happening – the disgusting, interminable war, the riots, the tensions in the Middle East, and the tensions at home between hawks and doves, between parents and their children – I was confused and not at all as self-assured as I may have seemed to my students in class. I was acutely aware of how fast the world was changing, and that the pace of change had accelerated dramatically that year. I could not tell where my life was going. Would I get drafted? Would I continue to teach? Would I move back to Boston as I had always dreamed I would from the day my family left there? Would I get married? To whom?

As 1967 ended I was very apprehensive about what lay ahead, not just for me, but for the country. Nineteen sixty-seven had shown that we were in for a long, gruesome war in Vietnam, that racially fueled incidents would continue to happen, and that tensions between the generations would only get worse. The seeds of the terrible events of 1968 — the brutal Tet Offensive in Vietnam, the assassinations of Dr. Martin Luther King, Jr. by the racist James Earl Ray and the killing of Bobby Kennedy by Sirhan Sirhan who was angered by Kennedy's support for Israel, the riots at the Democratic Convention in Chicago – all were sown in 1967.

But, there was also a bright side. The Red Sox were going to be fun to watch; music and television would be more interesting. And, during the year I had started seeing a girl I really liked and would finally marry in 1970. For me, that was the most important thing that happened in the maelstrom of events that rocked 1967.

THE ENCOUNTER

TWO YEARS AFTER THE DETROIT RIOTS I INVITED
A MILITANT LEADER IN THE BLACK COMMUNITY
OF DETROIT TO VISIT MY CLASS. OUR SCHOOL
PRINCIPAL WOULDN'T ALLOW ME TO HAVE A
"DISRUPTIVE SPEAKER" DURING THE SCHOOL DAY,
SO MR. FRANK DITTO HAD TO COME AT NIGHT.
THIS IS MY ACCOUNT OF WHAT HAPPENED THAT
NIGHT IN 1969.

We sat waiting in our modern, well-equipped classroom. I was
the teacher, a twenty-five-year-old from a middle class family that
had always lived in the white suburbs. The other twenty people
were my students, boys and girls seventeen-years-old in a wealthy,
all-white, mostly Jewish suburb of Detroit. In a few minutes our
visitor would arrive and we were anxious to meet him and hear
his views. We were also rather nervous. We had seen this man on
the evening news and he looked rather formidable.

Heavy footsteps sounded in the hall and soon a stocky black
man with an "Afro" haircut and a full beard stood dominating
the doorway. He was wearing a khaki paramilitary uniform and

heavy boots. With him was a young man of eighteen similarly attired except for the addition of a black beret with a red star.

"You must be Mr. Ditto" I heard myself saying, "We're glad you could come. Welcome!"

"I had to be careful," he said, clomping into the room, "It's not safe out in the suburbs at night."

We all laughed. The inner city was no place to be at night, but surely our town . . .

The look Ditto gave us said he wasn't kidding. "More than once black people have been beaten, maimed and even killed in white suburbs. In a racist society like this black people have to stay where they have been put. If they venture beyond the line they get into trouble, and I don't need to tell you whose side the police would be on if there was a fight."

As I looked around the room I could see several of the students bridling at Ditto's remarks. I, too, had been caught a little off guard by his "strange" assertion. It was almost a matter of faith in white society that blacks were perpetrators of violence, that whites were risking their lives if they ventured into black neighborhoods. But, surely, no black man needed to be afraid to come here.

Ditto seemed to be reading our minds. "One of the myths of this racist society is that it is the black man who is violent. Ha! Every black man knows through experience that it is the *white* man who has proved again and again that *he* is the violent one. Your teachers probably never tell you about the lynchings that took place in this country around the turn of the century and the fact that there are still lynchings of black people today. The white press and the white government do a good job of covering it up, but in almost every city almost every day some black man, woman or child is either beaten or killed by a white. And many of the times that white man is a policeman!

"People sometimes ask me how I got started working for black rights and organizing people in the black community. Well, I came from Chicago over ten years ago. When I lived there I was a typical "Uncle Tom Nigger." You all know what an "Uncle Tom Nigger" is. That's a black man who has some crappy little job sweeping floors for some white man for the puny salary he gets. Then, when he goes home, he steps aside for white people and truly believes that the white government and the white police and all the white laws are doing the best that can be done for him.

"One day, though, as I was coming home from my job, I saw a group of brothers and sisters – only I didn't call them brothers and sisters then, just other 'Negroes' – picketing a movie theater. They were protesting the fact that the theater required black people to sit in a special black section. Even though I was an Uncle Tom, I believed that what these people were protesting against was wrong – that all people have a right to sit where they please in a public place. So, I began walking back and forth with them. Pretty soon someone handed me a sign. Suddenly I began to realize that I was feeling proud – proud that I was doing something for justice, proud that I was standing together with my own people, proud that I was black. Yes, black! Not brown, not a "Negro," but BLACK!

"Then the police came. They pulled up in a van with a blue light blinking on top and came out swaggering the way cops do and told us we were breaking the law, that we were committing vagrancy. One of the brothers answered that we were only assembling peacefully like the constitution says we can. After that bit of "insolence," the cops started grabbing everyone and saying we were all under arrest. Some of us started to resist; nobody wants to be thrown in jail, especially a black man because we had all heard what it was like – how the guards kicked you and forced you to live in filth. So, the police started using their clubs and pretty soon several of us were sitting in the van with bloody gashes on our heads. That day I vowed I would never again bow like a slave to white people, that I would stand tall and be proud of my race, and that I would do whatever I could to help my people fight against white oppression."

One girl in the group had heard enough. Her face was flushed as she said, "You make it sound as though all white people are out to get Negroes and that police are always looking for a chance to beat up Negroes. Even if that was once true, you have to admit that it isn't *that* bad any more."

Ditto gave a bemused smile. "You're right. It isn't that bad any more. . . . It's worse. In spite of everything you've heard about the Civil Rights Acts and all that crap, the persecution of black people in our society has *increased*. More black people than ever are rotting in prisons, many of them just waiting for their trials and their slim chance at justice. More black people than ever are beaten for little or no reason by police or by other whites while the police stand by and do nothing. That's why my organization carries on a constant police watch. We no longer count on the laws to protect us. Racism knows no laws. We have to watch the police ourselves. We have radios and we listen to police calls and send our men to wherever the police are going. We want some black person to be there to be able to give the black version of any incident that occurs, or to lend a hand to a brother being illegally treated by the police!"

The young man with Ditto was sitting quietly through all this, his eyes looking blankly ahead. His black beret brandishing its red star seemed to add a threatening overtone to all that Ditto was saying. Although Ditto was not a "Black Panther," he still presented as a militant black man who led a group of militant young men. The girl with the flushed face was flushed more than ever now and I sensed that Ditto was taking a quiet satisfaction in seeing her and the rest of us growing increasingly uncomfortable with what he was saying. I remembered Malcolm X's amusement in his autobiography at the way white people turn red when they are confronted. Many of us felt that some of Ditto's stories were exaggerated, but we were not sure how much. We were all very aware that he knew the black situation first-hand and that even if his accounts were only partly true, they made us ashamed of being white.

Then one of the boys in the class asked the inevitable question, "Well, what can *we* do about this? We have tried to do things to improve race relations, like the tutoring program we run for kids in the inner city on Saturday mornings. Is there anything else?"

"You have no place in the inner city tutoring black kids," he said. "Even if you do teach a few of them how to read – which I doubt – you do irreparable harm in the process. You simply enforce the image they have been brought up with that the only people who know anything or can do anything that requires brains are white. Leave the teaching and the day-care centers and all the other things like that up to black people. We take pride in developing our own community, in picking ourselves up. We don't need Whitey. You are only giving comfort to your own consciences by going down there to tutor.

"If you really want to do something to help cure this racist society you should do your work right here in the suburbs. The main thing you can do is help get rid of racism. You've got to talk to people out here and tell them that they are wrong when they assume black people are violent. Ask them who started the only two world wars that were ever fought; read about the lynchings; read what Eldridge Cleaver, Malcolm X, and some of the other brothers and sisters have to say. Most important, every time you hear a racist statement or meet someone who is a racist, you must confront that racism and do what you can to stamp it out.

"Of course, before you can do that you have to stamp out the racism in yourselves. I'll bet a lot of you, when you are down there in the inner city tutoring on Saturday mornings, are thinking to yourselves — hopefully subconsciously — 'I'm gonna teach these dumb little black kids how to read.'"

"You mean we should give up our tutoring program?" the boy asked.

"Yes. The black community don't need no white missionaries."

Then another boy in the room blurted out, "How come you wear military uniforms? Couldn't you do your work for the black community without them? Don't you think it gives your group a bad image – especially the red star which some people might take to mean your group is communist?"

"The uniforms help our group achieve solidarity," Ditto responded. "They are a symbol of unity and pride. The people associated with us take pride in what they are doing. In fact, giving people pride is one of our biggest accomplishments. As far as the star is concerned, if white people want to associate communism with that, that's their problem. Maybe we *are* communists. Black people in this society certainly are not capitalists!"

By this point, as I looked about the room, I could see that several of the students were either extremely uncomfortable or very angry. The girl with the flushed face had gone. Yet, a couple of students, in particular one boy with long, straggly blond hair and metal-rimmed glasses, were smiling in appreciation at nearly everything Ditto said.

"Well," Ditto concluded, "I hope I have given you folks something to think about." He glanced at his silent partner and they started toward the door. A few students went up to him to shake his hand or ask him one last question. The boy with the long blond hair enthusiastically thanked him for coming and shook hands with him in the fashion of black solidarity: right hands straight up, thumbs interlocked, fingers grasping the other's wrist.

And then he was gone. As the students put their coats on to leave and stood in small groups talking with each other and with me, I could see that our speaker had made a strong impression. Some of the students felt hostile to the man. They had thought they were in the vanguard of the civil rights movement and now he was telling them that there *was* no civil rights movement. Instead, there was a black power movement that was going to challenge the degraded image black people had of themselves because of the attitudes of white racists and white "liberals."

As I thought about it and talked with the students I realized that Frank Ditto was right. Even the so-called enlightened people were all racist. We all had the attitude that we were going to "uplift the backward peoples." As Ditto said, we were just like missionaries. Now we were told to eradicate racism in ourselves and in our own neighborhoods – a much more difficult task.

When the last student had left the room I stood there for a moment contemplating what had happened that night. There might be some repercussions, I thought. Irate parents might call the principal and complain that their kids had been exposed to a violent black man. (None did.) Yet, no matter what repercussions of that sort developed, I felt that the whole evening had been a profitable learning experience for everyone. Ditto had given us a quick glimpse of what it is like to be black. More important, he had held a mirror before us and invited us to examine ourselves – our own attitudes and motives. The end result of Ditto's visit, I concluded, was not a confrontation with a black man, but a confrontation with ourselves.

* We *did* continue the tutoring program for the remainder of that school year, but after that we ended it and focused on bringing black artists and black history events to our school.

Billy G., Booker T, and Me

I WOULD NEVER HAVE EVEN LIKED AMERICAN
HISTORY IF I HADN'T MET THESE GUYS!

In 1860, William Lloyd Garrison was in his thirtieth year of publishing his anti-slavery newspaper, *The Liberator*, and speaking to scorning crowds about the horrors of slavery and the need to abolish it immediately. In *1960,* I was in my junior year of high school and very content to be a disinterested high school kid who only learned American History because he had to. Suddenly, in January of that year, I met William Lloyd Garrison in a mental time warp created by the story of how he was nearly lynched by a mob in Boston. I was able to put myself in Garrison's place and evaluate whether I would be able to act as principled and as bravely as he did. His life and his feelings became so familiar to me that I began to see him as a friend. As a sign of our friendship I began jokingly to refer to him as "Billy G." even though I knew no one in his own time would have called him that.

I read several biographies of Garrison, including the account of his life written by his children. Enthralled by the stories of how he became aware of the plight of the slaves in the South and vowed to fight for their freedom until he died or freedom came, I used him as an entry into the whole story of how the disputes over slavery led to the Civil War and to the emancipation of the slaves.

After "Billy G." sparked my interest in biography, I went on to read *Up From Slavery*, the autobiography of Booker T. Washington. Washington's story of his quest for an education after freedom came inspired me. Even more inspiring was his creation of his own school, Tuskegee Institute, which he and his students constructed brick-by-brick. By 1900, he was the spokesperson for millions of African-Americans across the country. Many people, even in his own day, criticized his willingness to forgive white people for slavery and to accept the segregation laws. But I understood Booker T. Washington's belief that his people needed to establish a strong economic and social base on which they could build their futures, and I sympathized with him as he suffered mounting criticism from people, black and white, who disliked his accommodating attitude. It was so easy to put myself in his place and to identify with his struggles that I began to see him as a friend, as well. I called him "Booker T."

Billy G. and Booker T. became my portals into the entire study of American History. Their stories demonstrated that history is the story of real people – people we can get to know, understand, and evaluate if we appreciate their humanity. As I went on to study history in college and became a history teacher in several high schools, it became my passion to make the humanity of the people we study in history palpable to myself and to my students.

In the last ten years of my teaching career, I began writing books about people I had met in my studies. My purpose was to help my students, and anyone outside my classroom who chose to read my books, to enter into a love for American History the same way I had – through coming to know and appreciate the human beings whose stories are the fabric of our nation's story.

Naturally, my first book was about William Lloyd Garrison. I realized partway into the project that Garrison's crusade ended in success only because of the skills of Abraham Lincoln, a consummate politician who, for many years, had no use for disruptive radicals such as Garrison. Thus, I decided to analyze how Lincoln came to join Garrison in the anti-slavery cause. I ended up writing a dual biography: *The Agitator and the Politician; William Lloyd Garrison, Abraham Lincoln and the Emancipation of the Slaves.*

My second book delved into the history of the twentieth century through a study of the lives and leadership styles of two major leaders: Douglas MacArthur and Dwight D. Eisenhower. *Leaders in Dangerous Times* gives its readers the history of the two world wars, the Cold War, the Korean War and the 1950s through the stories of two very interesting, yet very dissimilar men.

My most recent book has the title *American History – It's More Than the Crap You Learned in High School.* In this latest attempt to help people appreciate American History I show how some people in our nation's story have been great role models we can emulate, and others have led lives that are cautionary tales. Some of our presidents have shown leadership skills from which all of us who aspire to be leaders can profit. I believe this book proves that American History is full of stories of interesting people and interesting events from which we can learn many worthwhile lessons.

My sixteen-year-old self in 1960 could never have imagined liking American History so much that I would teach it for fifty years and write books about it. It all happened because I found two friends: "Billy G." and "Booker T."

EXPERTS DISCUSS HOW TO MAKE A GREAT SPEECH

THESE GREAT ORATORS ARE NO LONGER WITH US. BUT WE CAN IMAGINE THEY ARE AND LEARN FROM THEM.

If you want to learn how to make a great speech you should follow the advice of people who have delivered the most memorable speeches in American history. Those people spoke words so powerful that they changed the course of events by giving people the courage and motivation they needed to accomplish remarkable things. It can be very instructive to examine the stylistic and verbal elements that went into reaching people at intellectual and emotional levels and inspiring them.

To help us do this, I have imagined a gathering of five men who delivered speeches that became famous and asked them what they did to make an impact on their audiences. Our gathering includes Patrick Henry, well known for his "Give me liberty or give me death!" speech to the Virginia Assembly on March

23, 1775; Abraham Lincoln, whose most famous speech, the Gettysburg Address, inspired the country in 1863 to continue supporting the Civil War; William Jennings Bryan whose "Cross of Gold" speech rocked the Democratic Convention on July 9, 1896; Franklin Roosevelt, who rallied the depression-stricken nation with his inaugural address on March 4, 1933; and who inspired the country again with his address to congress after the Pearl Harbor attack in 1941; and Martin Luther King, Jr., who inspired a quarter of a million marchers with his "I Have a Dream!" speech on August 28, 1963. These men have all passed away, so they are free of any fears that they might appear to be immodest if they tout their own excellence.

Their conversation might go like this:

Lincoln: I think we would all agree it is impossible to give a great speech if you don't have anything meaningful to say. Your speech must have a clear purpose, a theme. If it doesn't, all the rhetorical gimmicks in the world won't save it. Before you begin to write your speech, decide on your theme. I decided that the purpose of my address at Gettysburg was to convince people that the thousands of men who had died there, many of whom were close relatives of the people who would be gathered to hear me, had died for a noble and important cause. That cause was to give the nation a "new birth of freedom," a very noble cause indeed! What was the purpose – the theme – of each of your addresses, gentlemen?

Henry: My theme was America's need – or even divine responsibility – to take a stand for freedom and to be ready to fight and die for it if necessary.

Bryan: I was focused on the inequalities in the economy and my solution to that problem, which was to expand the amount of money available to the people by adding silver to the nation's coinage.

Roosevelt: My theme in my first inaugural address was that the people, and their government, had to banish paralyzing fear and move forward with programs that would battle the depression as if it were an enemy in time of war. The theme in the Pearl Harbor address was to alert the people to the dangers that confronted us and to assure them that we would fight back hard and win through to victory. It was very important, in each of those speeches, to show the people that their leader was not the least bit afraid.

Dr. King: My goal, after one hundred years of segregation and degradation, was to inspire the Negro people to fight for their God-given rights and to offer them a vision of the better life that awaited them if they worked together with energy and unity.

Bryan: Very good! We all had significant goals to accomplish. Now let's discuss what we did in those speeches to achieve our goals.

Lincoln: I think one of the first rules of a great speech is that it is no longer than it needs to be. At the dedication of the Gettysburg Cemetery, Edward Everett spoke at great length – over two hours — about the importance of the battle that had been fought there. Then I stood to "make a few remarks." A few days later I received a very gracious letter from Mr. Everett in which he said, "I should be glad if I could flatter myself that I came as near to the central idea of the occasion in two hours as you did in two minutes." Brevity, achieved without sacrificing the soul of the speech, is very difficult. It requires many hours of thought and the selection of just the right words and phrases. I once wrote a very long letter to a friend and said at the end of it – "Please excuse the length of this letter; I didn't have time to write a short one." By the way, I did not scribble the Gettysburg Address on the back of an envelope as the myth would have it. I spent many hours writing, re-writing and revising my talk to hone it down to exactly what I thought would reach my audience effectively.

Roosevelt: I completely agree with being concise, and I would emphasize your comment that doing that often requires choosing exactly the right words. Mark Twain once said, "The difference between the right word and the almost right word is really a large matter; it is the difference between the lightning and the lightning bug." Just before I gave my Pearl Harbor speech I crossed out the word "history" in the first sentence and substituted "infamy." That made all the difference. No one would have remembered "a date which will live in history." Everyone remembers "a date which will live in *infamy.*"

Dr. King: You are both absolutely right. Finding a word or a phrase that captures everyone's imagination and will be easily remembered will give a speech great impact. It is especially effective if you can find a graceful way of repeating the phrase several times with a rhythm or cadence. Who can forget my "I have a Dream" speech? That phrase appeared on bumper stickers and was repeated in various settings countless times. It spoke to the deepest aspirations of the African-American community.

Lincoln: That's right, Martin. I believe I achieved the same thing with my conclusion at Gettysburg: ". . . that government, of the people, by the people, and for the people, shall not perish from the earth." Everyone remembers those words, and they served as an inspiration to the people across the North who needed an important reason for all the sacrifices they were making in the Civil War.

By the way, you notice that my opponent in the war, Mr. Jefferson Davis, never made *any* memorable speeches. That's why he was a freakin' LOSER! Oh, pardon me, gentlemen. I've been listening to the new President, Mr. Trump, a little too much!

Bryan, wincing: Back to the topic. I think it's crucial that your memorable word or phrase has a *visual* image that captures people's attention and dramatically illustrates your point. Everyone remembered my metaphor in the speech I gave to the convention in 1896. Speaking to the rich men of the nation who were only there in people's imaginations I shouted, "You shall not press down upon the brow of labor this crown of thorns; you shall not crucify mankind upon a *cross of gold*!" Who will ever forget my "Cross of Gold Speech?"

Dr. King: That's very true, Mr. Bryan. Visual metaphors greatly help to add impact to a speech and I used them as often as I could. I was constantly referring to "valleys of despair," "mountain tops of exhilaration," "deserts of poverty," and "oases of hope."

Henry: I totally agree with everything that has been said about the importance of choosing the right word or phrase and using vivid metaphors and colorful imagery. But I would add that it is important to organize your speech so that each point proceeds logically from the points made before. Do not jerk your audience this way and that. Also, build your speech gradually to a dramatic and powerful conclusion. If I had said, "I know not what course others may take, but as for me, give me liberty or give me death" at the beginning of my speech rather than at the end, no one would have remembered it.

Roosevelt: So, you think I made a mistake when I said at the start of my inauguration speech, "So, first of all, let me assert my firm belief that *the only thing we have to fear is fear itself*!"?

Henry: No, not at all. Calm down, Franklin. In your situation the people in the country were in a panic about the ever-worsening depression. You had to reassure them *right away*, so it was good to put that powerful line right at the beginning. But, generally it is better to have your most powerful image at the end. By the way, you are often misquoted. People think you said, "We have *nothing* to fear but fear itself." That would have been lame and not memorable.

Roosevelt: Right! That sounds like that loser Hoover. Oops, I, too, have listened too much to Mr. Trump! But recalling Hoover, we haven't spoken at all about the delivery of the speech. A beautifully written speech with great visual images and metaphors and abounding in powerful repetition of important words and phrases falls flat as a flounder if it is delivered in a bland way. Many speakers talk flat with no inflection in their voice, or they talk way too fast, hurrying through their words as if they are ashamed of them and want to get the whole thing over with. Instead, you should show confidence in your ideas and pride in each word you have chosen. Speak slowly, emphasizing the important words, so that your audience gets the full impact of what you have so diligently planned to say to them.

Bryan: *So right*!! And – I would add – SPEAK IN A LOUD AND POWERFUL VOICE. LET EVERYONE HEAR YOU AND FEEL THAT YOU ARE CONFIDENT IN WHAT YOU ARE SAYING!!

Dr. King: Got it, Bill. But don't try to speak so loudly you end up screeching like a hyena.

Roosevelt: Exactly right, Dr. King. As I spoke I always tried to imagine that I was speaking personally with each man and woman in the audience – having a fireside chat, if you will. The personal touch makes all the other devices we have discussed even more effective.

Dr. King: Well, gentlemen, I think we are almost finished, but before we go silent, I feel I must say something that has been troubling me during our entire conversation. All five of us are men. Surely many women have delivered important speeches and could offer great advice on how to reach an audience.

Roosevelt: Right you are, Martin! I must say that my wife, Eleanor, was more than a little annoyed when she heard there would be no women here today. She herself gave some memorable speeches to the troops overseas during the war, and on human rights at the United Nations.

Bryan: Yes! And, in my day there was Mary Elizabeth Lease, the fiery populist from Kansas. When we speak of memorable images and phrases, how about her takeoff on Mr. Lincoln's "of the people" line: "Our government is a government of Wall Street, by Wall Street, and for Wall Street." And her famous, "Farmers should raise less corn and more hell!" Those images, I must say, were surely as evocative as my "cross of gold."

Dr. King: Of course, for many years it was considered inappropriate for women to speak in public. Many women's rights speakers such as Susan B. Anthony, and abolitionists such as the Grimke sisters suffered garbage and rotten eggs being thrown at them when they tried to address audiences. Now that it is finally considered acceptable for women to speak in public, I'm sure we will see many more women give speeches that are truly memorable.

Henry: You are surely right, Dr. King. In my day Abigail Adams could have delivered speeches fully as powerfully as her cranky husband. When she wrote to him at the Continental Congress prodding him to "remember the ladies," she must have felt truly annoyed that she could not be at the great meetings to speak for *herself*!

Lincoln (chuckling): My wife, Mary, delivered some great speeches to me about my clothes, my table manners, my roughhousing with the boys, and countless other annoyances. It's unfortunate those addresses were not recorded; they would have been great examples of some of the principles we have discussed – imagery, metaphors, repetition, peaking at the conclusion!

Roosevelt: Seriously, though, I think the next gathering of people who gave great speeches will be almost all women. The future belongs to the women. Just look at how many are getting into politics these days, and the law schools have a large majority of women. That is probably a good – I mean *great* – thing. Men have been in charge for seven thousand years and look where we are now.

Henry: Well, I hate to sound like a psychiatrist, but I see our time is up. We need to walk off, or (nodding toward Roosevelt) wheel off into the mists of the past.

LAST NAME FIRST, PLEASE

WHERE HAVE ALL THE FAMILY NAMES GONE?

I'm not sure exactly when it happened, but sometime in the last two decades it seems that everyone has gotten to know each other well enough that we are *all* on a "first name basis." No one uses last names anymore; there seems to be no such thing as a surname or a family name. In the film *You've got mail*, Meg Ryan gets exasperated with Joe Fox (Tom Hanks) who has just told her to "call me Joe." "Joe," she says with annoyance, "'Just call me Joe,' as if you were one of those twenty-two-year-old girls with no last name. 'Hi, I'm Kimberly.' 'Hi, I'm Janice.' What's *wrong* with them? Don't they know you're supposed to have a last name? It's like they're a whole generation of cocktail waitresses." Right, Meg! And that film was made in 1998. It's gotten worse since then.

A student in one of my classes apparently knew Abe Lincoln personally because she was on a first name basis with him and referred to him as "Abraham" throughout her research paper. For all my students that year the President was "Barack" and, presumably now is "Donald" . . . or "The Donald."

Recently a twenty-something woman I was working with at a book signing gave me an alphabetical list of the people signed up for the event. I looked to see if my friends the Cooks were on the paper and had pretty much concluded they were *not* there when I noticed that Amy Cook was listed at the very top of the list —as an "A", of course — and Doug Cook was separated from his wife down among the "D's!" The woman had made up the alphabetized list by the people's *first* names!

Now I observe that every alphabetized list I see is by the people's first names. The ultimate example of this is the latest edition of the textbook we used in my Advanced Placement American History course. I got a sample copy and was looking through it to see what treatment the authors gave to my hero, William Lloyd Garrison. In the "G" section of the index I couldn't find him and I started to feel annoyed. Then, on a hunch, I checked into the "W's" and there he was, under "William." Then I was even more annoyed. The entire index used first names – Lincoln was in the "A's" for Abraham, Grant was in the "U's" for Ulysses, and so on.

This first name thing is totally pervasive. One day I had my students arranged in groups and I instructed the leaders of the groups to list the members of their groups by *last* names because we had a number of duplicate first names in the class – three Kaitlyns, for example. In every group I overheard the leaders asking the others in their little circle what their last names were. They had no idea!

This all represents a complete reversal of the way it was in the "olden days." When I was in high school in the sixties everyone used *nothing but* last names to refer to each other. I was always "MacDougall" or "Mac." When I went to college I was amazed, and a bit gratified, when all the professors referred to me as *Mr.* MacDougall. Today the professors would probably call me "Bobby!" Puleeze!! My uncles called me "Bobby" when I was six, but no one has since then.

My children, in their thirties, scoff at me when I rant about this: "Get over it, Dad! It's not a big deal." I suppose they're right, it isn't . . . EXCEPT if it is a symptom of a deeper issue. Could it be that young people today have given up on their last names because they have given up on their family identity? With the divorce rate as high as it is, and with the number of families with multiple fathers growing, maybe people don't feel connected to their family name. One of my students had three brothers and two sisters and every one of them had a different father. In that kind of chaotic situation why would you NOT use only first names? Or, to put it another way, which family name would you use?

So, it is more than just confusing (which "David" did you mean?), disrespectful (President Abraham!) and annoying (alphabetizing by first name). It is also rather sad.

UNCLE SAM VERSUS APOLLO

WHEN UNCLE SAM TAKES ON THE GREEK GOD OF THE SUN, WHO WINS?

First of all, none of us – I hope – truly believes that "daylight saving time" really extends the amount of daylight we enjoy. The earth will take the exact same amount of time to rotate on its axis causing the sun to appear to move across the sky for a certain duration of time regardless of how we mere humans measure it. The sun will rise at exactly the same time it has always risen on March twelfth whether we call it 6:03 or 7:03 and it will set at the same time it always has on that date whether we call it 5:46 or 6:46. As the Greeks saw it, Apollo drives his blazing chariot across the sky in his own time. So, how did the absurd notion come about that we could actually save ourselves an hour of daylight by setting our clocks ahead?

In the United States the absurdity began during the First World War when Congress bought the notion that we could boost production of agricultural and factory goods by moving our clocks ahead by an hour, thus giving farmers and factory workers an hour more daylight time to complete their work. Say what? No one asked the cows about this, and the farmers were the first to complain about its absurdity. As for factory workers who were working twelve-hour days to produce the weaponry and vehicles needed to defeat the Kaiser, they were ambivalent about whether it was dark when they went to work or dark when they went home in the summer, and it was dark during both trips in the winter. As for saving coal needed to provide lighting, the lights had to be on for twelve hours whether those hours were called morning or evening. A propaganda poster of the time showed Uncle Sam just waking up with the sun already risen. The caption read: "Your enemies are already awake and at work! When will you get going?" I think the whole idea was just another way – along with victory gardens and saving cork and coffee grounds – to get non-combatant Americans to *think* they were contributing to the war effort.

The foolish idea of saving daylight was abandoned after that war, but it came back again during World War II (along with victory gardens and saving cork). It has bedeviled us ever since. At various times Congress has changed the starting and ending dates of "daylight savings," bringing it from April to October to its present March to November. States are free to opt out of the nonsense and remain on standard time and two of them actually do: Arizona and Hawaii. The way it stands now a plane flying in summer could get from Amarillo, Texas to Tucson, Arizona in no time – literally.

Those of us who are "morning people" enjoy the way we gradually get more daylight for morning activities as we go through February. Then March 12th comes and the federal government orders us back into the darkness. If you are a night owl who never knew there was a six o'clock *in the morning*, then I guess DST (daylight saving time) is one of the best things the United States Government ever dreamed up. I think it is an abomination, right up there with "Form 1040" and traffic rotaries.

LIBERAL LITMUS TEST

WOULD YOU CALL YOURSELF A LIBERAL OR A CONSERVATIVE? CONSIDER YOUR ANSWERS TO MY TEN QUESTIONS BEFORE YOU ANSWER.

At the risk of seeming simplistic, I would like to make ten "liberal" statements and pose ten questions based on the way traditional "liberalism" has been defined in American history. If you can truthfully answer "yes" to all of them then you are, indeed, a true American political "liberal." If you answer "no" to more than five of them then you are leaning toward the right – the conservative side of the spectrum. I will reveal how I would answer the ten questions at the end. Here we go:

1. A speaker I heard once told a story about his grandfather who would always say, when pie was being served, "Cut me a 'liberal' slice!" One of the children at the table asked, "What do you mean by that, Grandpa? He replied, "'Liberal' means 'generous.'" In politics, a liberal is a generous person. He is generous with his money: willing to pay high taxes to enable the government to

help the people in our society who are less fortunate. He is generous in spirit: accepting and welcoming all people, regardless of their color, their faith, their gender, their age, or their sexual orientation.

Question 1: Do you agree with grandpa's definition of a "liberal?"

2. Franklin Roosevelt's "New Deal" with its government programs such as Civilian Conservation Corps (C.C.C.) and Works Progress Administration (W.P.A.) was designed to "put people to work". It was the ultimate expression of "liberalism" and saved the country from complete disaster during the "Great Depression."

Question 2: Do you agree with this assessment of F.D.R. and his presidency?

3. The American economy has resulted in fifty percent of the wealth being controlled by one percent of the population. As William Jennings Bryan said in his great "Cross of Gold" speech, the theory that if you make the rich richer the wealth will filter down to those on the bottom is false. The way to reduce income inequality is to make sure that the lower classes have money and that money will eventually work its way to the top.

Question 3: Do you agree that "trickle-down economics" is a fantasy concocted by the wealthy to justify cutting their taxes and do you believe that redistribution of wealth through raising taxes and creating government aid programs for the poor people in society is the proper course?

4. The United States has a second-rate health care system. To improve it, the government should fulfill the dreams of F.D.R., Harry Truman, L.B.J., Hillary Clinton and Barack Obama and

institute a federal "single payer" system in which everyone's health care is covered by the government.

Question 4: Do you agree with this statement about American health care?

5. For three centuries the treatment of African-Americans in this country has been a disgrace. The civil rights acts of the 1960s were steps in the right direction, but much more needs to be done if this country is going to make it true that "black lives matter."

Question 5: Do you agree that this country's treatment of African-Americans has been and continues to be a disgrace? Do you support vigorous enforcement of the anti-discrimination laws and, if needed, the passage of additional legislation? Do you support the use of the slogan "Black Lives Matter?"

6. The new frontier in the struggle for civil rights is the protection of the rights of LGBTQ people in our society. More legislation needs to be created to make sure that those people have all the protections they are entitled to.

Question 6: Do you agree that new laws are required to advance the rights of LGBTQ people in American society? Do you support same sex marriage?

7. Historically, American capitalists have been careless, or even rampantly disdainful, of the environment. Global warming is a reality that needs to be dealt with. Stricter laws and regulations need to be enacted to protect the air and the water that are so much endangered by population growth and unfettered expansion of cities, suburbs and industrial plants.

Question 7: Do you agree that new environmental regulations and a strengthening of the E.P.A. are necessary for the long-term health and wellbeing of our society?

8. The 1973 Supreme Court ruling in *Roe v Wade* was an enormous advancement for the right to privacy and the right of women to have control over their reproductive health. Since then, the efforts of many states to restrict the right to choose have gone from annoying to disgraceful. *Roe v Wade* should be upheld, and the states should stop interfering with the fundamental right so clearly established in that landmark ruling.

Question 8: Do you agree with the ruling of the 1973 Supreme Court that there is "an implied right to privacy" in the United States Constitution that precludes any power of the states to interfere with a woman's right to choose to have an abortion?

9. Ours is a nation of immigrants. Every one of us is a descendant of immigrants. We should open the gates to immigration as wide as possible within acceptable limits of security. Cities that have designated themselves as "sanctuary cities" are properly protecting the rights of people who come into contact with the local law enforcement agencies within their borders.

Question 9: Do you agree that immigration restrictions should be as limited as possible and that the concept of "sanctuary cities" should be supported by the people and accepted by federal authorities?

10. In the decades since the Second World War the United States has been the strongest military power on earth. We have met challenges by the Soviet Union and China in the Cold War, but

we have unwisely attempted to interject ourselves into regions where we should have kept out: Southeast Asia and the Middle East.

Question 10: Should the defense budget be as limited as possible and U.S. intervention in global regions be restricted to only those areas that are truly vital to national security?

My Views:

I surprised myself as I wrote this because I found it fairly easy to express the liberal point of view in almost every case since they represented some of my basic thoughts. However, I could never be classified as a "liberal" because I have serious issues with four of the statements (3,8,9, and 10) and I don't fully agree with any of them without at least a few reservations.

On the abortion issue (#8), I totally disagree with the statement; I can only reproduce it above because I've heard it shrieked by multiple "pro-choice" fanatics. I believe another life is involved in a pregnancy – I find it very hard to see how anyone who has had her or his own baby can fail to understand that – and that that incipient life is worthy of protection by the government. *Roe v Wade* cites the 14th Amendment as one of the sources of the *implied* right to privacy, but that same amendment requires the states to guarantee that no person shall be deprived of *life* without "due process of law." If there is a choice to be made between privacy and life, I choose life.

On economic matters (number 3), the William Jennings Bryan concept works better for me than the "trickle down" theory, but only because "trickle down" seems to have failed the two times it has been tried in recent decades (the 1986 tax cuts and the 2001 tax cuts), and because I hate to see poor and exploited people ignored on the hope, probably misplaced, that the wealthy people will some day "distribute" their fortunes. On the other hand, when I visit the mansions in Newport and other such places, I think of how many people were put to work doing the construction of all those beautiful buildings. None of those jobs would have existed if Vanderbilt and the others hadn't had the money to hire all the contractors and workers that it took.

The tax reform act passed by the Republican-controlled Congress and signed by President Trump is once again premised on "trickle-down economics." If it works, if many new, good-paying jobs appear and the welfare rolls shrink, then I might conclude that the liberal concept of federal aid to the lower classes is a lot of sappy, bleeding heart nonsense that should only be used during dire emergencies such as a huge depression.

The last two statements which deal with the security of the country also gave me pause. I do not completely agree with them, and I do think that some liberals live in a fantasyland in which all military action is wrong and every restriction on immigration smells like fascism. During the Vietnam Era I saw medal-bedecked generals talk about how we could win in Vietnam if we "killed enough Cong," and now I know that military men cannot always be relied upon to give an objective evaluation of how successful we can be going into regions we know nothing about, and killing all the "bad guys" we believe are going to hurt us. But, as a student of history, I also know that wars are best avoided by making it very clear to potential enemies that annihilation awaits them if they "mess with us," and by having a strong military that supports that understanding. Appeasement – or any kind of wishful thinking that the people who want to do our country harm are going to cooperate and be nice – has never worked in the past, and we shouldn't take any chances with the idea that it will work in the future.

As for immigrants, I do agree with liberals that we should be as open to newcomers as possible; we should live up to the Emma Lazarus poem on the Statue of Liberty: "Give me your tired, your poor, your huddled masses yearning to breathe free, the wretched refuse of your teeming shore. Send these, the homeless, tempest-tossed to me. I lift my lamp beside the golden door." We should "liberalize" our immigration legislation to allow for refugees from oppression to come into our country in large numbers. Yet, I do think immigrants need to obey the laws like everyone else and those who have violated the immigration laws should be sent back to their homelands.

I think "sanctuary cities" are unconstitutional and I am surprised they haven't been forced by the federal courts to change their policies. The United States Constitution clearly states: "This Constitution, and the laws of the United States which shall be made in pursuance thereof . . . shall be the supreme law of the land; and the judges in every state shall be bound thereby . . . " If a person who has committed a crime is stopped by local law enforcement authorities — even for just a traffic violation – the officer involved always checks for other violations for which the detained person may be responsible. It would seem totally legal and appropriate that a detained person who is wanted for a crime, even one of illegal immigration, should be turned over to the proper authorities.

All the issues I have discussed here are subject to constant discussion and debate. I think it is clear that except possibly for the abortion issue, I might be amenable to a change in my opinion – perhaps even a drastic one, if someone with an opposing view could persuade me that his or her view was more logical or "righteous!" The give-and-take of concepts and ideas is vital in a free society. That is why I am more than a little annoyed, sometimes, by phrases such as "safe spaces," "hate speech," "micro-aggressions," "politically correct," and more. The word "snowflake" has most commonly been used referring to liberals, but I think such people exist on both ends of the spectrum. If you are going to melt or be so upset you simply cannot go on if you are exposed to views that are different from your own, and you want all such talk silenced or "thrown off campus," or even made illegal, then you are truly to be pitied. Free and energetic discussion of all points of view should be encouraged and you should be eager to defend your own views and to listen to the views of others. Lately, we seem to be forgetting what always was a guiding principle on college campuses and in political dialog: "I do not agree with what you say, but I will defend to the death your right to say it."

Some of the best times I ever had at college were at the "point-counterpoint" presentations that were held in the 1960s at the University of Michigan. At those events, conservatives such as William F. Buckley would debate head-to-head with liberals such as Gore Vidal. Each man would say things that outraged the other side, but the other side's job was to formulate and pronounce rebuttals, not riot in the streets and try to get the offending speaker thrown off campus!

We need to get back to civil discussions of ideas, to debates with no holds barred, and then to following the debates with convivial celebrations of the fact that we are free people in a free society who have the privilege to speak our minds: think President Ronald Reagan and House Speaker Tip O'Neil toasting each other at a party after a day in which each one lambasted the *policies* of the other in strong language! Can we do that?

WEST POINT

ALL AMERICANS, LIBERALS AND CONSERVATIVES, CAN LOVE THIS PLACE.

April 26, 2018

I have just returned from the annual trip my brother and I take to West Point. We tour the campus, watch a few athletic events, and absorb the beauty of the Hudson Valley. It always reassures us that the future of our country is in good hands when we watch the industrious and dedicated cadets at the premier military academy in the United States compete in sports, march in military formation, and stride briskly across campus on their way to classes. West Point is the only place I've ever been where a young man or woman comes toward me on the sidewalk and says, without a trace of irony or condescension, "Good morning, sir!"

The history of the academy is a storied one. Many of America's most famous leaders went through the famous "beast barracks" hazing as Plebes, and then put in their four difficult years of rigorous classes and torturous training. At the end, they marched in formation the day before graduation and tossed their hats in the air on graduation day when they received their commissions. The storied list includes:

Robert E. Lee who placed first in his class, served with distinction in the Mexican War, but unfortunately took his talents south during the Civil War.

Jefferson Davis who, along with Lee, used his skills to break apart his country by attempting to preserve slavery.

Ulysses S. Grant who placed in the middle of his class but, in the Civil War, forced Davis to flee for his life from Richmond and took Robert E. Lee's surrender at Appomattox.

John J. Pershing, who led American forces to victory in World War I.

Douglas MacArthur, who was a ranking and much-decorated officer in World War I, led American forces to victory over Japan in the Pacific in World War II, led U.N. forces in Korea, and governed post-war Japan with skill and compassion.

Dwight David Eisenhower, who led Allied forces in Europe in World War II, served as Supreme Commander of the N.A.T.O. Alliance, and served two terms as President of the United States, presiding over a decade of peace and prosperity.

George C. Marshall, who was Army Chief of Staff in World War II, and later Secretary of State and Secretary of Defense.

Omar Bradley, who was commander of American forces in World War II and later served as chairman of the Joint Chiefs of Staff.

George Patton, who served as a tank commander in World War I, and served as commander of the American Third Army in Europe in World War II.

William Westmoreland, who served as commander of American forces in Vietnam.

This list is really just a start; there are hundreds of other West Point graduates who made major contributions to our nation.

That list would include General Norman Schwarzkopf, commander of U.S. and coalition forces in the 1991 Gulf War. It surprises many people to hear that Edgar Alan Poe attended West Point; it does not surprise them to hear that he dropped out.

What other college in the country has produced such a distinguished list of alumni? Certainly no other institution can claim as many graduates who have dedicated their lives to the service of their country rather than to making large salaries! The motto of the academy, "Duty, Honor, Country," is etched on stone in several places around the campus. It is no mere collection of words; it is the code by which every cadet lives and breathes.

If a person wishes to capture the full spirit of the West Point Military Academy, he or she should listen to the farewell address delivered by Douglas MacArthur to the cadets assembled in the dining hall in 1962. MacArthur had graduated from West Point in 1903, he had served with great distinction in the Philippines, Mexico and in France during World War I; he had served as superintendent of West Point in the early 1920s. In the 1930s, he was Army Chief of Staff in Washington. In World War II he led American forces in the Pacific and followed that by serving as military commander of Japan for five years. In that capacity, he led the rebuilding of the nation he had defeated, wrote a new constitution for Japan, and inspired a devotion among the Japanese people that continues to this day. Finally, he led American and United Nations forces against the communist invaders from North Korea for a year before his removal by President Truman.

Now, in the twilight of his life, the old general spoke to the young cadets. Many of them, although they did not know it yet, were about to serve their country in Vietnam. MacArthur extolled the values they held and the commitments they had made while at the academy. Those values were so well expressed in the motto, "Duty, Honor, Country," which he employed as his theme.

He described in moving detail how those values had inspired his own life. By the time he was finished, there was not a dry eye in the room. MacArthur had a gift for colorful speech and a flair for the dramatic; this was one instance in which he used both to powerful effect . . . because he was so genuine.

The speech can be found on YouTube and it is worth taking the time to listen.

We call West Point — and Annapolis, the Air Force Academy, and others – the "service academies." It is important that we appreciate the full meaning of the word "service." The men and women who attend those great institutions are not just entering the "service" (which many people use as a synonym for the military). They are dedicating their lives to serving others, to serving their country. Many people volunteer their service on occasion. They serve meals at soup kitchens or march against hunger – which is all very good. But the young people at the service academies are dedicating their entire lives to real service, the kind that might even require them to sacrifice life itself.

It is encouraging to see and to meet those people. I recommend that you go to West Point for a visit. Stay at the Thayer Hotel right next to the campus, walk along the bluffs overlooking the Hudson River, watch a baseball game or a track meet, go into the Grant Building cafeteria that is open to the general public, talk to a few cadets, and, generally soak in the atmosphere of one of America's greatest institutions of higher learning. You will certainly be inspired.

NEVER MAKE A JUDGMENT IN A HURRY

MAKING A DECISION BEFORE YOU KNOW ALL THE
FACTS IS VERY UNWISE. LEARN THIS FROM HISTORY
RATHER THAN FROM LIFE. IT'S EASIER.

In my most recent book (*American History; It's More Than the Crap You Learned in High School*), in the chapter on leadership principles, I make a major point of showing how successful leaders always take the time to get a decision right. As President Eisenhower once said, he never wanted to make a mistake in a hurry. One example I offer in the book is how John F. Kennedy made a big mistake early in his presidency when he gave the order to launch the invasion of Cuba without giving the plan careful consideration. That order resulted in the disastrous Bay of Pigs debacle. He learned his lesson and showed more mature leadership a year and a half later when he found out the Soviets were installing missiles in Cuba. Then he waited until he had all the facts, he dismissed panicked advice that he should immediately invade or order air strikes, and brought the country – and the world – through the crisis safely.

I have said in some blog posts early in President Trump's administration that he has made some mistakes in a hurry – indeed, he makes them almost daily when he tweets on a whim or in a pique. But I also feel the American people would be making a mistake in a hurry if they judged the President as a failure at this early date. The jury should still be out on President Trump and, I must say, there have been moments that have given me reason to think that it just might be possible that this simplistic, egocentric and childish man might actually accomplish some things that his much more erudite and articulate predecessors could not.

Every Saturday morning, I always get a laugh or two out of listening to N.P.R.'s "Wait, Wait, Don't Tell Me!" radio broadcast. This show always features jokes and comments that take shots at conservatives, but recent shows have taken the bashing of the conservative "right" to a new level. The host, Peter Sagal, and the guests never miss a chance to demean President Trump and call him stupid. They never refer to him with any sort of respect; it is always just "Trump," said with a definite tone of contempt. It sometimes irritates me that these self-righteous, pseudo-intellectuals feel no need ever to support the man who is representing our country on diplomatic missions when world peace may actually be at stake. A few years ago, it likewise irritated me when Rush Limbaugh and other "far right" political commentators would demean President Obama and never even credit him with having honorable motives as he traveled abroad.

President Trump is probably right when he says that a large majority of the people in the media hate him and are always ready to pounce on any shred of evidence of wrong-doing in his administration and elevate it to "smoking gun" status for impeachment charges. As one of the President's few defenders on MSNBC said, "Trump could say 'I love puppies,' and the headline would read 'Trump hates kittens.'"

As President Trump has traveled abroad this past year we have seen a President who is accorded a great deal of respect and almost adulation in some places. Is it possible – could it possibly be – that this simplistic man who seems to overlook the nuances and intricacies of global politics (possibly because he is not aware of them?) might just be able to go to the core of issues and get deals made? Two examples of his seemingly heavy-handed, "bull-in-a-china shop" approach that could possibly yield results:

He told the assembled nations of the world that we would annihilate North Korea if Kim Jong Un tried anything nasty. Everyone knows that is true, but he had the audacity to break with tradition and bluntly say it. Perhaps President Trump has made Kim and his friends, as they contemplate what could happen to them in a war, nervous enough to give up saber-rattling, to try to act civilized and to try being responsible leaders for once. He announced that the United States would recognize Jerusalem as the capital of Israel and we would move our embassy there. This makes the Arab nations and the Palestinians, in particular, positively catatonic. But perhaps the Palestinians will realize that they are in danger of ending up with no state at all, and thus accept what has long been a possible solution for them: a Palestinian state on the West Bank with East Jerusalem as *its* capital.

The history of previous administrations illustrates the point that it is silly to make a final evaluation of a President in the first year or two of his time in office. The best example is the history of Abraham Lincoln's presidency. After Lincoln was elected President he did not have thousands of people marching in the streets of Washington shouting "Not *my* President!" No, it was much worse than that! He had seven states immediately leave the Union rather than live under his presidency; four more left the Union a month after he took office, and four others thought seriously of joining the mass exit. Almost all the newspapers were dubbing his presidency a failure because his cabinet seemed to be in disarray and the whole situation seemed completely out of control. His top cabinet officer, William Seward, even offered to take control of the government because Lincoln seemed incapable of handling things. By the time Lincoln had been in office for a year and a half, conservatives were outraged because he had not made a compromise peace with the southern states and radicals were outraged that he had not yet freed the slaves. In those days they did not take public opinion polls, but if they had, Lincoln's rating almost surely would have been below thirty percent.

Of course, Lincoln weathered the storms, pulled the country along with him, and at the end of his first term he was re-elected by a wide margin. I am not predicting that Donald Trump will have a similar kind of trajectory. For one thing, he is not anywhere near as eloquent as Lincoln was. In fact, his lack of eloquence is one of his biggest problems. Yet, as he has proven several times, sometimes it is just his simplicity that carries the day. Perhaps, in a couple of years, we will see that some problems such as job creation or peace in the Middle East are solvable if they are reduced to their basics and not overly embroidered. For example, he could say to a company CEO: I'll give you lower taxes and a friendlier business climate, so move your business back to the United States. He could say to Middle East leaders: Stop getting all whipped up about small stuff and make a "two-state" deal.

All the facts about Donald Trump's presidency are not yet in. From a historian's perspective, it is clear we need to back off and give the new guy a chance. We need to pray that his outsized personality and simplistic thinking are just what the country and the world need right now. The chance that this is true grows slimmer by the day as we witness government by whim and chaos, but we need to ask ourselves, "Would a disastrous presidency be a good thing for the country?"

DAMN THE TORPEDOES!?

BOLD, COURAGEOUS LEADERSHIP IS BEST. USUALLY.

During the Civil War Union Admiral David Farragut was commanding a fleet that was advancing into Mobil Bay in Alabama. One of his officers warned him that the waters of the harbor were infested with "torpedoes" – water mines. In what has come to be regarded as an act of bold courage and strong leadership, Farragut barked out, "Damn the torpedoes! Full speed ahead!" The Union fleet successfully sailed past the forts protecting the entrance to the harbor, defeated the Confederates and seized the port, winning one of the most important victories in the Civil War. No Union vessel struck a mine and went to the bottom, so Farragut was hailed for his bold command.

Farragut joins the ranks of several other military heroes who defied danger and led their men to great victories. There was Teddy Roosevelt who walked calmly back and forth in front of his cowering men at the foot of San Juan Hill as Spanish bullets whistled by his head. There was Douglas MacArthur who strolled the length of an airfield on a Pacific island as Japanese snipers lurked in the jungles waiting for the chance to get off a fatal shot. These leaders seemed to be charmed and invincible; their leadership inspired their men and gave them courage.

But then there is General John Sedgwick at the Civil War battle of Spotsylvania Courthouse. He spoke boldly to his men and assured them three times that the Confederates "couldn't hit an elephant at this distance." Within five seconds of the last time he made this bold statement a Confederate bullet struck him right in the face and killed him. He lay sprawled on the ground, his face a bloody, unrecognizable mess, as his horrified men looked on.

So, what are those of us who aspire to learn the lessons of history to think? Should a person who hopes to lead and inspire his followers defy the odds and put himself at risk? Or should we heed the example of General Sedgwick and not chance putting our followers in a position of seeing their leader ignominiously gunned down?

Of course, I am speaking metaphorically here. Usually our leadership does not put us in a literal line of fire. Personally, I think all the leaders in these examples exposed themselves to needless risks. Sedgwick paid the price; the others went on to fame and glory . . . and, along with their followers, accomplished great things. But, really, if a Spanish soldier atop San Juan Hill had aimed his rifle just a little more to the right, TR's head would have exploded in a shower of blood and brains; he never would have taken the hill, become governor of New York, Vice President of the United States or President of the United States. We would not have the "Pure Food and Drug Act" or the extensive national park system, and there would be only three presidential faces on Mount Rushmore. Perhaps these heroes could have accomplished their military goals without putting themselves in mortal danger.

In the ordinary moments when leadership is required – when lives are not necessarily at stake – we need leaders who will use a reasoned approach, who will proceed slowly and carefully, who will not insist on reckless, all-or-nothing approaches to complex problems. President Lyndon Johnson once quoted Isaiah (1:18): "Come now, let us reason together." At the time I disliked Johnson and questioned his sincerity, but in recent years I have learned to appreciate his plea. Instead of shouting "Damn the torpedoes, full speed ahead!" we need calm heads to prevail.

PLEASE PARDON
A FEW RANTS

AM I HYPERSENSITIVE AND SHALLOW?

Perhaps it's the weather today (July 13, 2017) but I feel like deviating from my usual historical essays and indulge myself in a few rants about things that bug me in *today's* world. These same things may have annoyed people in the past as well, but my guess is not as much.

I am very annoyed by:

1. People who take the principle that pedestrians have the right of way to absurd levels by simply stepping into the crosswalk (or just onto the road where there is no crosswalk) without looking in either direction. They force drivers who might be in the vicinity to slam on their brakes, at which point the indignant pedestrian might look over and give the motorist a blistering, self-righteous look. Of course, they *are* right; in Massachusetts, and almost everywhere else in the United States, pedestrians *do* have the right of way. But some day they might be *dead* right. In many other countries there is no such concept as "pedestrians' rights" and people stepping off a curb are supposed to follow the old admoni-

tion, "Look both ways before crossing the street." If you go to any city in Europe or the U.K., you better forget about your "rights" as a pedestrian. The drivers there act as if they would run you over just as soon as look at you if you stepped into the street in front of their car.

2. Pedestrians who cross the street while drivers are waiting for them and meander along as if they have no reason in the world to pick up their pace so the drivers can get on with their rush to the hospital or wherever they may be going. Those strollers are very selfish, self-righteous, self-centered and . . . well, you get my drift.

3. Cashiers who make change for you at the store by handing you the bills first and then precariously balancing the coins on top. They should give you the coins first and then the bills. Employers: please teach your checkout personnel how to make change.

4. Drivers who come up fast behind you on the highway in the left lane when you are going 75 and immediately blink their lights to demand that you move over and get out of their way. I always *do* move over; they might be armed.

5. People, especially men, who wear shorts in the middle of winter when it's five degrees outside so everyone will be sure to see the tattoos on their legs.

6. Teachers who proclaim at the beginning of the course that they do not want to lecture — that they want everyone to participate — and then proceed to talk incessantly through every class that follows.

7. Parents who simply will not believe that their children could ever possibly do *anything* wrong.

8. Fit-bits and every other gadget that micro-analyzes everything the wearer does. If people want to know how far they ran or walked, they should measure out routes of various distances

in their cars and then do the one each day that gives them the mileage they want. Or, they can time their pace for a mile on a track some day – let's say 16 minutes — and then, every time they walk after that, tally up a mile for every 16 minutes they walked. It really is so very simple!

9. Weight loss programs that claim to help you lose weight fast without diet or exercise. They swindle the unsuspecting public out of millions each year. Along with this come the expensive government studies, dozens of them, that conclude that "diet and exercise are the keys to weight loss." Astounding!

10. People who walk toward you on a sidewalk and don't make the slightest effort to make room for you. If *you* did the same thing you would smack right into them! So, you step aside and let them march by looking as if they don't even know you are there. Of course, if they are on their #%*& phone, they probably *don't* know you're there!

11. Gigantic SUVs and "camping" vehicles. I hate to offend you if you own one, but you should realize that your vehicle – especially in a parking lot – blocks the view of anyone who is driving a normal-sized car. When a super-sized SUV is parked next to me when I back out it's like trying to get clear of the U.S.S. Enterprise before I can see what might be coming.

12. Finally, overused, vague or simply stupid expressions, such as:

"Have a good one!"
Have a good what? Day? Night? Vacation?

"at the end of the day"
at the end of the day is midnight

"the bottom line is . . . "
is everything a financial statement?

"'mornin'"
is it too much effort to say *"good morning?"*

"If I don't see you, have a good trip!"
Can I have a good one if you *do* see me?

"Their food is to die for."
Really – you would *die* just to eat there?

Now that I've vented, I feel better – and very, very shallow. What would Abe Lincoln's rant look like?

Lincoln: I'm hugely annoyed by:

1. Generals who send thousands of our young men up a hill against entrenched enemy sharpshooters and cause fifteen to twenty thousand men to die on a single day.

2. War profiteers who charge the government ten times the normal price for uniforms and equipment and produce shoddy goods to boot!

3. "Copperheads" in the North who think the country would survive just fine if we let the secessionists go and slavery to continue.

4. Generals who defeat the Confederates in battles and then rest on their laurels for three months while the enemy escapes and prepares to fight another day.

5. Orators who go on for two hours when a simple speech of two minutes would be so much more effective.

Now, *those* are things to be more than just annoyed about!! Ouch, I feel so petty!!

PERSPECTIVES ON PEOPLE AND EVENTS

My Personal View of Things
That Have Happened and the People
Who Were Involved

HISTORIC APRIL

IN THE SPRING THE WEATHER GETS WARMER AND STUFF STARTS HAPPENING!

April 1, 2017

This month marks the one hundredth anniversary of the United States' entry into the First World War. On April 2, 1917, in response to the unrestricted submarine warfare on American shipping being waged by Germany, President Woodrow Wilson went before Congress and asked for a declaration of war against Germany and its ally, Austria-Hungary. Two days later, by a vote of 82-6, the Senate passed a war declaration, and on April 6, 1917 the House voted for war by a margin of 373-50. Thus, the United States entry into World War became yet another historic event that occurred in April. There have been so many others that April should be ranked as the number one month for the making of American history.

The list of major events that occurred in April is impressive:

The American Revolutionary War began at Lexington and Concord on April 19, 1775. The Continental Congress did not vote to declare independence for another fourteen months, but the die was essentially cast on that April day when the "Minute Men" stood their ground on Lexington green, and the patriots at Concord bridge fired the "shots heard round the world."

After the War for Independence was won, the newly created country struggled with an inadequate government created by the Articles of Confederation. In 1787 the current constitution was written and, under its terms, George Washington was elected the first President. He took the oath of office in an elaborate ceremony in New York in April of 1789. Thus, the government of the United States that has had an unbroken succession of Presidents for the 229 years since Washington took the oath had its beginnings in April.

As the people of the United States moved westward and settled regions that were not even under United States control, difficult relations with foreign powers arose. In the 1830s, the Americans who had settled Texas, then the northeastern province of Mexico, revolted. After a small garrison of Texans was massacred at the Alamo, Sam Houston led an army of Texans in a successful campaign against the Mexican general, Santa Anna. That campaign ended in victory for the Texans in the decisive battle of San Jacinto on April 21, 1836. The humiliated Mexican general signed an agreement giving Texas its independence.

Nine years later the United States annexed Texas and made it a state – an act that led directly to the Mexican War that began with an incident on the Rio Grande River on April 25, 1846. The U.S. defeated Mexico in that war and took another large chunk of Mexico, including California, where gold was discovered in 1848. Thus, in a war that started in April, 1846, the United States took half of Mexico's territory and a large quantity of its wealth.

In 1860, after Abraham Lincoln was elected President, southern states began seceding from the Union. When he took the oath of office in March, Lincoln asserted that no state had a lawful right to secede and vowed to maintain federal government installations in all the seceded states, including Fort Sumter in Charleston, South Carolina. In April, 1861, when Lincoln sent a supply ship to Sumter, the guns of the Confederacy along the shore opened fire on the fort and bombarded it for two days, April 12th and 13th. Lincoln issued a call for volunteers "to put down the southern rebellion," and the civil war that everyone had been dreading for thirty years was now a reality.

The Civil War ended in April, almost exactly four years later. On April 9, 1865, the Confederate commander, Robert E. Lee surrendered to the Union general, Ulysses S. Grant, at Appomattox, Virginia. Sadly, five days later, on Good Friday, April 14, 1865, John Wilkes Booth, a Southerner intent on avenging the South, crept into the President's box during a play at Ford's Theater and shot Lincoln in the back of the head. Lincoln lingered through the night and died on the morning of April 15, 1865.

There were other important events in April of 1865. In fact, there were so many that had long range implications that the historian, Jay Winik, has written a book focused only on that month: *April, 1865.*

On April 25, 1898, after months of hesitation and diplomatic maneuvering over Spain's treatment of her Cuban subjects and the blowing up of the battleship *Maine*, President McKinley asked Congress to declare war on Spain. The resulting "Spanish-American War" netted the United States the Philippines, Guam, and Puerto Rico, and made Theodore Roosevelt a hero, soon to be President.

On April 15, 1912 Americans in New York were anticipating the arrival in a few days of the gigantic, luxurious new passenger liner, H.M.S. Titanic. They did not yet know that at 11:40 the previous night the ship had struck an iceberg and had gone to the bottom at 2:20 that morning sending over 1,500 people to frigid, watery deaths. It was the biggest civilian maritime disaster in history.

Five Aprils after the Titanic sank, as I've recounted above, the United States finally got fed up with ships being sunk by submarines and we declared war on Germany.

In the late 1940s, the United States awakened to the realization that our new adversary was our old ally from World War II, the Soviet Union. To deal with this our policy makers took two major steps toward setting in place a policy of "containing" Soviet expansion. On April 3, 1948, President Truman signed an act creating the European Recovery Program, legislation to send massive economic aid to Western Europe. This program was first proposed by Secretary of State George Marshall and became better known as the "Marshall Plan." A year later, on April 4, 1949, twelve nations signed the agreement creating the North Atlantic Treaty Organization (N.A.T.O.), an alliance that committed the signatories to come together for mutual defense if any of them were to be attacked by a foreign power, presumably the Soviet Union.

In 1961, just three months after he took office, John F. Kennedy ordered the launching of the invasion of Cuba by 1,200 Cuban exiles. It had been planned by the CIA under President Eisenhower. On April 17th the attack began and within two days Castro's army had killed or captured every one of the invaders. To his credit, Kennedy took responsibility for the disaster and vowed, within himself, never to take the advice of so-called military experts at face value in the future.

On April 4, 1968, Dr. Martin Luther King Jr., was in Memphis, Tennessee, where he had gone to support a strike by sanitation workers. As he stood on the balcony of his hotel room a shot rang out and a bullet hit Dr. King in the head, killing him instantly. The assassin, a racist named James Earl Ray, had fired from another building over a hundred yards away. He was arrested several weeks later. The death of Dr. King at age thirty-nine silenced the voice of moderation in the struggle for African-American rights and, ironically, set off a wave of violence in the streets.

Throughout the month of April in 1975 the Vietcong communists and the North Vietnamese regular army closed in on Saigon as the South Vietnamese army disintegrated. Finally, on April 30th, the communists entered the city, the remaining Americans and the few fortunate Vietnamese who could go with them, fled the city, and the war was finally over. The American twenty-year struggle to keep communism from spreading into South Vietnam had failed.

More recently, on April 15th, 2013, as runners were streaming towards the finish line of the Boston Marathon on Boylston Street, two "pressure cooker bombs" exploded killing three people and severely injuring hundreds of others, dozens of whom lost legs. Surveillance cameras caught images of the perpetrators – Tamerlan Tsarnaev and his brother, Dzhokhar – and they became the subjects of a massive manhunt. The search ended in Watertown where Tamerlan was killed and Dzhokhar was captured. The brothers were motivated by Islamic extremism. Dzhokhar was tried and convicted of first degree murder in a federal court and sentenced to death.

Each year, as we approach another April, we might ask ourselves, "What significant event in the history of our country will take place this April? The list of April events I have just recounted is pretty impressive: the start of the American Revolution, the inauguration of the first President, the Battle of San Jacinto, the beginning of the Mexican War, the start of the Civil War, the end of the Civil War, the assassination of Abraham Lincoln, the start of the Spanish-American War, the sinking of the Titanic, the entry of the United States into World War I, the inauguration of the Marshall Plan, the signing of the N.A.T.O. Treaty, the failed invasion of Cuba, the assassination of Dr. Martin Luther King, Jr., and the bombings at the Boston Marathon.

One event is certain to happen every year in April: we will all be filing our federal and state income taxes on April 15th.

THE "BOWL OF CHERRIES THEORY OF HISTORY"

WHAT MAKES THINGS HAPPEN?

Among historians there is an ongoing debate between two major camps. There are those who believe that history is largely made by consequential people such as George Washington who *make* events happen – the "Great Man Theory of History." (Sorry, ladies, but that's what it's called!) The others are those who believe history is the result of thousands of private decisions and emotions, such as migrations, made by ordinary people. In this view "great men," as Lincoln famously said, do not control events but are controlled by them. The true talent of a great man, in this view, is to stay on top of a powerful wave as it breaks. This argument has been going on among history geeks for many years, but I believe there is another explanation for historic events.

History is sometimes driven by seemingly inconsequential occurrences (such as sudden storms) or mundane objects (such as an innocuous piece of paper on the ground) that set off significant sequences of events. These small things can have such huge consequences that some people believe they were put in place by God to guide human events in the path He chooses. The Greeks used this concept in their dramas and they had a term for it: "Deus ex machina" — a contrivance sent from God. The Japanese also used the concept to explain the defeat of the invading armies of Kublai Khan in the thirteenth century. Khan's ships were blown away by a sudden, unexpected typhoon and Japan was saved. The Japanese called the storm a "kamikaze" ("divine wind"). In 1945 they tried to replicate that salvation using airplane pilots, but their "great men" were no substitute for the divine.

I call this concept — that seemingly random and unexplainable things determine some events — the "Bowl of Cherries Theory of History" because there was a very important episode in American History in which a small bowl of that fruit greatly affected the outcome of an enormous crisis. The year was 1850 and the Union was teetering on the verge of civil war. Senator Henry Clay, (the "Great Compromiser") had devised a compromise to keep the northern and southern sections of the country from shedding each other's blood, but one very key individual stood in the way of getting the compromise passed — President Zachary Taylor. Taylor was vehemently opposed to Clay's plan and he vowed to veto it if it passed Congress and came to his desk for his signature. It seemed as if the entire compromise process was being held hostage to the President's whims.

In the midst of the crisis, President Taylor attended a dedication ceremony for the new Washington Monument that was being erected near the White House. The day was extremely warm so, when Taylor returned home, he sought some refreshment and found it in a bowl of cherries which he devoured. Shortly afterward the President began to feel ill and by the following day he was deathly sick and vomiting. His condition grew steadily worse;

doctors were summoned, and they followed their customary procedures in such cases: they bled the President by applying leeches to his skin hoping to draw the toxins out of his system. With this kind of care poor old Zach steadily weakened and finally died.

Politically, Taylor's sad demise was a godsend to the compromisers in Congress because the Vice President, Millard Fillmore, supported the compromise and the process moved forward with the assurance that he, as the new President, would sign it. Thus, a tainted bowl of cherries saved the Union and civil war was postponed for ten years.

Those historians who believe in the "great man theory" of history and who refuse to accept "deus ex machina" – or any other chance determiner of events – have long believed that Taylor was deliberately poisoned. There were several possibilities regarding the poisoner, but the chief suspect came to be the author of the compromise proposals, Henry Clay. It wouldn't be the first time a good man committed murder in the national interest. Suspicion of Clay was heightened when a search of White House records revealed that Clay had visited the executive mansion on the morning of the 4th. Thus Clay had the motive and the means to commit the crime. Incredibly, historians received permission from the Taylor family to exhume the old general so his remains could be tested for the presence of poison. So, on June 6, 1991, researchers dug up the ancient coffin and what was left of the old man was tested for the presence of arsenic or other types of poison available in 1850. They found none. So, Clay was cleared and, in my mind, the "Bowl of Cherries Theory of History" was vindicated. It was a completely chance occurrence that allowed the great Compromise of 1850 to pass!

There are, I believe, more instances in American History in which my theory applies beyond the one involving an *actual* bowl of cherries. Let me present a few for your consideration.

THICK FOG SAVED A REVOLUTION

In July of 1776, the Continental Congress had just declared American independence, but our fight for freedom was already heading for a humiliating defeat. On Long Island, New York, British General William Howe gave George Washington's so-called army a sound thrashing and was closing in for the final blows. The American rebels were "toast," what with their backs up against the Hudson River, Howe's army closing in from the east, and several huge British warships about to sail up the Hudson from New York City to close the trap.

But then, a miracle occurred. On the night of August 28th, a fog denser than anyone who was there had ever seen at that time of year rolled up the river. Visibility was reduced to only a few feet. In the dead of night Washington's men rowed across the murky waters and evacuated Long Island while the British army on the east side of the river sat blissfully unaware that their prey was escaping, and the British warships sat helpless in the thick gloom only a few miles down river.

Without that fog the fledgling American nation might very well have been killed in its infancy. As it was, Washington's army lived to fight on and, a few months later, crossed another river – the Delaware – to defeat the Hessians on Christmas night and revive hopes for the revolutionary cause.

ICE DOUBLED THE SIZE OF THE COUNTRY

In 1802 the French Dictator, Napoleon, who dreamed of nothing, not even women, so much as he dreamed of empire, decided to make a strong statement about what he would do in America. The slave rebellion against the French army in Haiti had been successful and the Spanish had just turned over Louisiana territory to France, so he decided the time had come to send an enormous French force across the Atlantic to reassert French control over Haiti and occupy Louisiana, at least the area around New Orleans. In the fall, his force was ready and it was the biggest French force ever assembled for overseas duty. But, just as it was prepared to sail out of the harbor at Helvoet Sluys in Holland, a sudden cold snap occurred that froze up the harbor and made movement of his ships impossible. As they sat ice-bound for six weeks, the French soldiers consumed all the supplies and made the ships unable to sail in the spring without being re-supplied. Frustrated – a feeling he hated even more than anyone else does – the impulsive little Napoleon decided to sell all of Louisiana to the Americans for fifteen million dollars. When President Jefferson heard the news, he was aghast. Once he got over his shock – and his scruples over buying territory when the U.S. Constitution does not explicitly provide for such a thing – he leaped at the chance to double the size of the nation. The Louisiana Purchase, the greatest land deal in history, was made possible by the early arrival of thick ice in a Dutch harbor.

MARMALADE HELPED DOUBLE THE SIZE OF THE COUNTRY . . . AGAIN

In the hot summer of 1847 the American Army under General Winfield Scott, known to his men as "Old Fuss and Feathers" for his by-the-book orders and his grandiosity, was winning victory after victory and closing in on Mexico City. As he sat sweltering in his tent, Scott received a pompous message from another egomaniac, Nicholas Trist, who informed the General that he had been sent by President Polk to accompany the American army and begin peace negotiations with the Mexicans as soon as it seemed propitious to do so. Scott was enraged. He did not want to have some nitwit from the State Department tagging along and possibly talking peace with the enemy before he, the great General Scott, had made his grand entrance into the capital.

When the two men finally met, Trist was as annoyed as Scott had been. He was also unimpressed with the General. In his diary he wrote that the General was an imbecile and probably the dumbest man he had ever met. The relationship between these two egocentric men clearly had nowhere to go but up.

Then Trist became ill – very ill (Montezuma's revenge?). Scott took pity on the ambassador and decided to make an effort to cheer him up. In his storehouse he found a jar of guava marmalade and he sent it to Trist along with a note wishing him a return to good health. Unknown to Scott, guava marmalade was Trist's favorite delicacy in the whole world and that enticing jar, along with the kind words from the General, started him on the road to recovery. Scott visited Trist's bedside, the two men had long conversations, and gradually became fast friends.

A few weeks later Scott made his long-anticipated grand entrance into Mexico City on his huge white horse. Trist began negotiating with a group of moderate Mexicans who did not want to see the war dragged out with the Mexican army resorting to guerrilla tactics. Trist could speak fluent Spanish and the talks got off to a promising start.

But then Trist received a message from Washington. President Polk, wary of what Trist might do, terminated his mission and ordered him to return to Washington at once. Nicholas Trist was outraged. A treaty was very much in the making. So, he decided to ignore Polk's recall and continue his negotiations. Surprisingly, in this very insubordinate act he was supported by General Scott who was, ordinarily, a stickler for protocol.

The result of Trist's talks was the Treaty of Guadalupe-Hidalgo (named for the leafy suburb in which the treaty was signed). It gave the United States nearly half the territory of all of Mexico, including California, where gold was discovered nine days before the treaty was signed. This was clearly a spectacular deal for the United States. It nearly doubled the land size of the country and added incalculable amounts to the nation's supply of gold. It might also have been a good outcome for Mexico because its army was virtually annihilated and there was a strong movement in the U.S. Congress to annex the entire country of Mexico to the United States. What might *that* have meant one hundred and seventy years later to presidential candidate Donald Trump?

Without that jar of guava marmalade General Scott very likely would *not* have befriended Ambassador Trist and would have been delighted to send him home when Polk's order arrived. After that, who can say what kind of treaty would have ended the Mexican War?

CIGARS WRAPPED IN PAPER HELPED FREE THE SLAVES

In the summer of 1862, the Civil War was not going well for the Union cause. The Confederates had driven the Union army away from their capital city, Richmond, and they had inflicted a stunning defeat on Union forces at the Second Battle of Bull Run, replicating what they had done a year earlier in the same place. Desperate to strike a telling blow against the South, and convinced that Britain would help the Confederacy if he did not act soon, Lincoln had decided to make emancipation of the slaves a war aim. Following the advice of Secretary of State William Seward, Lincoln decided to wait for a Union victory before he proclaimed emancipation lest his announcement appear to be an act of desperation rather than one of righteousness made from a position of strength.

In September, General Robert E. Lee led his Confederate forces north into Maryland in hopes of striking a decisive blow on Union soil that would entice the British to recognize the Confederate States of America and cause the people of the North to demand peace, even if it meant the end of the Union and independence for the Confederacy. It was a desperate strategy, but it had a chance of succeeding and winning the Civil War for the Confederacy. Lee was a great strategic planner. The Union general in command of the Grand Army of the Potomac, George McClellan, was notorious for being slow and indecisive, qualities that had brought about his defeat earlier that year when his army was within thirty miles of Richmond but he had flinched and retreated.

On September 13th, the Twenty-Seventh Indiana Volunteers, a very small part of McClellan's huge army, was camped near Frederick, Maryland. The southern forces had passed through the same area a day before. Incredibly, in the tall grass near an abandoned campfire that the Confederates had left, Corporal Barton W. Mitchell noticed a small bundle of cigars wrapped in a piece of paper. At first the corporal's attention was focused solely on the fragrant cigars, but then he turned his focus on the paper which was covered with tiny, cramped, but legible handwriting. The corporal's interest in the paper turned to excitement as he gradually realized that the writing was battle orders for Lee's force, the Army of Northern Virginia. He sent an emissary with the paper to McClellan's headquarters where the cautious General concluded that the orders were authentic, and that he had in his hands what every general dreams of – every detail of his opponent's strategy.

In the days that followed, McClellan was able to meet every maneuver the Confederate army made and finally, on September 17th, along Antietam Creek near the town of Sharpsville, Maryland, the two armies met and engaged in one of the bloodiest battles of the 19th century. For two days the struggle continued, and when it was over twenty thousand men lay dead or wounded. Neither side had won a decisive victory, but Lee had been stopped from achieving his objectives, and on the morning of the 19th, his Army of Northern Virginia retreated across the Potomac to resume its defensive positions outside of Richmond.

In Washington, Lincoln was burdened by the heavy casualties and his increasing irritation with McClellan who did not follow Lee's army to strike a final, mortal blow. However, even though the Battle of Antietam (as it was called in the North) was not the kind of victory he had hoped for, Lincoln felt it was a victory enough to make his announcement of an emancipation policy appear to be made from a position of strength. On September 22, 1862, President Abraham Lincoln issued his "Preliminary Emancipation Proclamation," stating that on January 1, 1863, all slaves "in areas in rebellion against the Union" would be henceforth and forever free. Thus, the Union army's performance in the Battle of Antietam made possible the abolition of slavery in the rebellious states.

As cautious and indecisive as he was, General McClellan might not have been able to fight a pitched battle with the wily Robert E. Lee unless he had known Lee's plan of attack. In an incredibly fortunate sequence of events McClellan learned those plans because a careless officer in Lee's command chose to wrap his cigars in the only paper he had available – the orders of the day from commanding general Robert E. Lee.

A WHITE HANDKERCHIEF
MADE T.R. PRESIDENT

At the Republican National Convention in 1900, the party bosses were fed up with the egotistical, self-righteous, reform-minded governor of New York, Theodore Roosevelt. When he had returned from Cuba two years earlier "T.R." had ridden his fame as the "Rough Rider" hero of San Juan Hill to the governor's office in Albany. Now he was riding roughshod over the traditional politics of the "Empire State" and annoying every "good old boy" in the state's Republican Party with his holier-than-thou reforms. The party bosses needed to get *rid* of him and they thought they had the perfect plan to do so. They would nominate him for Vice President on the ticket with President William McKinley who was running for a second term.

Everything went just as the bosses planned. McKinley won re-election and T.R. was relegated to the most innocuous job in the world – Vice President of the United States — whose only constitutional function is to preside over the Senate and vote if there is a tie. The bosses rubbed their hands together in glee at the thought of how they had put the overly ambitious reformer on the shelf. But Marc Hanna, party leader from Ohio and a close friend of McKinley, was not so sure. "Now only one life," he warned, "stands between that mad man and the White House."

In September, 1901, six months into his second term, President McKinley traveled to Buffalo, New York, to attend the Pan-American Exposition that was being held there. At the Music Hall, a building chosen for its easy access for a large crowd, a reception was arranged for the President to shake hands with as many people as possible. It was a hot day, and many of the people who waited in line to see the President were carrying handkerchiefs to dab at sweat on their faces. Thus, no one paid much attention to the white cloth the man approaching the President had wrapped around his right hand.

The man was Leon Gzolgosz, an anarchist. He was convinced it was his duty to kill the President who was an enemy "of the good people, the good working people." As he drew near to McKinley, the President, apparently thinking the man's right hand was injured, reached out his left hand. At that moment Gzolgosz fired two shots from the gun that was hidden under the white cloth. The first bullet grazed McKinley, but the second tore into his abdomen. Police and armed guards, appalled that this had occurred right under their eyes, swarmed over the assassin and wrestled him to the ground. McKinley slumped forward but still had the presence of mind – and the Christian heart – to say, "Do not harm him!"

McKinley lingered, clutching to life, for eight days. In fact, for a time, he appeared to be recovering. But then internal infection caused a severe turn for the worse and on September 14, 1901, President William McKinley became the third President in thirty-six years to die from an assassin's bullet. When Marc Hanna heard the news he exclaimed, "Now that damn cowboy is President!"

In the aftermath of the assassination grief-stricken security men and soldiers who had been guarding the President lamented that there were so many people crowding into line and there were so many white handkerchiefs out that they did not see the danger the President was in until it was too late.

Almost immediately Theodore Roosevelt, the nation's twenty-sixth President, began making a name for himself as a reformer – the very thing the bosses had feared. They must have cursed white handkerchiefs from then on.

A LIGHT GRAY SUIT MADE JFK PRESIDENT

The presidential election of 1960 was the closest of all time. Only a little more than 100,000 votes separated John F. Kennedy from Richard Nixon out of 70 million that were cast. The gap in the Electoral College was considerably larger, but if the states Kennedy won by very narrow margins were close wins for *Nixon*, Nixon would have won. A tiny factor that might have changed only a few voters' minds might have made the difference. Thus, it is very possible that the visual appearance of the two men on the night of their first nationally televised debate may have swung the election to Kennedy. We do know that the Vice President had a slight lead in the polls going into the first debate, and that Kennedy emerged with a moderate lead after that debate.

Everyone who watched the first debate (four were held) agreed that Kennedy *looked* much better than Nixon. Not only was he a better-looking man than Nixon to begin with, he seemed more robust and confident. Kennedy was tanned, he looked rested and relaxed, and he exuded self-assurance and confidence. Nixon, by contrast, looked washed-out. He had only recently recovered from a bad case of the flu, so he was pale and wan. On top of that he had chosen – probably because of the warm weather – to wear a light gray suit. Every time the camera was on Nixon he disappeared into the gray background. The telecast was in black and white; Nixon was pale gray. Kennedy was wearing a dark suit so, when the camera was on him, he stood out and was clearly focused.

The people who listened to the debate on radio mostly felt that Nixon had the better arguments, had presented his views more clearly, and had, by a small margin, won the debate. However, the much greater number of people who watched on television felt, by a wide margin, that Kennedy had clearly won. My parents were Nixon Republicans and I remember their dismay as the debate was flickering on the TV in front of them. Their candidate looked bad and they sensed that this might be the beginning of the end for him. It was.

Nixon learned a tough lesson that night. He never again wore a light suit on television even when, as a President disgraced by the Watergate Scandal, he said a tearful good-bye to the White House staff on a hot August day. Perhaps, at that moment, a light gray suit that made him disappear might have been a *good* idea!

A HELMET BROUGHT DOWN A PRESIDENTIAL CANDIDATE

When George H.W. Bush, Vice President under Ronald Reagan, ran for President in 1988, his Democratic opponent was the Governor of Massachusetts, Michael Dukakis. Dukakis – or "Duke," as he was called in his home state – was a short, scholarly man . . . a "policy wonk" who liked to dig deep into complex issues and devise plans for the ways government could work to improve things. It seemed that his policies had worked economic miracles in Massachusetts, and he was basing his candidacy on the idea that he could do the same for the whole country.

Polls showed the race to be very close, but Dukakis was clearly at a disadvantage against George Bush in the areas of foreign affairs and military experience. Bush, besides being Vice President for eight years, had served as U.S. Ambassador to China and head of the C.I.A. In 1942, at age seventeen, he had patriotically volunteered for service in the Naval Air Corps and had been shot down in the Pacific during a bombing run. He clearly knew foreign affairs and the military very well!

To try to level the playing field, the Duke's campaign advisors decided to stage a photo opportunity that would bolster his image with military-minded voters. On September 13th, at Sterling Heights, Michigan, the Duke took a ride in an A1M1 Abrams tank. To complete the image, he donned a bulky tank commander's helmet. The tank driver took the vehicle around the grounds and past the gaggle of ninety print media and television reporters. The massive video cameras of the day followed the tank and its passenger as it rumbled past. Peering over the edge of the driver's hole, the would-be commander-in-chief looked like a child with his dad's helmet on. It was the most absurd footage any of the reporters had ever seen and it evoked loud laughter and guffaws.

The next day film of the event was on every newscast in the country and around the world. Still shots appeared in newspapers and magazines. It was the 1988 version of going viral. In every photo, Presidential candidate Michael Dukakis, Governor of Massachusetts, looked like an excited child getting his first ride in a real tank!

Considering Vice-President Bush's stature and the strength of the economy that fall, it was likely that George H.W. Bush would have won the election of 1988 tank helmet or no tank helmet. But, to this day, Mike Dukakis, who teaches politics at Northeastern University, believes he may have lost the election the moment he donned that helmet. A few years ago, Barack Obama, when offered a hat to wear during his campaign, remarked that it was "Politics 101" not to put on *a hat*. For Donald Trump, of course, that's just one more silly rule to be ignored.

This piece could go on for many more pages with examples of times in American history when a small, seemingly inconsequential item, statement, or event turns out to have enormous consequences when the complete story is in. The concept was part of a well-known ancient proverb that Ben Franklin published in *Poor Richard's Almanac* in June of 1758:

For want of a nail, a shoe was lost
For want of a shoe, the horse was lost

For want of a horse, the knight was lost
For want of a knight, the battle was lost
For want of a battle, the kingdom was lost
So, a kingdom was lost, all for want of a nail.

This piece must conclude with a caveat, however. Those of us alert to the ways history is made are always on the look-out not only for consequential men or women, or trends in society, but also for insignificant items or occurrences that turn out to drive events much more than anyone could have expected. But, we can sometimes be deceived or be unaware of other factors that will supersede the one we are focused on. Many of us, for example, thought Monica Lewinsky's blue dress would be the evidence that drove Bill Clinton out of the White House and would join Taylor's bowl of cherries, McClellan's wrapped cigars, Nixon's gray suit, and all the other artifacts in the "Bowl of Cherries Museum." It did not. It *is* famous, but it did not drive Bill Clinton out of office because other factors proved to be more important: Bill Clinton's likability ("Great Man Theory") and the booming economy at the time ("Thousands of Decisions Theory"). I do like the "Bowl of Cherries" concept, however, and I am always on the lookout for the next one.

JOHN ADAMS DESERVES BETTER

HE NEEDED A POET LIKE PAUL REVERE HAD OR A
BROADWAY MUSICAL WRITER LIKE ALEXANDER
HAMILTON HAS HAD.

Poor John Adams! He knew history would not treat him kindly and, in this one instance, he was correct. Rather petulantly he predicted that future generations would learn that Ben Franklin smote the ground with his electrical rod, George Washington rode forth on his great white steed, and the United States was born. No one would pay any attention to the hard work John Adams did lining up votes for independence in the Continental Congress. His diplomatic missions to France and Holland would go unnoticed and, of course, his eight years as Vice President would be completely ignored. In the history of the world, no more useless job had ever been created. Finally, his presidency would be lambasted because rather than achieve great victory in a war he had, instead, avoided war. What glory was there in that?

Even the portraits we have of John Adams do not impress us. We see him as a rather portly, middle-aged man (his enemies called him "his rotundity") who cannot seem to suppress a rather priggish, sanctimonious look that makes the viewer certain that Adams was an arrogant and self-righteous man.

The truth is that John Adams was one of the most able of the founders, and certainly the one whom twenty-first century students should admire. It is not a minor point that not only was he one of the few founding fathers who did not own slaves, he vigorously condemned the institution – to the faces of his slave-owning colleagues, I hasten to say. He was a man of high principle who conducted his affairs in accord with strict moral standards and integrity. Beyond that, a simple summary of his achievements during a long life of public service will establish his stature.

In 1770, after the so-called "Boston Massacre," he employed his legal credentials and courtroom skills to defend the British soldiers who fired into the mob because he believed every man is entitled to a fair trial. He presented the evidence in a compelling manner and won acquittals for all of the soldiers but one, whose sentence was a brand on his hand. This success did not make Adams popular in Boston, but John Adams never cared a bit about the "bubble popularity."

Between 1774 and 1776 he worked tirelessly for independence at the Continental Congress and finally achieved success when his fellow delegates voted for independence on July 2, 1776. Two days later the Congress adopted the Declaration of Independence that had largely been written by Thomas Jefferson who, in the minds of every generation to come, would be thought of as the "Father of American Independence." Adams predicted that in future years great celebrations with fireworks and parades would take place on the day independence was voted – July 2nd. Of course, he lost this battle of history just as he did many others.

In 1778, Adams helped secure French assistance for the American Revolution and he encouraged the French to send a naval fleet to the Americas, which they did – a move which proved decisive in the climactic Battle of Yorktown. George Washington, of course, received all the credit for that victory and became known as the "Father of Our Country."

In 1780, John Adams personally wrote the new constitution for the Commonwealth of Massachusetts. Many of the principles he worked into that document, including separation of powers, checks and balances, and a two-house legislative body, served as models for the new constitution of the United States which was written seven years later. James Madison wrote the minutes of the Constitutional Convention and much of the document itself, so he became known as "Father of the Constitution."

In the 1780s, Adams served as the United States ambassador to Great Britain. It was no small matter for the instigator of the revolution to present his credentials to the monarch he had attacked vigorously for over a decade and who would have ordered him hanged if the revolution had failed. Adams carried out his duty with dignity and aplomb and earned the respect of the king and his government for the new United States of America.

In 1788, Adams received the second highest number of votes for President – behind George Washington, of course – and thus, under the terms of the original constitution, became the first Vice-President of the United States. For eight years he occupied that thankless post, carrying out the Vice-President's only constitutional duties: presiding over the Senate and standing ready to assume the presidency if the great man died. Good Puritan that he was, Adams took that job seriously and assiduously tried to keep order in the often unruly Senate chamber.

Finally, in 1796, John Adams was elected President of the United States. Much of his term was preoccupied with an undeclared naval war the country was fighting with France. In 1798, during the notorious "XYZ Affair" in which three anonymous French officials (dubbed MR. X, MR. Y., AND MR. Z) demanded a bribe from American diplomats, Adams could easily have secured a declaration of war against France from an enraged Congress. The American people, furious at the insults to American honor from the French, would have hailed Adams's decision, united behind him, and re-elected him resoundingly in 1800. But, Adams knew our fledgling nation needed time to build its strength and that a war at that time would be a disaster. So, he put duty over popularity and national survival over his own re-election. Instead of sending a war message to Congress, he sent a peace delegation to France. A peace agreement with France was signed in 1800 and, later that year, Adams lost his bid for re-election to his old frenemy, Thomas Jefferson.

Through all of these momentous events, John Adams was a devoted family man who deeply loved his wife, Abigail, and his six children. He was not the "father of his country" or the "father of the constitution," but he was the father of John Quincy Adams, who became a diplomat, a member of Congress, Secretary of State, and was President of the United States in 1826 when John Adams died on July fourth. On the day he died, poor old John was wrong one last time. As he was passing away he muttered, "Jefferson still lives." Jefferson had died in his Monticello home in Virginia a few hours earlier.

When the esteemed writer of history, David McCullough, was researching a dual biography he intended to write about John Adams and Thomas Jefferson, he soon decided to drop Jefferson and write only about John Adams. The reason: Adams was by far the more admirable of the two men, and McCullough wanted to give him the attention other historians had not. At long last John Adams had an admirer. He deserves one . . . and many more.

THE ART OF THE DEAL 1790 STYLE

IN GOVERNMENT, NOTHING GETS DONE WITHOUT
A DEAL . . . EVEN IN THE OLDEN DAYS!

President Trump sees himself as the ultimate dealmaker and he has implied he will teach the clueless politicians in Washington how it's done. The fact is, of course, deal making has been going on in Washington –- or Philadelphia – since the government began, and Mr. Trump might learn something by seeing how some true masters of the art solved one of the country's thorniest problems when the government was only a year old, meeting in makeshift quarters in Philadelphia, and looking for a capital.

Alexander Hamilton, as the new Secretary of the Treasury, felt it was necessary for the federal government to pay off not only its own debts but also the debts of each of the states. It was important for the new country to have good credit and to establish a reputation of being financially sound and secure. The problem was that some of the states, all in the south – Virginia,

North Carolina, Georgia and Maryland – had already paid their debts and they were loathe to pay taxes to the federal government in order that the debts of the northern "deadbeat" states could be covered. Hamilton's plan was placed before Congress as the "Assumption Act – an act for the federal government to assume the debts of the states." By a three-vote margin the southern representatives sent the bill down to defeat, a stunning blow to the new Secretary of the Treasury. Hamilton was convinced that the credit of the United States, and therefore the functioning of the United States government itself, was in great jeopardy.

Hamilton was so distraught about the situation that he worried himself to a frazzle. Thomas Jefferson, the Secretary of State who was usually at odds with Hamilton, encountered him on the sidewalk in front of President Washington's house. The Treasury Secretary was dejected and haggard, "even his dress was uncouth and neglected," Jefferson wrote later, and it was clear that Hamilton thought the country was on the verge of collapse. Jefferson was inclined to favor the southern congressmen who opposed Hamilton's assumption scheme; his good friend, James Madison, was the leader of that faction. Yet, he did see some wisdom in Hamilton's plan – and he felt a bit sorry for the Treasury Secretary who seemed to be on the verge of a breakdown.

To resolve the crisis Jefferson invited Hamilton and Madison to dinner at his house to discuss the assumption issue. If everyone remained inflexible, Jefferson argued, there would be no bill passed for funding the public debts and that could very well mean the end of the newborn American government. It was as if Jefferson extended his arms toward his dinner guests and asked plaintively, "Can't we all just get along?"

The key to the solution, of course, was more than just cajoling. Jefferson needed a workable compromise, and he had one. If Madison would accept the Assumption Bill, his friends from the southern states that had already paid their debts would receive in return a promise to locate the new national capital in the

South – specifically in a new location along the Potomac River between Maryland and Virginia. Both sides showed flexibility. They agreed to the compromise and, by the end of 1790 the federal government had assumed the state debts and plans were being made to locate the national capital in a "District of Columbia" on the Potomac River.

This all came about because of Jefferson's "compromise dinner." Each man who came to dinner certainly would have agreed with what Jefferson wrote privately – that "men of sound heads and honest views needed nothing more than explanation and mutual understanding to enable them to unite in some measures which might enable us to get along."

If political leaders of the stature of James Madison, Alexander Hamilton and Thomas Jefferson could work out the thorny issues of their day over a hastily arranged dinner, surely politicians of our own day can do the same. Early in his first year President Trump held a dinner for senators to discuss health care. That seemed promising, but all the guests were Republicans. If he is to learn from Jefferson, he needs to invite leaders from both parties and have a meaningful meeting of the minds. He needs to serve a steak dinner and a good red wine to Mitch McConnell, Paul Ryan . . . and . . .Chuck Schumer and Nancy Pelosi, and see what happens.

THE ART OF THE DEAL, 1850

SOMETIMES REACHING A DEAL IS A LIFE
OR DEATH MATTER.

My essay "The Art of the Deal, 1790" described how Alexander Hamilton, Thomas Jefferson, and James Madison were able to forge a compromise regarding Hamilton's plan to have the federal government assume the debts owed by the states. The deal showed how many thorny problems in government can be solved if there are people willing to listen and be flexible enough to bend when it is clear that bending is the only way to keep the peace and keep the country moving forward.

On another occasion the political skills of a small group of United States senators kept the country together and probably saved the lives of thousands of young men. The Senators were Henry Clay of Kentucky, Daniel Webster of Massachusetts, and Stephen Douglas of Illinois. The issue was slavery and whether it should be allowed to exist in California or in any of the other territories the United States had recently annexed after the Mexican War.

In late 1849, the territory of California, in the middle of a massive gold rush, held enough people to qualify for statehood. The territorial government applied for admission to the Union with a state constitution that did not allow slavery. Lest the reader think that the Californians were kind-hearted folk who hated slavery, it should be pointed out that they did not want slavery in their state because they did not want to compete with slave labor and they also did not want black people living in their state, slave or free.

Immediately a huge crisis arose in the United States Congress because California's admission as a free state would upset the balance of power between slave states and free states which currently stood at fifteen each. Southerners were outraged that they would now be outnumbered in the Senate, just as they already were in the House. If California came into the Union as a free state, a congressional action to limit or even abolish slavery might not be far off! California becoming a state that outlawed slavery — the South would have none of it! Led by the acerbic John C. Calhoun of South Carolina, Southerners proclaimed their states would leave the Union and create their own slave republic if such an outrage occurred. Calhoun's home state was a special case. Partly because its slave population equaled its white population, and partly because Calhoun had, since 1831, proclaimed that slavery was a "positive good" for both races, South Carolina had long been the "state most likely to secede."

The man everyone looked to when crises such as this arose was Henry Clay, Senator from Kentucky. In 1820, he had been the major force that kept the Union together when Missouri applied for admission as a slave state. In 1832, he had crafted a compromise to keep South Carolina in the Union when that irritable state threatened secession over the tariff issue. Now, after an illustrious career in the Senate and three failed presidential attempts, Clay was being called upon, once again, to save the Union.

On February 5, 1850, Clay rose in the Senate to deliver an oration on his compromise plan. He began by pleading the cause of compromise itself which he described as "a measure of mutual concession – a measure of mutual sacrifice" in which each side relinquishes its extreme demands. The basic elements of his plan were that the South would give up its demand that slavery be legal in California in return for the North being willing to accept a strong fugitive slave law that made it a federal offense to assist runaway slaves. There was also a provision to pay Texas ten million dollars for her claims to land in the "Mexican Cession" (today's New Mexico), and another provision to allow slavery into the Mexican Cession until the region was ready for statehood, at which time the people who lived there would vote on whether to keep slavery or outlaw it. One further section called for banning the slave trade, but not slavery itself, from Washington, D.C.

Clay spoke for two hours on the 5th and another two hours on the 6th. It was an exhausting effort for the seventy-two-year-old man who often broke into fits of coughing brought on by the tuberculosis that would kill him two years later. Clay soldiered on because he knew, as he warned passionately in his speech, that failure to compromise would lead to secession, that secession would lead to war between the seceding states and the Union, and that such a civil war would be terribly bloody.

Clay's address was followed by the most dramatic six months in the history of the United States Congress. On March fourth, John C. Calhoun, within days of dying of tuberculosis, sat wrapped in blankets as Senator James Mason read his speech. The frail, dying man scowled as Mason read his words of contempt for any action short of allowing slavery without restrictions into California and all the territory taken from Mexico. The South would surely secede, he warned, if its rights to "property" were ignored.

Three days later it was time for the dynamic senator from Massachusetts, Daniel Webster, to take the floor. What he said in what has become revered as the great "7th of March speech" was so powerful and eloquent that it was required reading for students in American History classes and "Rhetoric" classes for many years. The "God-like Daniel" was also in the twilight of his career, but he looked powerful and imposing in his traditional blue coat as he began, "I wish to speak today not as a Massachusetts man, nor as a northern man, but as an American and a member of the Senate of the United States. . . . I speak today for the preservation of the Union. Hear me for my cause!" He went on to urge support for the compromise proposal in a dynamic speech that lasted three hours.

What few people knew as Webster spoke was that back in January, Henry Clay, coughing and wheezing, had trudged through a snowstorm from his hotel in Washington to Webster's lodgings to try to convince the man who had often been his adversary to support his compromise plan. Webster knew that supporting the plan with its provision for a strong fugitive slave law would deal a deathblow to his political future in Massachusetts, the bastion of the anti-slavery movement in the country. Nevertheless, he made the decision to support Clay and put the country ahead of his personal success.

The speeches delivered that winter by Clay, Calhoun, and Webster were the finale for the "Great Triumvirate," as they were called. Two years later, all three were dead. The United States Senate would never see their likes again.

But important legislation cannot be passed only by the power of speeches, magnificent as they may be. Legislating requires skillful maneuvering, daily attention to recent turns of opinion, cajoling and, quite frankly, deal making. During the spring and early summer of 1850 Clay made seventy appearances on Capitol Hill to work the halls, the cloakrooms and the offices drumming up support for his five-part plan. He even visited the White House to convince President Taylor, who loomed as a major obstacle because he would veto the bill if it came to him for his signature. Fortunately for Clay, Taylor died of food poisoning and the new President, Millard Fillmore, was much more amenable to compromise.

(Taylor's "convenient" passing came under suspicion in 1990, an incident I deal with in another essay.)

By August of 1850, sick and feeling every one of his seventy-two years, Clay felt too tired to continue. He retreated to the Delaware coast for a few weeks of recuperation at the seashore, leaving work on the compromise plan in the hands of the young senator from Illinois, Stephen Douglas.

Douglas devised a strategy of dividing the compromise plan into its five components and bringing them to the floor one at a time. This enabled senators to avoid voting for parts of the plan that would kill their re-election chances back home. Northerners could vote for the admission of California as a free state, for example, but be absent or abstain when the federal fugitive slave law was up for a vote. As the process unfolded, each component of the compromise package passed. It was legislative maneuvering at its best.

By the end of 1850, the Compromise was passed, the secession movement in the South collapsed, and the Union was saved . . . for the time being. During the next ten years repeated crises between the North and the South eroded the moderate middle. Clay and Webster both died in 1852, and in 1861 civil war did finally come with all the blood Clay and Webster had predicted.

During those ten years the North experienced a tremendous growth in population. Concurrently, its industrial capacity and railroad mileage doubled and then doubled again. Thus, when the war did come, the Union was better able to prevail and slavery was abolished. The skillful maneuvering of Henry Clay, Daniel Webster and Stephen Douglas in 1850 achieved more than just a legislative "win." It changed the course of history.

In 2017, in a very dramatic moment, Senator John McCain returned to the chamber after being away for several weeks being treated for terminal brain cancer. In a short address to the Senate, the institution that has been called "the world's greatest deliberative body," McCain commented that the Senate has not "been overburdened with greatness lately." He went on to say that while compromise is not glamorous or exciting, it is "usually the most we can expect." We need to stop listening to the bombastic loudmouths – especially those in the media – and say, "To hell with them!" Instead of just trying to "win" we need to work together to get something done.

McCain's speech did not rank in eloquence with Clay's and Webster's in 1850, but it ranked very high in drama. Perhaps it takes an octogenarian who is terminally ill to show his Senate colleagues the way. I do not wish illness on the members of Congress, but perhaps if they all could *pretend* they are dying and have no political futures they could finally put their country's interests ahead of their own. Maybe it takes a man knowing he is about to *be* history to compel him to do what it takes to *make* history.

THE LAST TIME BOSTON WAS A SANCTUARY CITY

ONCE BEFORE BOSTON WAS A PLACE WHERE
FUGITIVES FROM FEDERAL LAW COULD BE SAFE.

Mayor Marty Walsh has not only declared Boston a "sanctuary city" for undocumented immigrants, he has even declared that the city will allow immigrants threatened with arrest to seek refuge in city hall if necessary. Some people regard the mayor's stand as an outrageous flouting of federal law and, to some extent, it is. But this is not the first time in its history that Boston has defied federal law to take a stand for what its leaders see as moral justice.

In 1850, Congress passed the Fugitive Slave Law. As part of the compromise with the South over slavery in the territories, the law required states to hold runaway slaves and allow federal agents to apprehend them. The law also gave federal marshals, rather than local judges, authority to preside over cases of suspected runaways. The marshals would be paid ten dollars if they ruled in favor of the slave owner who was trying to reclaim his "property," and five dollars if they ruled that the person being held was, in fact, a free citizen. Clearly the law was weighted in favor of the slave owners demanding the return of their "property."

Throughout the North, and particularly in Massachusetts, people were outraged by the new law. In the first year of its existence a rescue mob in Boston successfully broke into a federal courtroom and spirited away a runaway slave named Shadrach and sent him safely to Canada.

A group of Boston abolitionists formed a "vigilance committee" to be on the lookout for slave owners or slave catchers who might be scouring the city in search of runaways. The committee, led by notable men such as attorney Wendell Phillips, also warned people in the black population to take due care and to seek out committee members if they felt threatened.

Then, Anthony Burns came to town. Burns was an African-American slave who escaped from his owner in Virginia in March of 1854 and made his way to Boston where he kept a low profile, told no one he was a runaway slave, and got work in a clothing store. Unfortunately, Burns wrote an indiscreet letter to his brother that revealed his whereabouts. Before Anthony could truly begin life as a free man, his master showed up, identified him as his property, and secured his arrest by federal marshals.

While Burns was being held in jail awaiting his appearance before a judge, a mob of abolitionists and free African-Americans attempted to break into the jail and rescue him. In the ensuing melee one of the guards was stabbed to death and the crowd was driven back. Dozens of Bostonians had broken federal law, had even caused a deputy federal marshal to be killed, and Anthony Burns was still a captive.

President Franklin Pierce sent a contingent of United States marines to keep order and Boston was placed under martial law. After the judge ruled that Burns was indeed the "property" of the man claiming to be his master (a man named Charles Suttle), preparations were made to ship Burns back to Virginia. On the appointed day (June 1, 1854), a thousand soldiers lined the streets between the jail and the harbor. They held back over fifty thousand irate citizens who screamed with rage at the soldiers and wept bitter tears at the sight of a man in chains shuffling down to the harbor where the ship was waiting to sail him back to the horrors that surely awaited him in the South. A brief moment of ironic levity occurred when Burns said to his captors, "awful lot of people came out to see a black man walk down the street."

The city, indeed the entire state, went into a period of mourning after the Burns tragedy. Even Burns's return to Boston in 1855 after abolitionists had purchased his freedom did not lift the pall that hung over the state because of the injustice of the Fugitive Slave Law. The Massachusetts State Legislature, responding to the mood of the people, passed the "Personal Liberty Act." This legislation virtually made the fugitive slave laws unenforceable in Massachusetts. From that year until the start of the Civil War six years later, the houses and barns that had long been "stations" on the "Underground Railroad" had the sanction of the state government. Almost every Bay State city and town can point to at least one house that had false walls or basement storage bins for runaways to spend the night on their way to Canada. Boston and every other town in the commonwealth were, in effect, sanctuary cities.

All of us today applaud the citizens of Boston – and the city of Boston – for defending the freedom of people seeking refuge from slavery in the 1850s. One man at the time who did *not* applaud was Abraham Lincoln. In the year 1850 — and always – he believed all citizens should obey the law, even if it was obnoxious and they hated it. After he became President, during the first year of the Civil War, he ordered federal troops to obey the law and return runaway slaves to their masters. He did that partly to prove to the South that, as President, he would enforce all the laws and he had no intention of interfering with slavery where it already existed. His fundamental belief was the rule of law. The laws should always be obeyed . . . until we change them.

Lincoln ultimately concluded that the South, itself, had violated the law by seceding, waging war against the government, and refusing all entreaties to return to the Union. Only then did he feel legally justified in seizing southerner's property, their slaves.

Today, if we applaud the concept of "sanctuary cities," we are taking the same position as the vigilance committees of the 1850s and opposing the views of Abraham Lincoln. As it turned out, the vigilance committees were "on the right side of history" (as the current saying goes). They were on the side of what would eventually be regarded as the right, the morally righteous position. And so, we honor them; we have erected statues commemorating the heroics of Wendell Phillips in Boston.

Will Mayor Walsh and the mayors of San Francisco and dozens of other "sanctuary cities" one day be seen the same way? Will Governor Brown become a hero for making California a "sanctuary state?" Or, will historians in the future conclude that those leaders should have obeyed the federal laws? Will Walsh and Brown one day be scorned as public officials who not only violated their sacred oaths to enforce the law, but also sacrificed the peoples' safety for the sake of soft-headed, misplaced sympathy? It is not so easy to make a call such as that when events are happening around you in real time and the issues under debate affect you or people you know personally.

AND THE WAR CAME

POLITICAL LEADERS IN THE 19ᵀᴴ CENTURY COMPROMISED OFTEN. SHOULD THEY HAVE DONE IT AGAIN?

President Trump's chief of staff, John F. Kelly, made a statement about the Civil War that everyone who managed to stay awake in high school American History class knows is only partly true. He claimed that an "inability to compromise" caused the Civil War. The fact is that the political leaders of the northern and southern sections of the country compromised and avoided conflict on at least four occasions over a seventy-three-year period. Finally, in 1860, they needed to do it again but, by that time, the deal on the table would have required one side to yield far more than it was morally willing or able to do.

The compromises that were made during those seventy-three years left many people on each side nauseated, but they worked . . . for a while.

At the Constitutional Convention in 1787, the delegates from the southern states threatened to leave the hall and take their states out of the proposed new union if the slaves were not counted as population for the states' representation in Congress. Conversely, the southern delegates did *not* want the slaves counted for purposes of taxation. This was the first instance — of many that were to come — in which the South threatened to break up the Union if its views on slavery were not accepted. The compromise that was finally agreed to disgusted many people at the time and has disgusted even more people since, but it did keep the southern states in the fold. The crisis was resolved, the framers were able to produce a new constitution, and all was well. The deal that was struck allowed the southern states to count *three fifths* of their slaves for both representation and taxation. This cynical calculation was the most egregious of the several ways slavery was glossed over – indeed, not even mentioned by name – in the new constitution. But, the union was held together and the slavery issue, with its enormous moral and economic implications, was put off to another day.

In 1818, Missouri applied for admission to the Union as the second state to be carved out of the Louisiana Purchase. The first was Louisiana which came into the Union as a slave state in 1812. As Missouri's application came up for a vote there were eleven slave states in the Union and eleven free states. The balance in the number of slave states and free states was beginning to loom as critical, especially to Southerners, because the North was beginning to leap ahead of the South in population and thus in its numbers in the House of Representatives. Maintaining at least equality in the Senate was important to the South if it were going to be able to block legislation inimical to its interests – legislation such as tariff increases or, God forbid, a bill to outlaw slavery

The issue grew more heated – indeed ominous to Southerners – when Representative James Tallmadge of New York proposed an amendment to the Missouri Bill that would effectively end slavery in the state after twenty-five years. The "Missouri

Debates" became very tense, even threatening to turn violent within Congress itself. Finally, Henry Clay and others came up with a proposal that saved the day. Missouri would enter the Union as a slave state and the balance of slave states to free would be maintained by breaking Maine away from Massachusetts and bringing it into the Union as a free state. The remaining territories still to be settled in Louisiana would be closed to slavery north of Missouri's southern border (the 36 degrees, 30 minutes line of latitude) and open to slavery south of that line.

The "Missouri Compromise" of 1820 resolved, for the foreseeable future, the question of whether slavery would be allowed in the federal lands west of the Mississippi River. But many people were uneasy. Thomas Jefferson, living in retirement on his plantation in Virginia, wrote that the Missouri Debates woke him "like a fire bell in the night" and filled him with alarm. John Quincy Adams wrote in his diary that the debates were a prelude, the opening chapter to a "great and tragic volume."

The third major compromise came about because of a dispute over the protective tariff but, as some historians have shown, the real issue was, once again, slavery. Southern political leaders wanted to set a precedent of "nullification" – the right of a state to nullify a federal law — in case they would ever need to nullify a law that interfered with slavery. They hoped to establish that precedent with a nullification of the tariff. In 1832, South Carolina's legislature voted to nullify the protective tariff that had recently been passed by Congress. The reaction from the White House was swift. If the politicians in the Palmetto State had any notions that the President, a native son of their state, would be sympathetic to their action, they were sorely mistaken. President Andrew Jackson threatened to lead an army into South Carolina to enforce federal law and proclaimed he would hang every "nullifier" he could find from the nearest tree. It looked as if civil war were about to begin.

Once again cooler heads prevailed. Henry Clay of Kentucky, who was gaining stature as "The Great Compromiser," proposed a new tariff which would gradually lower over a ten-year-period, giving the northern manufacturers time to become more competitive with foreign producers, and Southerners the promise that the tariff rates would, ultimately, come down. President Jackson, on the one hand, and the southern "firebrands" led by John C. Calhoun, on the other, accepted the deal and the storm blew over. Of course, everyone who thought about it realized that the real issue — whether a state had the right to nullify a federal law or, indeed, secede from the Union — had not been resolved.

At about the time of Clay's tariff compromise William Lloyd Garrison and others were launching their abolitionist crusade. From the mid-1830s onward, an increasing number of Northerners were beginning to see slavery as a terrible evil that needed to be, at the very least, contained. In reaction, an increasing number of Southerners were embracing slavery more than ever and steeling themselves to resist not only abolitionism but also any attempts to impede slavery's growth.

The fourth time the political leaders of the nation were able to compromise came in 1850 and it was probably the most dramatic because this time civil war was a very real threat. With South Carolina leading the way (of course), southern states threatened to secede from the Union unless the new state of California became a slave state. Since the Missouri Compromise of 1820 the balance of slave states and free states had been maintained and now stood at fifteen slave and fifteen free. To allow California to be a free state, which it proposed to be, would give the North the majority in the Senate as well as the House where the North held a huge advantage. In the early months of 1850 it truly looked like civil war was about to start and most observers predicted that such a war would be very bloody.

In this crisis, Henry Clay – and the timely demise of his major foe, President Zachary Taylor – saved the day. Clay proposed a compromise that would allow California to enter the Union as a free state and, to balance the scales, the South would get the right to bring slaves into the "Mexican Cession" lands of the Southwest and a strong federal fugitive slave law requiring Northerners to return runaway slaves to their "rightful" owners. The issues were debated through most of the year 1850. Henry Clay, who was now in his seventies, was left exhausted when it was finally over. The debates and maneuvering made the reputation of Stephen Douglas, who did much to get the deal passed. Conversely, the debate destroyed the reputation of Daniel Webster who made a dramatic speech supporting the compromise despite the fact that it contained a fugitive slave law that his constituents in Massachusetts despised. After Webster spoke for it, they despised *him*!

The "Compromise of 1850" was one of the biggest political compromises of all time. Had the Congress not reached an agreement there surely would have been war between the slave states and the free states in that year.

Thus, General Kelly is not correct when he says the political leaders suffered an "inability to compromise." They got it done four times! But then came 1860. Perhaps it is the period from November, 1860 to April, 1861 to which General Kelly is referring.

It all started on November 6, 1860, when Republican Abraham Lincoln of Illinois won the presidential election with only 39.5% of the popular vote, but a clear majority of the electoral votes. His electors were *all* from northern states. Lincoln and his party had made it very clear where they stood on the slavery issue. They opposed slavery and thought it was wrong and immoral, but they felt it was up to the states to decide what to do about it within their own borders. Republicans wanted the *federal government* to ban the *spread* of slavery into federal territories, and that was *all* they proposed to do. The individual states could keep slavery as long as they wished. The Republican platform was not an abolitionist manifesto, and Lincoln said many times that he, personally, was not an abolitionist.

Without even waiting to see what the new President might do, South Carolina's legislature called a special convention which voted the state out of the Union by passing an "Ordinance of Secession." It invited other slave states to join it in the creation of a "Confederate States of America," a new nation that would guarantee the right to own slaves in perpetuity. "The state most likely to secede" had finally actually done it!

Henry Clay had died in 1852, but the man who held Clay's Senate seat, John J. Crittenden, attempted to fill "the Great Compromiser's" shoes. He proposed what has come to be called the Crittenden Compromise. The deal would be this: The old 36-30 line would be re-established by constitutional amendment, making it nearly permanent, and it would be extended all the way to the Pacific Ocean. Every territory south of that line, including land that might come into the Union in the future, would be open to slavery. There were several other components to Crittenden's plan, all designed to reassure the South that the newly empowered Republican Party would only ban slavery from northern territories, nothing more.

Through the early winter of 1861 there was panic in Washington as one southern state after another declared itself out of the Union and somber congressmen such as Senator Jefferson Davis delivered speeches of farewell to their colleagues. The man at the center of the crisis, newly-elected Abraham Lincoln, stayed at home in Springfield, Illinois, growing a beard and waiting for the right moment to ride the rails to Washington to take the oath of office. (Inauguration day was March 4th at that time.) When he received word of the Crittenden proposals he wrote to an old friend and fellow Republican, Senator Lyman Trumbull. "Have none of it," he said simply. "Stand firm as a chain of steel. The tug has to come, and better now than any time hereafter."

At this point we reach the moment when General Kelly may be right. If Lincoln had embraced the compromise, if he had traveled swiftly to Washington to reassure Southerners and halt the process of secession and the preparations for war that were going on in the South, civil war might have been avoided . . . again, for the moment.

I have often wondered, if Lincoln knew at that time that 650,000 lives would be lost in the war if it came, would he have accepted Crittenden's plan? I believe that even had he been aware of those grotesque numbers he *still* might have rejected the compromise. The moral issues had become too great to be compromised. Slavery was a moral evil; declaring it so and banning it from federal territories was the very least that should be done. Crittenden's plan would allow that awful institution into New Mexico and Arizona and any future lands the U.S. might acquire – Cuba, for example. Lincoln had been elected on a platform of *non-extension of slavery*. Could he renege on that promise before he even took office?

In his inaugural address he assured the South – now a seven state "Confederate States of America" – that he had no intention to interfere with slavery where it already existed and would even support a constitutional amendment to that effect. If reason had prevailed, it was the South that should have accepted his offer, stayed in the Union, and avoided war. But no. Many Southerners, as we say these days about jihadists, had become radicalized. They were determined to throw down the gauntlet, take a stand for what they saw as the moral righteousness of slavery, and fight for a slave republic. On April 12, 1861, Confederate guns opened fire on Fort Sumter in Charleston harbor and the bloodiest war in American history began.

Why the American Civil War started has been the subject of hundreds of books. As usual, the person who put it most succinctly was Abraham Lincoln himself. In his second inaugural address, delivered as the long and bloody war was entering its final weeks, he said: "Both parties deprecated war, but one of them would make war rather than let the nation survive; the other would accept war rather than let it perish. And the war came."

Yet, truly, if "Honest Abe" were a little *more* honest in his second inaugural he would have said: "One party would make war rather than allow slavery to be condemned and restricted; the other would accept war rather than praise slavery and allow it to expand. The secessionist slaveholders started the war and now the lovers of freedom have finished it."

"OLD BUCK"

SHOULD THIS SCOTSMAN'S REPUTATION
BE BETTER THAN IT IS?

If you can answer the question "Who was James Buchanan?" by saying "He was the president just before Lincoln," you are ahead of the majority of your countrymen. Most Americans have never heard of him and, if they have, they think he is one of those Presidents who never did anything worth mentioning – men of the Franklin Pierce, Benjamin Harrison, Chester A. Arthur, and James A. Garfield ilk. The textbook I used in college one semester – *The American Pageant* by Professor Thomas Bailey – described the three hundred-pound Buchanan as "the blubbery James Buchanan," and went on to say that he had exceedingly small feet of which he was "inordinately proud." (Donald Trump, take note!) His nickname was "Old Buck" and he was the only life-long bachelor to occupy the White House. It was all trivia all the time with this guy. But, perhaps he has been underappreciated.

Some very important things happened while "Old Buck" was in office. He had just been sworn in when the Supreme Court ruling in *Dred Scott v Sanford* was announced. For most of his time in office Northerners and Southerners were engaged in a bullet-riddled feud over slavery in Kansas. He was still President when Lincoln was elected, and seven southern states seceded from the Union. Surely, in the midst of all this, he must have done something!

Recently the reputations of various Presidents have been greatly enhanced. New biographies have been written that rehabilitate the reputations of Dwight D. Eisenhower, William Howard Taft, William McKinley and, most recently, Ulysses S. Grant. Perhaps we need to take another look at "Old Buck;" perhaps he deserves a grade higher than the "D" that most historians have assigned him.

Let's examine his record:

When he ran for president in 1856 the country was embroiled in the controversy that would eventually split it – the issue of whether slavery should be allowed to spread into the western territories. As a Democrat, his position was that of Senator Stephen Douglas (D – Illinois) – "popular sovereignty." The people who lived in a territory should be allowed to decide the issue. His opponent in that election was John C. Fremont, the first presidential candidate of the new Republican Party whose platform was to *ban* slavery from the territories. Buchanan won almost all of the southern states and enough northern states to win the White House, but the Republican Party had done surprisingly well in its first run and had shown itself a force to be reckoned with, at least in the North.

As he prepared to take office Buchanan was asked his view on the territorial issue. He answered that the Supreme Court would soon be announcing a ruling in a case that would settle the matter for all time. In fact, Buchanan had surreptitiously been in contact with a justice of the Court, had convinced him to broaden the ruling beyond the particular facts of the specific case, and he knew very well what the Court was going to announce. Two days after "Old Buck's" inauguration, the Supreme Court announced *Dred Scott*. In essence the Court ruled that because slaves were property protected by the 5th Amendment to the federal constitution, neither Congress nor a territorial legislature could deny a slaveholder his right to take his property onto federal land. Buchanan was hoping this would not only end the discussion of the accursed issue but also destroy the Republican Party by making its platform unconstitutional. On both counts he was hopelessly naïve and would soon be totally disappointed.

The issue that dominated most of Buchanan's four years in office was Kansas – whether it would enter the Union as a slave state or a free state. As a man with no moral feelings about slavery, he mostly did not care one way or the other and really just wanted the question to go away. When pro-slavery Kansans met at Lecompton, produced a constitution that allowed and protected slavery, and then finagled a fraudulent vote for it, Buchanan wanted Congress to get the whole thing over with by admitting Kansas as a slave state with the bogus "Lecompton Constitution." Senator Douglas was outraged at this attempt to make a travesty of his concept of "popular sovereignty." The Democratic Party split into Buchanan and Douglas factions and became virtually unable to accomplish much of anything for the next three years.

In 1857, an economic depression walloped the country causing massive unemployment in the North but not hitting the South especially hard because the price of cotton remained high.

This was a time in which the people did not expect the federal government to do very much to spur recovery from economic hard times, but Buchanan would have been ineffectual anyway, and the dispirited people turned against him dramatically.

By 1860, "Old Buck" was feeling really old and looking forward to retiring and returning to his home in Pennsylvania. But, leaving office quietly and going gently into the night was not to be his fate. The election of the Republican candidate, Abraham Lincoln, who won votes only in northern states just as Fremont had, set off a major crisis, and Buchanan was to be in office for four more long months. By Christmas, South Carolina had seceded, and by late January six other southern states had declared themselves out of the Union and into the new "Confederate States of America." Buck's handling of this "secession crisis" is what prompts most historians to take off points and give the big man with small feet a very low grade. From the White House he encouraged compromise efforts. He made a lame statement that he did not think the southern states had a constitutional right to secede, but he also did not think that he, as President, had a constitutional right to stop them! This spurred one congressman to exclaim, "Oh, for one hour of Jackson!" (When South Carolina nullified the tariff in 1832 Jackson screamed that he would personally lead an army into the state and hang every "nullifier" from the nearest tree.)

In January, upon learning that Fort Sumter in Charleston harbor was vulnerable, he sent the ship *Star of the West* to the fort with re-enforcements and supplies. When the ship was stopped at the entrance to the harbor he ordered it to return and he never made another attempt to resupply Sumter or any other federal facility.

After the Christmas of 1860, "Old Buck" mostly just waited for March 4th to come when he could hand over the whole secession problem to Abraham Lincoln. When that day finally came, Buchanan sat behind the newly inaugurated Lincoln and saw what true leadership was. In his inaugural address the new President made it very clear that there was no right to secede, that he would enforce federal law and maintain government facilities, and that if the South started a war he would certainly fight with every power available to him to preserve the Union. After the speech, Buchanan waddled off the platform and went away into oblivion.

To be fair, during his last four months in office Buchanan probably felt it would not be right to start a war with the Confederacy that the incoming President would be forced to deal with. With that in mind, I think historians have been a little harsh on the man. On the other hand, he certainly could have been more clear on the illegality of secession and on the strength with which the chief executive would fight it. There is some evidence that the southern leaders thought the incoming President, Lincoln, would be just as squishy as the outgoing one. It was not good for them to be so deluded.

James Buchanan was one of the most qualified men of all time to run for President. By 1856 he had been a member of the Pennsylvania legislature for two years, a member of the United States House of Representatives from Pennsylvania for ten years, a member of the United States Senate for eleven years, Secretary of State under James K. Polk (when the U.S. acquired California, the Mexican Cession and Oregon) for four years, and ambassador to Great Britain for three years. Clearly, he had plenty of legislative and diplomatic experience. The only things he did not have were a wife and children . . . which may partly explain why he was so inept in a crisis. Think about it.

On balance, after researching the man and trying not to be swayed by the fact that he was a fellow Scotsman, I would give him a B+ for his overall career in public service, but only a D for his presidency. The man did not seem to grasp the fact that the moral horrors of slavery were becoming a driving force in the minds of most Northerners and that the days of sliding past the issue and willing it to go away were over. He needed to be morally horrified at slavery (not "a northern man with southern principles" as he was sometimes called), and he needed to show more backbone. To put it bluntly, during his four years as President of the United States, James Buchanan was a disgrace to his tartan! What true, full-blooded "conquer or die!" Scotsman would allow such traitorous behavior as secession to go unchallenged?!

GRANT!

LIN MANUEL MIRANDA TURNED RON CHERNOW'S
BIOGRAPHY OF HAMILTON INTO A SPECTACULAR
BROADWAY MUSICAL.

*NOW I WILL DO THE SAME WITH HIS BIOGRAPHY OF
ULYSSES S. GRANT. OR, I SHOULD SAY, I WILL DO THE HARD
PART AND LEAVE THE EASY STUFF TO SOMEONE ELSE.*

**THESE WILL BE THE MAJOR SCENES WITH THE TITLES
OF EACH OF THE MAJOR SONGS:**

I. In 1837, fifteen-year-old Hiram Ulysses Grant works in his father's tannery in Ohio. His father, Jesse Grant, is a domineering type who speaks very loudly. They discuss Ulysses' future as Jesse sings: ***Don't Ever Have to Say, "I Coulda Been a Contender!"*** Jesse calls his son by his given name, Hiram, throughout the song. In the song Jesse refers to the fact that he, Jesse, is an abolitionist . . . but abolitionism is certainly NOT the path to riches or success for Hiram! He insists that his son, despite his lowly job as a tanner, has a great future ahead of him and he wants him to get to it.

II. Grant decides to attend the U.S. Military Academy at West Point. During his first year as a cadet, a distinguished visitor arrives – a hero of the War of 1812, General Winfield Scott. The general, 6'5" tall and dignified in a resplendent military uniform, inspires the young 5'7" cadet as he sings: **You're Bigger Than You Look, Cadet Grant**. Scott sees promise in the young cadet and he comments on how well Grant handles a horse.

III. Grant proposes marriage to Julia Dent in St. Louis. She is pretty and competent, but self-conscious about the fact that she is cross-eyed. Her father, Frederick, is a slaveholder. Julia and her father discuss the impending marriage and the groom as they sing: **What Sort of Man is This?** Dent despises abolitionists and says he will tell Ulysses he doesn't want his abolitionist father at the wedding ceremony. Julia mentions that her cousin, James Longstreet, will be in the wedding party.

IV. Grant serves in the Mexican War and questions the motives behind the U.S. war effort. He thinks it has been inspired by the slaveholders – particularly President Polk who owns slaves — as a way to take Mexican land and make new slave states. The officers Grant serves with include: Robert E. Lee, George Pickett, and James Longstreet, all of whom later become officers in the Confederate Army. They sing two songs: **Why Are We Here?** in which they discuss the purpose of the Mexican War and **We Will Meet Again**" in which they express assurance that they will fight together again, unaware that it will be on *opposite sides* of a great civil war.

V. Grant has resigned from the military, is living with his in-laws and is down and out with no prospects. He frequently drinks to drown his feelings of inadequacy. Wandering down the street despondently he sings: **What Am I To Do; Where Am I To Go?**

VI. The Southern states have seceded from the Union and fired on Fort Sumter, a federal fort in Charleston, South Carolina. Civil war has begun.

Lincoln, Secretary of State William Seward, and General Winfield Scott(dressed in uniform even more elaborate than the one he wore when he visited West Point in 1837) discuss the situation in Lincoln's office as they sing: **They Up and Did It!** They cannot believe the southern states have taken such a drastic step as to leave the Union and begin a civil war with the North.

VII. Grant, in command of a Union army in the northern part of Tennessee, captures Confederate Fort Donelson. The commanding officer of the fort asks for the terms of surrender and Grant replies "NO terms, just unconditional surrender." Grant sings: **No Terms!** Grant's top aid, Lt. John Rawlins, has taken on the responsibility of keeping Grant from hitting the bottle. He sings his own version of **No Terms!** as he tells the general he cannot have even *one* drink. (This song has many opportunities for double entendre and sarcasm about Grant's ability to be stern with others but not with himself.)

VIII. President Lincoln decides to free the slaves in the Confederacy as a military necessity to defeat the South. Frederick Douglass, a former runaway slave who is now an abolitionist, visits Lincoln in the White House. He is happy that Lincoln is finally making a move to eliminate slavery, but he urges him to do more, such as form black regiments, as he sings: **Let Us Fight!**

As Douglass sings Lincoln warms to the idea of black soldiers and finally says, "I'll do it!"

IX. Grant has besieged the Mississippi town of Vicksburg and the city has finally surrendered; all of its citizens are starving and wearing rags. As the exhausted and bedraggled southern prisoners file past them, Grant and William T. Sherman sing: *War is Hell!* They describe the ravages they have seen and the certainty that there will be more before the war is over.

X. President Lincoln finally makes Grant the commanding general of all Union forces. At a ceremony in the White House, he introduces him to top government officials as he sings: *I Like This Man, He Fights.* In one line of the song he orders his secretaries to find out what Grant drinks and to get some for the other generals in the Union Army. Grant stands on a sofa in order to be seen better by the crowd and sings: *On To Richmond!* In his song Grant declares he will fight Lee without let up, never let him off the hook, and wear him down. He concludes with, "I have twice as many men as you do, Lee. You're mine!

XI. Robert E. Lee surrenders to Grant at Appomattox. Grant tells Lee he will not be charged with treason. He and his men can keep their horses and their side arms. Grant sings: *Let Us Have Peace!* He espouses the need to have reconciliation and as little residual bitterness as possible.

XII. Lincoln, in a quiet moment, contemplates the cost of the war: 650,000 dead. He sings: *Was It Worth the Price?* He believes God has punished the nation for the sin of slavery.

XIII. Grant hears the news that President Lincoln has been assassinated. Grief stricken, he sings: ***The Best Man I Ever Knew.*** He extols Lincoln's spirit and his many kindnesses. He ruminates about how he might have saved Lincoln if he had accepted the President's invitation to go to the theater that night.

XIV. Three years after the Civil War Grant is elected President of the United States. Bedeviled by scandals in the administration and the endless demands on his time, Grant shares his sorrows with Julia and they sing: ***The Worst Job in the World!*** They complain of the job seekers, the corruption and the friends who turn against you. Julia, in an aside, admits she loves the status and the goodies that go with it.

XV. As President, Grant believes the Ku Klux Klan, with its viscous attacks on any black people who try to exercise their rights, is effectively putting the freedmen back into slavery. With his skillful Attorney General Amos Akerman, Grant moves to destroy the Klan and protect the "Freedmen." Akerman and Grant sing: ***Crush the Ku Kluxers Before They Steal the War!*** We can't let them take away the freedom we fought so hard to win! The song ends with the lament that even though the KKK may be squelched, the hatred of the blacks in the South and the tepid support for black rights in the North will result in the end of black freedom and equality. If that happens, all the bloodshed in the war will have been for nothing!

XVI. Grant, very ill with cancer and dying, is afraid he is going to leave his family destitute. Mark Twain encourages him to write his memoirs as a way to achieve financial security for his wife and children and a way to secure his reputation. Twain sings ***People Want to Hear Your Story!*** He recounts the great things Grant did: He won great victories in the west when the Civil War was going badly, he defeated the brilliant Robert E. Lee and captured Richmond, he served eight years as President and secured the hard-earned rights of the African-Americans. Twain promises to publish Grant's book and make his family financially secure. Grant replies, "Thank you, my dear friend. I can go now in peace."

There! I have done most of the work: I have outlined the story, set the scenes and named the songs that will excite the audience and make the musical *GRANT!* a big hit. All that's left to do now is *write* the songs – the lyrics and the scores . . . a simple chore for anyone with musical talent and access to a piano. Someone needs to grab the ball and run with it. I've done my part.

THE UNITED STATES VERSUS SPAIN

SPANISH SPEAKING PEOPLE DID NOT COME INTO
OUR COUNTRY. WE WENT INTO THEIRS.

As I discuss American history with people, I notice there is some confusion about the wars the United States has fought with Spanish-speaking people. In the 19th century we actually fought wars against Hispanics* on four different occasions.

1. In 1818, General Andrew Jackson led an American force into Florida in pursuit of Seminole Indians. In those days Jackson was always chasing Indians. He captured the Spanish fort of Pensacola, thus arousing the enmity of the Spanish government in Madrid. Secretary of State John Quincy Adams, in an unusual moment of support for Jackson whom he disliked, urged President Monroe to take advantage of the situation by demanding that Spain, if it was not able to secure its Florida border, should cede the territory to the United States. Within a year he had negotiated a treaty with

the Spanish under which Spain sold all of Florida to the United States. Thus, by invading Florida, Jackson made it possible for the United States to acquire a major territory from Spain.

2. In 1836, the Americans living in the northeast province of Mexico called Texas rebelled against Mexican rule. The Texans, mostly from the American South, were not happy with the Mexican government's new restrictions on their freedoms, particularly their freedom to own slaves! After the bloody massacre at the Alamo in which 180 Texans died, the Texans rallied under Sam Houston and defeated the Mexican army under General Santa Anna at the Battle of San Jacinto. Houston forced the unhappy Mexican general to sign a surrender document that gave Texas its independence. Texans lived in a state of limbo for the next nine years. They were an independent "Lone Star Republic" with their own government and their own flag, but they were seeking to become a state within the United States. The U.S. Government held them off because northern congressmen did not want another slave state in the Union and because no President wanted to provoke a war with Mexico.

3. In 1844, James K. Polk won the presidency on a platform of expansion. He would annex Texas (Mexico be damned!) and acquire California from Mexico as well. Even before he took office Congress annexed Texas through joint resolution. Then, when Mexico refused even to negotiate the sale of California to the United States, Polk provoked a war with Mexico by sending an American army into disputed territory along the Rio Grande river, virtually inviting the Mexicans to attack, which they did. In the ensuing war, the United States forces were victorious on every front. After General Winfield Scott's army marched into Mexico City, the Mexican Government surrendered. The Treaty

of Guadalupe-Hidalgo gave the United States everything Polk had been seeking, and then some. Mexico formally ceded Texas, with its border at the Rio Grande, and also California, and all of the territory in between them (today's Arizona, New Mexico, and large portions of Utah and Colorado). The U.S. thus took about half of the Mexicans' territory.

4. In 1898, Americans were wrought up about what was happening in the Spanish colony of Cuba, a mere ninety miles off the Florida coast. The Cubans were rebelling against Spanish rule and the Spanish government was resorting to harsh tactics to quell the uprisings. American newspapers were boosting their sales by printing lurid stories of the Spanish atrocities (some not wholly true or patently false – fake news!) and President McKinley sent a battleship, the *U.S.S. Maine*, to Havana harbor to protect American interests. In February, 1898, the *Maine* exploded killing 268 American sailors and the people were quick to blame Spain (unfairly, as it was discovered much later). McKinley was reluctant to go to war, but ultimately the public uproar was so strong and there were so many people within his administration advocating a military solution, that he finally pushed Spain into trading declarations of war during the last week of April. The war went extremely well – Secretary of State John Hay later called it a "splendid little war" – and after four months of fighting Teddy Roosevelt was the hero of the Battle of San Juan Hill in Cuba, Admiral George Dewey was the hero of the Battle of Manila Bay in the Philippines, and Spain had lost control of Cuba, Puerto Rico, Guam and the Philippine Islands. We gave Cuba its nominal independence but required that they include in their constitution the "Platt Amendment" that allowed us to interfere in their affairs whenever we felt like it. We took over the other is-

lands, but had to fight the Filipinos for three bloody years before they finally agreed to accept our benevolence.

So, there have been, in a sense, four Spanish-American wars. The result of all of them has been considerable territorial gains for the United States: Florida in 1819, Texas in 1845, California, New Mexico, Arizona, Utah and Colorado in 1848, and Puerto Rico, Guam and the Philippines in 1898. When we consider just these wars – let alone the numerous arrogant steps we took in Central America such as Teddy Roosevelt's maneuvers to take the Panama Canal Zone from Colombia – we must conclude it is a wonder we are not hated even more than we are in the Spanish-speaking world. How would we feel about the Canadians if Canada had seized all of our territory west of the Mississippi River, told us they alone would patrol the Great Lakes with their warships, and took the land to build a canal between Lake Erie and Lake Michigan?

- Technically "Hispanics" are Spanish-speaking people living within the borders of the United States. When these wars were fought the Spanish people involved were *not* living within the United States. But, after the wars were over, they *were*!

THE SPLENDID LITTLE WAR WAS HUGE!

BRIEF, DECISIVE, MANY HEROS, MANY SPOILS.
WHAT'S NOT TO LOVE?

One hundred and twenty years ago this spring the United States began its first large-scale intervention overseas by declaring war against Spain. Although the war would last only four months it would have enormous consequences. Indeed, it could be argued that the role the United States would play in world affairs for the entire twentieth century was determined by the Spanish-American War of 1898.

Predominantly the war was fought over Cuba, but there were other large issues involved as well. In 1895, the Cuban people began a rebellion against oppressive Spanish rule and Americans were sympathetic. After all, throwing off European rule was exactly what we had done in 1776. Our sympathies for their rebellion were heightened by stories of atrocities being committed against the Cubans by the Spanish authorities, particularly

General Valeriano Weyler. Tales of "reconcentration camps," starvation of suspected rebels, and rape of Cuban women appeared regularly in American newspapers. In New York City, a circulation war between William Randolph Hearst's *New York Journal* and Joseph Pulitzer's *New York World* resulted in lurid stories and cartoon drawings of Spanish atrocities, some of which were fabrications.

But, it was not just events in Cuba that were driving American policy makers. Many people within Congress and the administration of President William McKinley — the "Imperialists" — were hungry for a war that would demonstrate American naval power and give the United States a chance to catch up to the other great powers of the world who were acquiring colonies across the globe. Spain, with its far-flung colonies and feeble military provided an excellent target for the Imperialists.

President McKinley, a veteran of the Civil War, was reluctant to go to war with Spain. He had seen the "bodies piled up" when he was a young man and he had no appetite for new killing. The atrocities in Cuba and the chance for empire were not enough to persuade him. He did, however, send a battleship, the *U.S.S. Maine*, to Havana harbor to protect American interests on the island.

On February 15, 1898, the *Maine* blew up in a tremendous explosion that sent the ship to the bottom of Havana harbor and killed 268 American sailors. Newspapers immediately reported that the blast was likely the work of Spanish saboteurs who had planted "an infernal Spanish mine" (as the Hearst papers put it), and a huge groundswell of public opinion began clamoring for war. McKinley still hesitated. In exasperation, the Assistant Secretary of the Navy, Theodore Roosevelt, was said to exclaim, "The President has no more backbone than a chocolate éclair!"

Actually, McKinley was showing considerable backbone as he resisted the tremendous pressure for war. He tried to negotiate with the Spanish government and even managed to get the Spanish to agree to a certain measure of independence for the Cubans. But then McKinley's backbone began to become eclairish. In mid-April, congress passed a joint resolution supporting Cuban independence and demanding Spanish withdrawal from the island. McKinley signed it. On April 23rd, Spain declared war on the United States and on April 25th the U.S. responded in kind. The "warriors" in Congress and the military had won the day. They would have their war and some of them, such as Theodore Roosevelt, couldn't have been happier. Although he was thirty-nine-years-old, was married, had five children, and was Assistant Secretary of the Navy, T.R. itched to be at the center of the fighting. He resigned his position, volunteered for the army, and was soon organizing a cavalry brigade that came to be known as the "Rough Riders." He couldn't wait to get to Cuba and see action!

For war lovers, the Spanish-American War was all any devotee of guns, mayhem, and slaughter could hope for. On May first, less than a week after the declaration of war, Admiral Dewey sank the entire Spanish Pacific fleet in Manila Bay in the Philippines with the loss of only one of his men. Dewey had sailed from Hong Kong to Manila a few weeks before war was declared on orders from Assistant Secretary of the Navy Roosevelt who had taken it upon himself, while his boss was out of the office, to put Dewey in position to take control of Manila and perhaps all of the Philippines. Dewey's victory gave T.R. a payoff for his presumptuousness far beyond what he could have hoped for. The war to help the Cubans win their independence had quickly become more than that – a war to deprive Spain of all her colonies.

Back in the Caribbean, where one would expect this war for Cuban independence to be fought, events went equally well for the United States. Although the American army was not really prepared for combat – which was the case in all of our wars up through the Korean War – a hastily prepared force was ready by late June, landed in Cuba and began marching toward the Spanish stronghold of Santiago on the east end of the island. At San Juan Ridge, Teddy Roosevelt fulfilled his heart's desire for military glory by leading his "Rough Riders" up the hill (on foot, having had to leave their horses behind). He and his men charged through intense enemy fire and drove the "damn Spaniards" out. T.R. personally shot a Spanish soldier and excitedly exclaimed later that he saw the man "double up like a jack rabbit!" The newspapers back home reported every detail of Roosevelt's exploits and, within a few weeks, he was back in the United States ready to run for Governor of New York and begin his meteoric rise to the presidency.

A few weeks after the Battle of San Juan Hill, the Spanish Atlantic fleet was annihilated in Santiago harbor by a far superior American flotilla and by August the Spanish government, its entire navy in ruins and its army defeated on every front, was ready to sue for peace.

The treaty of Paris that ended the war gave the United States Puerto Rico, Guam, and the Philippine Islands. Cuba was given its independence, but the United States required the Cubans to include in their new constitution the so-called "Platt Amendment" that prohibited Cuba from making alliances with any other power. It also gave the U.S. authority to intervene in Cuban affairs and gave the United States a perpetual lease on a naval base at Guantanamo Bay.

Out in the Philippines, the islanders were totally dismayed to learn that the departing Spanish were going to be replaced by the arriving Americans. They had supported Admiral Dewey and the U.S. Army that came ashore after the Battle of Manila Bay in the fight against the Spanish. They had thought that the understanding was that the Philippines would become free just as Cuba was. When they learned that the Treaty of Paris called for their annexation to the United States they were outraged, and they began a rebellion to drive these new imperialists, the Americans, out.

The "War for Filipino Independence" lasted three years and was one of the ugliest wars in American history. It involved guerrilla tactics by the Filipino leader, Emilio Aguinaldo, and his men, and the use of torture by American troops to extract information from prisoners. Before the insurrection was over, five times more American soldiers were killed in the Philippines than had been killed in the war against Spain. Nevertheless, Aguinaldo finally surrendered, and the Philippines were forced to acquiesce to being an American possession.

By 1901 the United States was poised to play a significant role in world affairs. We had our own little empire consisting of Hawaii (which we had annexed during the war), the Philippines, Guam and Puerto Rico . . . and, also, Alaska which we had purchased from Russia in 1867, and Samoa and the Virgin Islands. We had naval bases in Hawaii, the Philippines and Cuba, and President Theodore Roosevelt was about to use strong-arm tactics to acquire land in Panama to establish a base and build an isthmian canal there. Meanwhile, Secretary of State John Hay was establishing our influence in China by announcing the "Open Door Policy" which called for free trade in China, making it clear we would not stand idle and be shut out of the China trade. We clearly were making our debut as a world power!

It took the American people quite a while to get used to their country's new status. Even in 1900 there were a sizable number of people who opposed any extension of American power and influence beyond our own borders. The "Anti-Imperialist" movement had many adherents. The Treaty of Paris which called for the annexation of the Philippines, passed the Senate with only one vote to spare. Throughout the rest of the twentieth century those who favored an "isolationist" policy would always be at least thirty-five to forty percent of the population. But those people were resisting a forceful tide because the United States was heavily invested in the Pacific and in Asia with several military bases and a considerable volume of trade, and we were recognized around the globe as a major world power. We allowed our military capacity to atrophy in the period prior to each of the world wars but, of course, we were ultimately dragged into both conflicts and we were the major force that determined the outcomes. By 1945 we were the most powerful nation on earth, a status we held, despite some challenges from the Soviet Union and China, until the end of the century.

All of this global involvement and accumulation of power began in 1898 when we challenged hapless Spain, destroyed the Spanish military and naval might, and built our own empire on the ruins of theirs. It is certainly fair to say that the Spanish-American War of 1898 set the stage for American foreign policy for the entire twentieth century.

WHAT IS A PROGRESSIVE?

FOX NEWS TELLS US PROGRESSIVES ARE BAD;
MSNBC SAYS THEY'RE GREAT. SO, WHAT ARE THEY?

One night, while channel flipping, I landed on Fox News and within a time frame of ten minutes I heard Senator Elizabeth Warren referred to as a "far left, liberal loon," a socialist, a loon ("liberal" implied, I guess) *and* a "progressive." In each case the label was supposed to be pejorative, an insult, a label at which all conservatives would nod in agreement that it was truly an awful thing. I understand how, from the conservative point of view, Warren is beyond liberal and even a socialist. I think even *she* might call herself "socialist." But, what I do not understand is equating "progressive" with those other labels, not to mention the implication that being "progressive" is dreadful.

When I taught American History, there was always a unit on "The Progressive Era, 1900-1920," that we usually got around to in March. It was always a relief to get there after the tedious post-Civil War stuff and the boring Presidents whose pictures looked like they belonged on cough drop boxes. (Young people update: You see there was this brand of cough drops called "Smith Brothers'" and on the box were drawings of the two brothers who each had long, ugly beards . . . as did all the Presidents after the Civil War: Rutherford B. Hayes, James A. Garfield, Chester A. Arthur, Benjamin Harrison – all bearded, all bland and colorless.) Anyway, after those guys, the "Progressive Era" came in like a breath of fresh air. There were reformers everywhere, most of them beardless, who were trying to make life better for everyone. And, there were consequential Presidents, most notably Theodore Roosevelt, the first of the "Progressive Presidents." He was followed by William Howard Taft and Woodrow Wilson who were also Progressives. T.R. and Taft were both Republicans, and Wilson was a Democrat, so the "Progressive Movement" clearly cut across party lines.

The Progressives at the turn of the twentieth century fought to clean up city, state and federal government. They tried to make government more democratic by advocating measures allowing citizens to propose legislation and to vote on laws in referendums. They even went so far as to advocate votes for women. They lobbied for legislation to protect the health and safety of factory workers and to provide for government regulation of the food and drug industries and the railroads. Their goal was to protect the public from nefarious, profit-hungry industrialists with their "public-be-damned" attitude. Theodore Roosevelt was one of the leading environmentalists of all time who personally took hundreds of thousands of square miles of forested land and natural resources away from private interests and placed them under the control of the federal government. In the first two decades of the twentieth century the Progressives confronted and often defeated the "malefactors of great wealth" – the plutocrats who made huge profits selling adulterated food and useless drugs to an unsuspecting public, treated their workers as if they were serfs, and controlled politicians as their errand boys. The reform politicians passed laws, such as the Pure Food and Drug Act, that protected the interests of the people.

I don't recall anyone in a college lecture or in a textbook saying very much negative about the "Progressives" and their movement. The message to us students was pretty simple and direct: the Progressives were good, honest political leaders who, at long last, brought in much needed reforms and made government serve the interests of the public. Of course, none of the business leaders and traditional politicians during the "Progressive Era" liked what the Progressives were doing, but the "fat cats" were the bad guys. Who cared what they thought? They were certainly on the "wrong side of history."

The sad conclusion to the Progressives' story came in 1920 when Woodrow Wilson's beloved League of Nations – which was an attempt to bring progressive ideals to the whole world – went down to defeat in the Senate. Later that year Warren Harding was elected President on a platform of returning to "normalcy" and the people made it clear they were sick of reform and were in the mood to party.

For the next eighty years the word "Progressive" lay dormant, even when its concepts flared brightly in the 1930s (The "New Deal") and in the 1960s (LBJ's "Great Society"). Now, in the twenty-first century it has re-emerged. But what does it mean in its latest iteration? And why do conservatives view it with such contempt? Do they really want to go back to the days of unfettered, "laissez-faire capitalism" and corrupt politics?

Today's "Progressives" seem to stand for the following:

- The right of every American to health services . . . provided by the federal government, if necessary.

- A federal government "safety net" to assure an adequate living for all Americans, particularly children.
- Taxes that adequately provide for the above, with wealthy Americans paying considerably higher rates than poor Americans.
- Federal regulations of business to protect the environment and safety of workers and consumers.
- Liberal immigration policies to allow refugees from war-torn regions and those who honestly seek a better life to enter this country with as few restrictions as possible.
- Laws protecting the rights of everyone regardless of religion, race, sexual orientation, or nationality. This includes "marriage equality" for homosexual and lesbian couples.
- Military spending restricted to that necessary to meet the needs of defending the nation. No foreign interventions for the purpose of expanding American power or economic interests.
- Protection of equal rights for women, including "reproductive rights."

The question is: Would the "Progressives" of Theodore Roosevelt's era agree with all the stands of the "progressives" today? If they would, then using that term the way it is being used makes sense. If not, perhaps the term "progressive" should be set aside as an historical artifact and we should stick to "liberal" ("loon" optional) and "socialist." Certainly the list above fits the "liberal paradigm."

Remembering that the overarching philosophy of the early twentieth century Progressive movement was the concept that the country needed to "make progress" toward a more healthy, fair and equitable society, I think a "T.R. Progressive" would agree with most of today's welfare programs and the Affordable

Care Act. They would fully support a graduated income tax (They were the ones who *created* it in 1916) and laws protecting the environment. Thus, on 1-4 above, the early Progressives would be sympathetic . . . with a caveat: T.R. once said that Progressivism was a "hedge against socialism," meaning that strict regulations by government would ward off demands for more radical approaches -- government *ownership* of business and a *complete* redistribution of wealth. Thus, any "progressive today who is actually a socialist (Bernie take note) would not be a Progressive of the T.R. brand.

T.R.'s Progressives would probably part company with today's "liberal agenda" from number five on. The Progressives of the early twentieth century were not particularly enthusiastic about immigration, they favored a strong military and T.R., Taft and Wilson all sent American forces to intervene in several places, particularly the Caribbean. Many of the Progressives were very racist; Wilson, in fact, reinstituted segregation in the federal government. And the concept of "gay marriage" would have completely eluded them.

So, I think referring to today's politicians on the left as "Progressives" is a little incorrect, at least historically. I would prefer to call them "liberals," "left," "far left," or, in extreme cases, "socialists." Leave the name "Progressive" to T.R. and the others.

As for loving the "progressives" as the people at MSNBC do, or hating the "progressives" as the people at Fox do, that's each individual's call. If you are wealthy, in the military or a veteran, or simply believe that government should tax, distribute money, and regulate as little as possible, you probably are a Republican and dislike today's "left-leaning" "progressive" politicians. But, you probably admire the Progressive Theodore Roosevelt — his *foreign* policies, not his domestic ones. So, where does that leave you since you like half of what the Progressives did but hate the other half? If you are a Democrat, you cheer T.R.'s domestic reforms, but hate his foreign policy. So, where does that leave *you*?

Wait a minute! As we reach the end of this discussion, I think I see where all this is leading. We need a *new* "Progressive Party," a party that stands for many of the progressive principles and cuts across party lines as the old one did. Ditch the far left "loons" on the one side and the neo-fascist racists on the other side and unite in a brand new party! T.R. tried to do this in 1912 with his "Bull Moose Party" and suffered defeat. But we need to see that election as a mere footnote to history. We can organize a new "Progressive Party" – and, yes, use the Bull Moose as our symbol – and this time carry elections and bring the country to new heights never dreamed of before!

FORGIVE ME, WILSON!

WHEN I WRITE ABOUT A MAN, I SHOULD PUT MYSELF IN THAT MAN'S SHOES.

In the movie, "Castaway," Tom Hanks, marooned on a desert island, "befriends" a volleyball he has found amidst the debris that has washed up on shore. He draws a face on it and calls the ball "Wilson" because of its brand name. For four years, through all his troubles trying to survive, he talks to Wilson and shares his innermost secrets and fears with him. Wilson reciprocates by always being there for him and listening without interrupting. But then, at a crucial moment when Hanks is making his escape from the island on a makeshift raft he has constructed, he falls asleep and Wilson is washed off the raft and floats away. When Hanks tries to swim out to retrieve Wilson and realizes he can't do it, he breaks down plaintively and cries out to Wilson begging him to forgive him for not returning his loyalty. Hanks' anguish is truly pathetic; he genuinely feels remorse for his lack of concern for Wilson the volleyball's wellbeing.

I feel similar remorse for my treatment of another mute Wilson – President Woodrow Wilson – during my years teaching American History. I always assessed his actions as President in a very judgmental way, never taking into account his tremendous personal struggles. In several instances where he made errors of judgment or held stubbornly onto positions that had clearly become untenable, I ridiculed him without considering his personal circumstances. Furthermore, I never gave him credit for the valiant effort he made to, quite literally, save the world. I certainly treated Wilson the President worse than Hanks treated Wilson the Volleyball.

Woodrow Wilson had to deal with a devastating personal loss and several severe health crises while he was President. Several other Presidents had to do the same, but I always took note of *their* struggles and sympathized with them. A few of them suffered the loss of beloved family members when they were in office or about to take office:

Andrew Jackson's wife, Rachel, died just after he was elected President in 1828, and he had to move into the White House without her. He dearly loved her and had once fought a duel to defend her honor. He sincerely believed the smear campaign that was waged against him during the election was what killed her. Besides being overcome with grief at his loss, Jackson carried a bullet around in his chest – placed there by his opponent in the aforementioned duel. The slug was too close to his heart to be surgically removed and caused him constant pain and indigestion. It's little wonder he was prone to fits of rage while he was in office.

President-elect Franklin Pierce's son died in a train crash just outside Andover, Massachusetts, as he and his family were traveling to Washington for his inauguration. Pierce was a very ineffectual President. Could his wife's and his own total despair over the loss of their son have had something to do with that?

Abraham Lincoln, who suffered through many personal trag-
edies during his life, endured the loss of his beloved son, Willie,
to typhoid fever in February, 1862, just when the Civil War was
at its lowest ebb. It was Lincoln's ability to carry on and make the
most consequential decisions of the Civil War in the year following Willie's death that mark him as a great leader.

Other Presidents have suffered health issues while they handled the toughest job in the country. Most notable in this regard,
of course, was Franklin Roosevelt who was afflicted with polio
and had to be carried or wheeled everywhere he went, and who
suffered considerable pain.

John F. Kennedy had suffered severe injuries to his back during
World War II and was in constant pain during his presidency.

But Woodrow Wilson's personal losses and health issues were
just as devastating as these and, until now, I have been unaware of
how tragic his situation was when he was handling the momentous crises that arose while he was in office. The recent biography,
Wilson, by A. Scott Berg, has brought Wilson's stories home to
me and made me feel the remorse I have mentioned above.

During the first week of August, 1914, Wilson's beloved
wife, Ellen, lay dying in the White House of "Bright's Disease"
(kidney failure). This was not just any ordinary week. War was
breaking out in Europe: Germany and Austria-Hungary, the
"Central Powers" were locking horns with Great Britain, France
and Russia, the "Allied Powers." On August sixth, as the massive armies of all those countries were mobilizing for war, Ellen
passed away. As she died, Wilson held her hand and wept openly.
He wept for the next four days as he moved in a daze through the
formalities of her funeral and her burial in her native Georgia.
For the next six months, just when it was his responsibility to
formulate American policies toward what soon became known

as "The Great War," he was completely and inconsolably grief stricken.

It might seem to the casual history scholar that American policy at the outset of the "Great War" was a simple matter. We would be neutral. But neutrality was never a simple matter for the United States. There were problems with it going back to the Napoleonic Wars one hundred years earlier. We are a country composed of people from many different nations and each group – the English, Irish, Italians, Germans, etc., is going to favor its homeland. Even though Wilson called on Americans to be neutral in thought as well as action, the people were going to find that level of neutrality difficult to maintain. It usually surprises many Americans to learn that there was a very large German population in the country who hoped to see the Kaiser's armies win, and a considerable number of Irish-Americans who also wouldn't mind seeing the British take a licking.

And then, there was the matter of foreign trade. This was always the bugaboo of American neutrality because each side in a European war believes that anything being shipped to its enemy – even something as seemingly harmless as cotton – is helping the enemy and is therefore un-neutral "contraband." For the first six months of the war, Wilson had to force himself to deal with these issues. What he really wanted to do after Ellen's death was crawl under a rock and die himself. He even considered resigning the presidency, citing mental lassitude.

Then, in the spring of 1915, just as the war in Europe was entering a critical phase and American neutrality would be tested to its fullest, Wilson fell deeply in love again. Her name was Edith Bolling Galt and the President was so in love with her that, like a schoolboy, he could barely think of anything else – even the sinking of the British passenger liner *Lusitania* and the loss of 128 American lives. It was all Wilson could do to stay focused on the crisis. He was busy composing ten-page love letters to Edith. The need to write diplomatic messages to the German government and to deliver speeches that articulated the American response to this outrage was an annoyance and an unwelcome distraction from what he *really* wanted to do – express his deep love.

He did handle the incident the way it probably should have been handled. The people of the United States probably would have responded well to a call for a declaration of war against Germany over the *Lusitania* and men such as ex-president Theodore Roosevelt were screaming for military action, but Wilson wanted the United States to remain neutral so we could be the arbiter of a fair and just peace agreement at the end of the fighting. In spite of his heart-throbs for Edith, he was able to steer a course that got the German government to apologize and promise to take greater precautions in its submarine attacks in the North Atlantic "war zone."

A year after the *Lusitania* incident the United States was still neutral, there were minimal German submarine attacks, and Wilson was preparing to run for re-election on the slogan "He kept us out of war." He married Edith and settled into his new life in the White House with his new bride by his side. As he headed into his second term he was going to need her in ways he could hardly imagine. He was going to have to respond to further, more unacceptable, German provocations; he was going to have to raise the largest American army ever assembled and send it into the country's first overseas war; and, he was going to bring to a conclusion the most devastating war in history, and try to do it in a way that would make another war impossible. Even a man with no distractions whatever would be daunted by those responsibilities. But distractions there would be.

In early 1917, Germany resumed "unrestricted submarine warfare" and in March German subs sent several American merchant ships to the bottom. Wilson finally felt compelled to go before Congress and ask for a declaration of war. As he entered upon this new and immense responsibility, his personal life was solid – his marriage to Edith was all he had hoped it would be – but a new issue arose that was going to make handling the war and the peace negotiations that followed very difficult. His health became fragile. Always prone to excruciating headaches, he began to suffer from them with increasing frequency as the war and its heavy responsibilities dragged on.

His goal, as almost everyone knows, was to make "The Great War" a "war to end all wars," and he thoroughly believed that his plan for the final peace treaty would accomplish just that. His "Fourteen Point Plan" for the peace, with its call for open agreements, freedom of the seas, reduction of armaments, free trade, self-determination of peoples, and, particularly, its fourteenth point – a "League of Nations" to resolve all future disputes – did stand a very good chance of preserving world peace through the coming generations if it had been adopted and approved by the United States and all the other nations exactly as written. But, world politics and domestic American politics can be very harsh and Wilson had to do battle with many strong-willed adversaries to get even part of his peace plan adopted.

First, he had to negotiate the peace treaty with the leaders of the countries involved in the war on the Allied side. (The Central Powers were not included in the peace conference – the first of many grievances the Germans were going to cultivate in the years to come.) After he decided to go personally to Paris to negotiate the treaty, Wilson made his first strategic mistake. He did not take a single Republican Senator with him to advise him on the negotiations . . . even though the Republicans had just won a majority in the Senate in the 1918 congressional elections. The Republicans felt jilted; they didn't have "any skin in the game," as we say today. Some historians have suggested that Wilson's frequent headaches were symptomatic of multiple small strokes and that his judgment was increasingly impaired. The failure to include Republicans seems very likely to have been the product of some sort of brain malfunction because, as a constitutional scholar, he had always believed that a parliamentary form of government was superior to a presidential form. In a parliamentary system, Wilson would not have even stayed in power following his party's loss of a majority in Congress. Surely, he should have known that it would be very advisable to include in his negotiating team the party that held a majority in the Senate – the very body that was going to have to approve the treaty by a two-thirds vote.

In Paris, he had to go head-to-head with the British Prime Minister, David Lloyd-George, and the very surly French Premier, Georges Clemenceau, the "Tiger of France." The French leader had scoffed at Wilson's fourteen-point plan by pointing out that even God had only ten points. Both European leaders felt that Wilson had no idea what their countries had suffered, that he represented a country that had come late to the cause, and that he should not expect them to accept a plan that did not extract severe penalties and reparations from the hated Germans. Wilson felt that these leaders were forgetting that their armies were beaten until the Americans arrived and that, without American help, it would be the Germans who were writing the peace treaty. This kind of head-butting made the peace negotiations much more difficult than anyone had predicted, and Wilson's constant headaches – along with the headaches anyone would suffer from dealing with stubborn men – made it a miracle he was able to get *anything* he proposed into the final treaty. The "Treaty of Versailles" that resulted was much more severe on Germany than Wilson wanted, but it did include a League of Nations and that, Wilson felt, was his major triumph in the negotiations.

But, there was still the Senate and the ratification process. The head of the Senate Foreign Relations Committee that would get the first crack at the treaty was Senator Henry Cabot Lodge of Massachusetts. Lodge had no use for Wilson (the feeling was mutual) and he was suspicious of anything that might interfere with American sovereignty. He was going to give the treaty all the scrutiny he could muster. Ultimately, he came up with fourteen "reservations" to the treaty – mocking Wilson's Fourteen Points – and it became very clear to impartial observers that Wilson would never get his treaty through the Senate without accepting at least one of the changes Lodge was proposing. The one Wilson needed to accept was the stipulation that the United States would not participate in any League of Nations missions without the approval of the United States Congress.

In the late summer of 1919, Wilson determined that the only chance he had of getting the treaty in its pure form through the Senate was to take his case to the American people. Against the stern warnings of Edith and his personal physician, he decided to make a speaking tour by train across the country. He would deliver dozens of speeches in cities from the east coast to the west coast and back again and convince the people to pressure their senators to vote in favor of the treaty. It was a campaign trip that would challenge the energies and health of even a young, healthy and vigorous person. Wilson was sixty-two-years-old and was constantly fatigued by those severe headaches.

At this point in the story I have, in the past, failed to see how heroic Wilson was on this trip. He said to Edith, his closest friends and advisors, "I have to do this to save the treaty and save the peace of the world." He truly believed it and, when we see what happened after the treaty was rejected we can easily conclude that he was right. In several of the speeches he delivered during that sweltering September trip he said that he believed that in twenty years there would be another world war if the nations of the world did not adopt this means (the League of Nations) by which to prevent it. Let it be noted that he said this in September, 1919; World War II began in September, 1939.

The trip totally exhausted him. Picture yourself delivering an energetic, hour-long speech in a stifling auditorium (no air conditioning then), and going on to deliver another one a few hours later, and another after that, and doing that for twenty-two straight days! It is a miracle that he staggered on and excited the crowds as long as he did. Finally, in Pueblo, Colorado, after he had delivered forty-seven speeches in twenty-two days, all of them in sweltering heat, he had to admit he could not go on and would be unable to complete the trip. The enormity of what this would mean to his beloved League was almost more than he could bear. His train took him straight back to Washington where, three days later, he suffered a severe stroke that left him mostly paralyzed on his left side.

For the next six months he was almost totally bedridden. Has there ever been a human being more miserable than Wilson must have been at that time? Those months, from October, 1919, to March, 1920, have intrigued historians ever since because, in effect, Edith was the President. She brought important papers into his darkened room, decided which ones he "needed" to see, and emerged with the ones he had "signed."

It was from his "sick-bed office" that Wilson made his final, crucial decisions about the Treaty of Versailles and its League of Nations. After the treaty failed to win the necessary two-thirds majority in the first Senate vote, it was clearer than ever that it would not pass unless Wilson relented and accepted Lodge's amendments. He refused; he instructed his fellow Democrats in the Senate to vote "no" on the treaty with the Lodge Amendments added to it. Some Democrats ignored his wishes and voted for the amended treaty because they knew that was the only way it would pass, but their votes were insufficient. The treaty went down to defeat. The United States would not be a signatory of the Treaty of Versailles, and the United States would not be a member of the League of Nations.

I have always thought that Wilson's stubbornness at this point disqualifies him from being included in the list of presidential greats. He should have known it was better to have the United States in the League under somewhat restricted circumstances than not to have our country in the League at all. But, Berg's biography makes me feel a little more empathy for Woodrow Wilson the man. We all know how cranky we can be when we are sick, and how difficult it is to think straight when we are in pain. Wilson truly was sick and in pain. From his point of view, a United States only half committed to the principles of the League would not be a worthy member. Perhaps he was hoping that the American people would wake up to their responsibilities when the presidential election of 1920 clarified them. If so, he was sadly mistaken. The Democratic candidate, James Cox, and his running mate, Franklin D. Roosevelt, campaigned vigorously on a platform that included the League. But, the Republican, Warren G. Harding, Senator from Ohio, captured the new mood of the country by adamantly opposing the League and advocating an end to efforts to save the world. He called for a return to "normalcy," and won the election easily. An intellectual such as Wilson must have cringed at the made-up word, "normalcy," and cringed even more when the people bought it!

How hard it must have been in March of 1921 for Woodrow Wilson to ride to the Capitol Building for Harding's inauguration sitting next to the President-elect who was the total antithesis of everything he believed in. In photographs of the event, Wilson looks as if he were about to vomit. I am more sympathetic to his plight now than I ever have been before. But really, when you get right down to it, the whole country, having elected Harding, should have said, in unison, "Forgive us, Wilson! We let you down when you were on the verge of giving the world a chance for peace!"

PURGING CONGRESS

**FDR WAS A SMILING, UPBEAT, POSITIVE PRESIDENT.
. . . BUT NOT ALWAYS.**

Two thousand eighteen marks the eightieth anniversary of President Franklin Roosevelt's attempt to destroy the political careers of congressmen in his own party who disagreed with him. Having won re-election in 1936 by the biggest margin in history (He won every state but Maine and Vermont.), FDR now wanted to consolidate his power and create a truly liberal Democratic Party. That meant getting rid of a few congressmen from his own party who were not on board with his programs. The press dubbed FDR's stratagem a "purge," the word then being used to refer to what was happening in Moscow at the time when Josef Stalin was shipping his opponents to Siberia.

For those of us who admire Franklin Roosevelt in most ways, the background for the purge was rather ugly. Roosevelt's ire was aroused in 1937 when he tried to "reform" the Supreme Court to make it more agreeable to his New Deal legislation. The Court had declared several New Deal measures unconstitutional and had particularly irked the President by wiping out the National Industrial Recovery Act and the Agricultural Adjustment Act. "What can we do for the industrial workers of America in this session of the Congress," he complained, "with any degree of certainty that what we do will not be nullified as unconstitutional by the Supreme Court?" He proposed to reform the Court by asking Congress to pass legislation (a "Court Reform Act") giving the President the authority to appoint additional justices (up to a total of fifteen) for every justice on the court over the age of seventy who would not retire. It was the justices from the "horse and buggy era," he believed, who were unable to see the modern day need for government action to manage the economy, and there were six of them on the court who clearly needed help.

Many members of Congress were quick to see that this reform bill would give the President nearly dictatorial powers. With huge majorities in Congress and a hand-picked Supreme Court, he would be free to do almost anything he pleased. This bill was an unacceptable meddling with the constitutional system of checks and balances. And it was not only Republicans who felt this way. When the "Court Reform Bill" came up for a vote, it went down handily, with many Democrats voting with the Republicans against it.

Roosevelt was beyond shocked; he was catatonic. By the end of 1937, he had a hit list of Senators who he felt had betrayed him, and he decided to support their opponents in the Democratic primaries; in states where there weren't any opponents he would recruit some. The Senators he marked for defeat were: Walter George of Georgia, Ellison ("Cotton Ed") Smith of South Carolina, and Millard Tydings of Maryland. On June 24, 1938, in one of his famous "Fireside Chats" on the radio to the American people, he called on voters in those three states to stay true to liberal principles and help create a truly liberal Democratic Party by voting for the Roosevelt candidates in the primaries. During the summer he even campaigned for "his" candidates but, in true FDR fashion, he did so with a smile and a generous dollop of praise for the men he was targeting for defeat. In Barnesville, Georgia, for example, he praised Senator George for his service, intelligence, and honor, but urged voters to cast their ballots for the other Democrat, Lawrence Camp, the "New Deal candidate." Besides getting more members of Congress who were more to his liking, Roosevelt was sending a message to all Democrats about what would happen to people who opposed him.

It is important to note that all of the targeted senators were from southern states. In 1938, seventy-three years after the Civil War, white Southerners hated the Republican Party – the party of emancipation – and very few black Southerners who would likely vote for the party of Lincoln were able to vote because of poll taxes, literacy tests, and outright intimidation. The "solid South" was solidly Democratic. Thus, winning the Democratic primary in a southern state was tantamount to winning re-election.

In South Carolina, the race issue in the Democratic primary was huge. In that race "Cotton Ed" was up against FDR's man, Olin Johnston. In one of his speeches "Cotton Ed" proclaimed: "Johnston endorsed the n——- and went one hundred percent for anything belonging to the New Deal, right or wrong, because he does not have the guts to disagree." On primary day Smith struck a heavy blow against FDR by beating Johnston 55.4% to 44.6%. After that, in true southern fashion, he beat the Republican candidate, J.D.E. Meyer, 98.9% to 1.1%! (How very different things are for the Republican Party in the South these days!)

The results were similar in Georgia and Maryland. In Georgia, Walter George smothered Lawrence Camp in the primary and went on to win handily in November. In Maryland, Millard Tydings crushed his FDR primary opponent in September and won handily over the hapless Republican fall guy in November. Thus, Franklin D. Roosevelt's effort to cleanse his party of congressmen who were lukewarm on the New Deal was a complete fiasco.

What lesson can we draw from FDR's attempt to purge members of his own party who opposed some of his policies? Most importantly, we can see that even a hugely popular President cannot dictate a local election. Members of Congress have their own appeal in their own states or districts. "Cotton Ed" certainly proved that axiom in South Carolina in his own obnoxious way. FDR carried South Carolina by a large majority in 1936, but the Palmetto State voters were not going to desert their man just because that liberal Yankee FDR asked them to!

But wait! There's more to consider here. Millard Tydings easily survived Roosevelt's attempt to purge him in 1938, but he suffered a far different fate in 1950. In that year Tydings had the gumption to stand up to Senator Joseph McCarthy, the Wisconsin senator who was gaining fame for his unsupported, yet terrifying, charges of communist sympathies by politicians in Washington. Tydings called out the Senator from Wisconsin for his smear tactics. McCarthy fought back by accusing Tydings of being "soft" on communism, a charge that was dynamite in 1950. McCarthy's charge caused the erstwhile Maryland senator to suffer a heart-breaking defeat. Thus, we see that if an outsider raises a strong enough issue – regardless of how invalid – he or she might be able to swing a congressional election.

In 2018, eight decades after FDR's rather ugly attempt, will President Trump try to purge Republicans who are not to his liking? Will the Democrats take advantage of a divided GOP? Will the 2018 election be like 1938 or like 1950? Will there be a purge of disloyal Republicans or a surge of anti-Trump Republicans? For historians and political junkies such as I am, the congressional elections in 2018 will be very interesting.

BREAD OR BULLETS

HOW SHOULD THE U.S. GOVERNMENT SPEND ITS MONEY?

In 1945, after Japan surrendered, General Douglas MacArthur took over that devastated country as the military governor. The Japanese people feared the worst because MacArthur was the American military leader whom their armies had driven from the Philippines only to see him return, drive them from the islands and liberate the thousands of American and Australian soldiers being held in squalid prison camps. Those prisoners of war had been starved for three years following the horrid "Bataan Death March." What mercy could the Japanese people expect from the American general?

But, instead of retribution, MacArthur ordered 3.5 million tons of U.S. Army food delivered to Japan and he set up army kitchens to feed the people. When the United States House of Representatives Appropriations Committee asked how he could justify the expense of such massive food distributions to our recent enemy who had shown no compassion for American soldiers, many of whom had starved to death, MacArthur replied: " . . . starvation breeds mass unrest, disorder and violence. Give me bread or give me bullets." In his memoirs MacArthur succinctly tells us, "I got bread."

He went on to bring order and democracy to Japan, and to write a new constitution for the nation, a document modeled largely on our own but with additional sections renouncing war as an instrument of foreign policy. He also oversaw a massive program of land reform, made sure that women were treated equally and got the right to vote (at long last!), and rebuilt the Japanese economy. To build better relations with the United States, he promoted Japanese baseball by attending games and sending a Japanese team on a tour of the United States. When he left Japan in April, 1951, having been removed from command by President Truman because of their Korean War dispute, the Japanese people cried tears of bitter sorrow as thousands of them saw him off at the airport.

In the sixty-seven years since then, Japan has been one of our most reliable allies. This was particularly important during the "Cold War" years, but it continues to be important today as we confront the dangers of a crazed dictator in North Korea who plays with nuclear weapons.

Once again, history informs us as we make our way forward. President Trump's recent budget featured massive cuts in many programs including the money for the State Department and "foreign aid." It also called for large increases in the defense budget, but perhaps the increases were not enough. Echoing General MacArthur, the current Secretary of Defense, James Mattis, stated, "If you don't fund the State Department fully, then I need to buy more ammunition, ultimately."

On several occasions President Trump has expressed admiration for General Douglas MacArthur. I suggest he read pages 306 and 307 of MacArthur's memoir, *Reminiscences*. The great general's full account of the story I have summarized above would convince President Trump, I am sure, to reinstate the funds for the State Department and, in particular, foreign aid. I am sure the President would agree that it is always preferable to spend money on bread rather than bullets.

STATUES AND MONUMENTS

Statues and Monuments Can Be Controversial

THE ENIGMATIC THOMAS JEFFERSON

SCHOLARLY YET SENSUAL, PRINCIPLED YET PRAGMATIC. THIS MAN IS HARD TO PIN DOWN.

I am writing on July 2nd, the day John Adams predicted would be celebrated in the future with parades and fireworks because that was the day, in 1776, when the Continental Congress voted to declare independence. Adams was instrumental in bringing that vote about so, naturally, he figured to be the founding father who would be the most honored every time the country celebrated its independence. But, alas for poor John Adams, all the honor went to his friend, future enemy, and future friend again, Thomas Jefferson, the author of the Declaration of Independence which was officially adopted two days later.

In my book American *History: It's More Than the Crap You Learned in High School,* I put forth Adams as a role model, but I do not include Jefferson in that chapter. Nor do I consign him to the chapter "Rogues and Cautionary Tales." To me, he is an enigma, the one Founding Father I cannot decide whether I like and admire, or dislike and disdain.

Most people – and most historians – hold Jefferson in high regard. He has his own memorial in Washington next to the Potomac River; he is one of the four faces on Mount Rushmore; the capital city of Missouri is named for him; and his profile adorns the nickel. In 1962, President Kennedy famously welcomed Nobel Prize winners to the White House by saying, "I think this is the most extraordinary collection of talent, of human knowledge, that has ever been gathered together at the White House, with the possible exception of when Thomas Jefferson dined alone." Clearly Jefferson is very well respected.

And yet, not long after I read Kennedy's remarks in the newspaper, I attended a lecture by my history professor at the University of Michigan, the well-known and acclaimed "Federalist Era" scholar, Bradford Perkins. The lecture was entitled "The Jefferson Fraud." For an hour Perkins tore into Jefferson's reputation saying, among other things:

He never had an original idea. Everything he wrote that he gets so much acclaim for was just a rehash of what others before him had said. The Declaration of Independence was simply a restating of the ideas of John Locke, the English philosopher who wrote his essays almost one hundred years before Jefferson ever put pen to paper.

He was a hypocrite who wrote about equality yet kept slaves and, not only that, took advantage of his dominion over those unfortunate human beings and probably fathered several bastard children. (When Perkins gave his lecture, DNA testing was unheard of and it was not proved until much later that there indeed were African-American descendants of Thomas Jefferson.)

Perkins used very strong language in this lecture; he truly believed Jefferson was a rogue and an evil person. Bradford

Perkins died just a few years ago still asserting (tongue firmly planted in cheek) that he was one of the country's few remaining Federalists (the party in the 1790s and early 1800s that opposed Jefferson's policies and attacked his character.)

I was very amused by Perkins's lecture, as were many students (some of whom were not even taking the class) who packed the hall that day. To some extent I agreed with him. Why, indeed, should Jefferson get credit for simply restating what had been said many times before? More importantly, he really was a huge hypocrite for writing about equality while simultaneously owning – and abusing – slaves!

On this day, 241 years after Thomas Jefferson wrote the famous declaration and fifty-five years since Professor Perkins delivered his lecture, I will give you my "take" on the man Thomas Jefferson by considering Perkins's two major points.

As for Jefferson being practically a plagiarist, I do not agree. It is true that the major concepts in the Declaration of Independence were well known long before 1776, but Jefferson explained them much better and more elegantly than John Locke or anyone else ever had. I could quote one paragraph from John Locke's treatise to show how pedantic and uninspiring the man was, but just one sentence will give you the idea. Locke wrote: "If man in the state of nature be so free, as has been said; if he be absolute lord of his own person and possessions, equal to the greatest and subject to no body, why will he part with his freedom?" Jefferson, by contrast, explained Locke's "contract theory of government" very succinctly in the famous words that many Americans can recite: "We hold these truths to be self-evident, that all men are created equal, that they are endowed by their creator with certain unalienable rights, that among these are life, liberty and the pursuit of happiness – that to secure these rights, governments are instituted among men, deriving their just powers from the consent of the governed . . . "

In essence what Jefferson did was get to the core of the complex theory and explain it in a way that was eloquent but also accessible enough that the average person could carry it into battle – both actual and metaphorical – in the six-year struggle for independence that lay ahead. Jefferson accomplished in 1776 what Lincoln was to accomplish four score and seven years later in his Gettysburg Address. He used beautiful, well-crafted words to place profound concepts into the culture.

On the second charge, that Jefferson was a hypocrite, I have to agree. First, however, hear what his defenders say:

He inherited his slaves and he was part of a society that accepted slavery as a long-standing fact of life. His wife, Martha, had died when he was still very young leaving him alone and desperate for female companionship. According to his most recent biographer, John Meacham, the slave, Sally Hemings, was "physically desirable" at age fourteen when she arrived in Paris as a servant to the Jefferson family. Sally was the half-sister of Jefferson's deceased wife – her father had impregnated one of his slaves, of course – and so Sally was light skinned and bore a resemblance to his deceased wife, Martha. Thus, the circumstances were perfectly aligned to lead to a sexual relationship between Jefferson (age 39) and Hemings (age 14). Er, yeah. . . . Well, enough for his defense!

Whether the relationship was consensual or not will never be known. In any event, Jefferson today would be charged with statutory rape. Furthermore, since Sally was his slave, we could make the charge of "institutional rape" because, as an enslaved woman, Sally must have felt she had no choice but to submit to the advances of her white master. If so, how degrading that must have been for her!

An interesting twist to the Sally Hemings affair was that under French law, Sally could sue for her freedom and she would probably have achieved it. This became an important card for her to play when she became pregnant just as Jefferson was preparing to leave France and return to the United States. She was strong-willed and bright – she knew the law – and she threatened to sue for her freedom unless Jefferson promised to give her many personal privileges, particularly one that stated that all of her children would be set free when they reached the age of twenty-five. Jefferson agreed to this and we know that she eventually had four children who lived to adulthood. Thomas Jefferson was the father of all of them.

Thus, we know for sure that what people were saying even at the time was true – that Thomas Jefferson was engaged in a sexual relationship with one of his slaves – possibly more – while he was Secretary of State, Vice President of the United States, and President of the United States. He thus joins a select group of Presidents who were engaged in what, in their time, was immoral behavior (is anything immoral any longer?).

As for slavery itself, Jefferson included in his original Declaration of Independence a sentence in which he stated that imposing the slave trade on the thirteen colonies was one of the King's offenses that justified rebellion. Much to Jefferson's chagrin, that sentence, at the insistence of southern delegates, was expunged from the document. We also know that Jefferson was very troubled by the institution but could not see any workable way to end it. "With slavery," he wrote, "we have the wolf by the ears and cannot safely hold on to it or let it go." So, I give Jefferson a sliver of credit for at least being uneasy about slavery and its immorality.

At the end of his life, Jefferson did not free his slaves – except for Sally Hemings and three members of the Hemings family (aside from his own children who were freed when they reached twenty-five). Part of the reason no slaves were freed was that his estate had to be kept intact to pay some of the many debts he owed when he died. He also felt that they would have a difficult time making their way in a country in which slavery was deeply entrenched. Of course, he could have at least given them a chance!

On balance, Jefferson was no better or worse in his handling of the slavery issue than most of his contemporaries, but in the realm of personal morality he must, at least, stand accused of using his power for his own sexual gratification. Even if Sally did truly love him – and since she did agree to return home with him, she *may* have – there was always the fact that the relationship started when he was the master and she was his slave.

So, is Thomas Jefferson, author of the Declaration of Independence – a rogue or a role model? I began by calling him an enigma and I have to finish with no clear and compelling answer. He had his strengths and his weaknesses. He was, in short, very human. He was a very scholarly and learned man; he was a consummate wordsmith; he sought constantly to improve himself; and he worked very hard to serve his country. He was extremely devoted to his wife, while she lived. Whether he would have indulged in the Hemings affair had his wife still been living is a question not worth asking. Oops, I just did!

The Hemings relationship can easily be described in a way that makes it very unsavory, especially to modern sensibilities. The ages of the two, alone, cause many people to recoil, as recent events in Alabama have shown. However, it can also be the story of two very passionate and physical people who were truly in love with each other for forty years – from 1787 until Jefferson's death in 1826. We can also note that fourteen was not considered as young then, when life expectancy was 40, as it is now. The movie "Jefferson in Paris" mostly takes this view.

I do dislike Jefferson's inability to attack slavery directly. There were some people in his day, John Adams for one, who were able to do that. A true hero and role model would have done more to attack that vile institution. His "wolf by the ears" metaphor does explain his reticence, but in my judgment, it does not let him off the hook entirely. He knew it was wrong.

In the end, if the scales on Jefferson were perfectly balanced between role model and rogue, the "role model" side for me would probably prevail when one final fact is thrown onto the role model side: Jefferson brought macaroni and cheese from Europe to dinner tables in America. The man who did that deserves a little slack on the other issues! . . . Oh, Please, lighten up!

LINCOLN THE MESSIAH

THE LINCOLN MEMORIAL IS LIKE A SHRINE.

I am writing on Friday, April 14th and it is "Good Friday," the day Jesus the Christ was hung on the cross. In 1865, April 14th was also "Good Friday" and that evening Abraham Lincoln was assassinated. The people at that time placed considerable significance on the fact that Lincoln was killed on the very day that Christians mark the crucifixion of the Savior.

"Father Abraham," as some had taken to calling him – his name, alone, so evocative of the Bible – had always used Biblical references to add impact to his speeches. Only six weeks before his assassination, in his Second Inaugural Address, he had made a Christ-like appeal to the nation to show compassion and forgiveness to the vanquished Southerners: "With malice toward none, with charity for all, let us bind up the nation's wounds." Could there be any doubt, people said, that this beautiful man, the savior of the nation and the liberator of four million enslaved souls, was the modern day "Messiah" suffering the same unjust fate as the real Messiah?

The deification of Abraham Lincoln began during the days immediately after his death, and much of that was because his assassination happened on Easter weekend. John Wilkes Booth hated Lincoln and wanted to destroy him. But the night he chose to do his awful deed was going to help make Abraham Lincoln a hero and a martyr.

Within two years of Lincoln's death a movement began to erect some sort of major memorial to Lincoln in Washington, D.C. Finally, in 1911 Congress created the Lincoln Memorial Commission with President William Howard Taft as president of the group. In 1913 Congress approved the design and the location, and work began on the construction of the memorial the following year. Daniel Chester French designed the statue of the seated Lincoln which was carved by the Piccirilli Brothers – famed marble cutters who had immigrated into the United States from Tuscany, Italy. The monument was completed in 1922 and dedicated by President Harding with Lincoln's only remaining son, 78-year-old Robert Todd Lincoln, in attendance.

Since 1922 the monument has been visited by millions of people from across the globe and has been the site of several major events that have advanced the cause of civil rights, most notably: Marian Anderson's concert that could not be held in Constitution Hall because the Daughters of the American Revolution's refused to allow a black singer to perform there in 1939, and the 1963 Civil Rights March on Washington at which Dr. Martin Luther King Jr., delivered his famous "I have a Dream" speech. How fitting it was to have Marian Anderson sing "My Country 'Tis of Thee," and Dr. King delivering his inspiring words with Lincoln peering over their shoulders.

Inside the building, on the marble walls surrounding the statue, are the words of two of Lincoln's most famous speeches: The Gettysburg Address and the Second Inaugural Address. Both speeches are rightfully acclaimed for their exquisite language and their profound sentiments.

There is no man or woman in American history more deserving of the largest and most architecturally magnificent memorial in the country than Abraham Lincoln. He started life as an adult believing that slavery was wrong, but also believing that it should only be confined to the South and that black Americans, as an inferior race, should be transported to Africa or a Caribbean island if they became free. As he dealt with the immense problems of the Civil War and met black Americans, he grew, and he began to believe that African-Americans should not only be free but also be set on a path of true political equality. Ultimately, he used his immense executive power to set the slaves free and his leadership skills to win the war that enabled them to keep their freedom. His contribution to the improvement of this nation was immense!

In another essay I will propose an idea whereby all statues and monuments can be preserved as long as historical honesty is maintained. Even this wonderful memorial could use a smattering of realism, as I will suggest in that essay. At the moment, however, I would like to let Lincoln's greatness stand and his beautiful memorial to be proclaimed "well-deserved!"

MR. GARRISON AND THE "RESPECTABLE" MOB

THE PEOPLE HANGING OUT, DRINKING
AND SMOKING, ON GARRISON'S STATUE ON
COMMONWEALTH AVE. SHOULD FIND OUT WHO
"THE DUDE" IS.

A statue of a seated William Lloyd Garrison resides on Boston's Commonwealth Avenue mall between Dartmouth and Exeter Streets. There is a bit of irony in memorializing Garrison in Boston because the leading citizens of that city once tried to lynch him.

Here is the story:

On the evening of August 21, 1835, Boston mayor Theodore Lyman presided over a capacity crowd meeting in Faneuil Hall. The speakers for the evening denounced abolitionists and declared their support for the perpetuation of slavery. The crowd cheered every word and then passed a resolution accusing abolitionists of trying to scatter "among our friends (the white Southerners), firebrands and arrows of death."

The resolution also denounced "the intrusion upon our domestic relations of foreign emissaries." The business and political leaders conducting the meeting were upset that Boston abolitionist and editor, William Lloyd Garrison, had invited George Thompson, an English abolitionist, to visit America on a lecture tour. The British Parliament had recently abolished slavery in the empire and Thompson had been instrumental in getting that done. Tall and charismatic, Thompson was already in the United States. The business leaders at Faneuil Hall were fearful that this invader would disrupt the union with the South. Implied in their speeches was the message that violence might be necessary against Thompson and Garrison.

Rather than fearing any action that the Boston pro-slavery faction might take, Garrison was delighted with the meeting. The Faneuil Hall speeches provided new fodder for his abolitionist newspaper, *The Liberator*. Garrison had been publishing it from a dingy printing office in Merchant Hall for four years but had not been able to generate a large subscription list. For most people it was far too radical with its demands for the immediate emancipation of the slaves without compensation to the slave owners. People were even appalled that Garrison had once asserted that a black man who fled from the police was much more likely to be shot than a white man! Perhaps if the good citizens of Boston read stories about the way the slave power was trying to suppress freedom of speech in the city they would at least feel some sympathy for the cause.

In person, William Lloyd Garrison did not seem like a dangerous radical. At thirty he was nearly bald, wore round, metal-rimmed spectacles, and spoke in a voice so calm and serene that one would expect he was a poet or a musician. But, in 1835, the people of Boston were convinced that his disruptive and dangerous demands were going to bring economic ruin on the city and quite possibly destroy the Union.

In *The Liberator's* first edition on January 1, 1831, Garrison had vowed to use strong language to denounce slavery, slave holders, and the "abettors of slavery," including the people of the North who condoned or passively tolerated it. Every weekly edition since then had lived up to its editor's promise, calling slave owners "man-stealers," "thieves," and "murderers."

Although few people subscribed to *The Liberator* and hardly any copies reached the South where local postmasters habitually burned them, Southerners had grown increasingly furious with Garrison's unrelenting attacks on them and their "peculiar institution." So angry was one group of Mississippi planters that they reportedly offered $20,000 for Garrison's head. Southern newspapers called on Bostonians to silence the raving maniac and incendiary. If Garrison continued to publish, they threatened, the South would be forced to sever its profitable commercial relationship with Boston, home to numerous shipping firms, many of which carried cotton, tobacco . . . and slaves.

Garrison was not surprised at the furor against him in Boston. He had long before realized that Bostonians were nearly as pro-slavery in sentiment as were Southerners. In the first edition of his paper he had said: "I found contempt in New England more bitter, opposition more active . . . prejudice more stubborn . . . than among the slaveholders themselves." For this reason he had decided to publish in Boston "to lift up the standard of emancipation within sight of Bunker Hill and in the birthplace of liberty."

Garrison expected that an immediate, active response would result from the pro-slavery enthusiasm generated at Faneuil Hall. "I assume our principle cities will be visited by assassins," he wrote almost hopefully. "It matters not. . . . If we perish, our loss will but hasten the destruction of slavery more certainly." The abolitionist editor was aware that the violent feelings aroused against him might result in his martyrdom, and he was prepared for it, almost welcomed it.

During October, 1835, Bostonians learned that Thompson planned to speak on the twenty-first at a meeting of the Female Anti-Slavery Society. The *Boston Commercial Gazette* took the lead in arousing public outrage and its editor predicted that "men of good property and standing" would prohibit the Englishman from speaking.

Two Boston merchants, Isaac Sterns and Isaac Means, commissioned apprentices at the *Gazette* to print handbills informing the public of the Englishman's planned visit and noting that this offered "a fair opportunity for the friends of the Union to snake Thompson out!" The notice went on to offer a $100 reward to "the individual who shall first lay violent hands on Thompson so that he may be brought to the tar kettle before dark."

On the morning of the 21st, these posts appeared on warehouse walls and in shops, hotel lobbies, and bars throughout the commercial district. Hundreds of men, including some of the most prosperous and respected in the city, made plans to be at the New England Anti-Slavery Society offices at 46 Washington Street in time for the meeting scheduled for three o'clock that afternoon.

Garrison had already decided that Thompson should remain out of town. During the previous six weeks the Englishman had been assaulted in Concord, New Hampshire, and elsewhere. Apparently unconcerned for his own safety, Garrison left his home on Brighton Street at two o'clock to attend the meeting. As he approached the door, he saw about one hundred men gathered in the street outside. On the stairway leading to the meeting room he had to squeeze past several menacing young men.

Inside, society members were trying to hold their meeting despite the jeers of several intruders at the rear of the room. As Garrison took a seat one man shouted, "That's Garrison!" The abolitionist turned and said, "Gentlemen, perhaps you are not aware that this is a meeting of the Boston *Female* Anti-Slavery Society." He asked them to leave unless, perhaps, some of them were women in disguise, in which case he would introduce them to the rest of their gender and they could be seated. His mocking words quieted the crowd only briefly. Soon, more men had forced their way from the stairway into the room.

The society's president, Mary Parker, suggested that Garrison leave to avoid offering the mob any pretext for violence. Garrison agreed and went into the office next to the meeting room. There he sat down to write an account of the incident for the next edition of *The Liberator.*

Meanwhile the mob outside had grown to several hundred people, filling Washington Street. Shouts of "Thompson! Thompson!" filled the air. Mayor Lyman arrived and tried to explain to the crowd that Thompson was not present, but the throng pressed forward anyway. Inside, some young men began to kick down the door to Garrison's office. The abolitionist saw them peering through the broken boards and cursing at him, but he continued writing, seemingly unperturbed.

The women continued their meeting despite the uproar, bowing their heads in prayer and unmindful of the noise. But Mayor Lyman, fearing for their safety, beseeched the members of the society to go home. His constables had cleared the stairway and, he said, if the women did not take this opportunity to escape, he could not guarantee their safety. The women agreed to leave, but only after they had approved, with proper parliamentary procedure, a motion to adjourn. Then they marched out together, white women paired with black, "thus giving," as society member

Maria Chapman later put it, "what protection a white skin could ensure a dark one."

With the women gone and Thompson absent, the mob's attention now focused on the abolitionist editor. "Lynch Garrison!" the men shouted as they pressed toward the door. Some of those in the crowd demanded that the sign reading "Antislavery Rooms" be torn down. In an effort to appease the mob the mayor ordered the sign thrown into their midst where it was promptly broken up and its pieces distributed as souvenirs.

The constables now managed to clear the door to Garrison's office, and the mayor ran in and begged the still-complacent young man to leave through a rear window. Outside, the shouts of "Garrison!" grew louder. Although loathe to show any fear of a mob, Garrison finally submitted and jumped from the window onto a shed roof and fell from there to the ground. He ran to a nearby carpenter's shop and tried to run through it to Wilson's Lane, but some in the crowd saw him. Although the friendly carpenters attempted to bolt the door and hide Garrison behind lumber on the second floor, the mob soon caught up with him. His assailants were prepared to hurl him out the window but relented at the last minute and allowed him to climb down a ladder to the crowd below.

Fortunately for Garrison, Dan and Aaron Cooley, brothers who ran a teamster's business on India Street, were the first to grab him. Although the Cooleys were well known as opponents of abolition, they shouted, "He shan't be hurt!" and they protected Garrison as the crowd swept them along. At one point a frenzied man tried to club Garrison, but one of the Cooleys raised his arm to deflect the blow.

The crowd pushed Garrison out Wilson's Lane onto State Street. Along the way his clothes were torn, and he lost his coat, hat and glasses. He was a sorry sight to onlookers who were nevertheless impressed with his calm serenity and seeming willingness to let the mob do what it would.

The Cooley brothers decided the safest place for Garrison was City Hall (the old State House). When they got there, with great difficulty they pushed him through the crowd into the south door and up the stairs to the mayor's office. As the mob screamed outside several men offered the bedraggled young man garments to replace those he had lost, giving him an old coat, pantaloons and a cap. Then Mayor Lyman decided, for safety's sake, to arrest Garrison for disturbing the peace and to lock him up in the Leverett Street jail. Once again Garrison was led through the angry crowd, this time to a horse-drawn carriage. Perhaps because the mob did not immediately recognize Garrison in his borrowed clothing, he made his way into the vehicle with little difficulty. But then the throng surged forward, making it almost impossible for the coachman to get the rig moving. Finally, the driver whipped the horses, the carriage lurched ahead and careened down the street with the mob in hot pursuit. Some of the crowd tried to grab the horses or hang onto the carriage wheels; others pounded their fists on the sides of the rig.

When the wild procession finally reached the jail, the few who had come the whole distance tried to grab Garrison, but he was rushed inside and locked safely in a cell. The men in the streets grumbled and cursed, but finally returned to the warehouses, offices and banks from whence they had come.

The mob having receded, Garrison enjoyed a pleasant night. Friends came to talk to him at his cell window. He sat on his bed musing contentedly on the renown he had achieved and the sympathy that was certain to be aroused by this vicious attack. For posterity he wrote on his cell wall: "William Lloyd Garrison was put into this cell on Wednesday afternoon, October 21, 1835, to save him from the violence of a 'respectable and influential' mob who sought to destroy him for preaching the abominable and dangerous doctrine that 'all men are created equal.'"

William Lloyd Garrison was released the next day and immediately set out to make the most of what had happened. In *The Liberator* he expressed outrage that *he* was arrested for disturbing the peace, but every member of the mob went free. He warned that such attacks, which attempted to deny a citizen his right to freedom of speech, were a natural consequence of slavery. The "peculiar institution" could only exist if thinking men and women were forced to be silent.

As Garrison predicted, sympathy for his cause *was* aroused. Within a month of the attack he was able to write to his wife, "New subscribers to *The Liberator* still continue to come in – not less than a dozen today. Am much obliged to the mob!"

For the next thirty years Garrison published *The Liberator* and called for the immediate emancipation of the slaves. Gradually, as the South continued to react violently and to demand the protection and extension of slavery, the sympathies of Garrison's fellow Bostonians began to change. By the 1850s new mobs were forming in the city, this time to protest the capture of runaway slaves. By 1861, throngs of young men were enlisting in the army to save the Union and, as they hoped, to free the slaves.

When emancipation finally came in 1863, Massachusetts promptly organized black regiments to fight against the Confederacy. One lieutenant of the black Massachusetts 55th regiment was William Lloyd Garrison's son, George Thompson Garrison, named for the Englishman so hated by Bostonians in 1835. As the young man marched by with hundreds of black men in uniform, the elder Garrison watched with tears in his eyes. Here was the fulfillment of everything he had spent his life working for. He stood on the corner of Wilson's Lane where, twenty-eight years before, he had been dragged and beaten by the "respectable" mob.

BOSTON'S FIRST INTEGRATIONIST

AFRICAN-AMERICANS HAD NO GREATER FRIEND THAN CHARLES SUMNER.

Few Bostonians walking along Boylston Street pay much attention to the statue of a determined looking man in the Public Garden. The pedestal inscription simply reads "Sumner." Occasionally pigeons perch discourteously on Sumner's head; in the winter he often wears a silly looking cap of snow. Some passersby probably assume he is the man for whom the tunnel is named; he is not. Clearly an explanatory plaque is necessary here.

If the spirit of Charles Sumner hovers around his bronze head he has watched with great interest the racial controversies that have bedeviled the city, particularly the school busing trauma that occupied much of the year 1974. Twice during his own career Sumner was a leader in struggles over racial integration.

During the 1840s, Sumner was a Boston lawyer and philanthropist. His reading of William Lloyd Garrison's *The Liberator* had made him a firm opponent of slavery and a staunch defender of equal rights for all people. In 1849, he took the case, pro bono, of Benjamin Roberts, an African-American who was suing the city of Boston for the right of his daughter, Sarah, to go to an all-white school. At the time two "colored primary schools" had been established by the city and Sarah was required to attend one, despite the fact that a white public school was within a few yards of her front door.

Sumner's main argument in the Supreme Judicial Court of Massachusetts was that setting black children aside tended to entrench them permanently in a lower "caste." "No matter what facilities are provided for black people," he said, "the separate school is not an equivalent. The matters taught in the two schools may be precisely the same, but a school devoted to one class must differ essentially in spirit and character from that common school where all classes meet together in equality."

The court did not agree. In his majority opinion Justice Lemuel Shaw wrote: "The plaintiff had access to a school, set apart for colored children, as well conducted in all respects . . . as the other primary schools; the objection is that the schools thus open to the plaintiff are exclusively appropriated to colored children, and are at a greater distance from her home. Under these circumstances, has the plaintiff been unlawfully excluded from public school instruction? The Court are all of the opinion that she was not." In 1896 this idea that separate schools could provide equal educational opportunities received the sanction of the United States Supreme Court in the case of *Plessy v Ferguson*. In that ruling the court cited the case *Roberts v City of Boston* as a precedent.

Justice Shaw went on to challenge Sumner's "caste" argument: "(Racial prejudice), if it exists," he said, "is not created by law." Indeed, Shaw concluded, prejudice might actually be strengthened by forcing black and white children to attend school together. In other words, if white children got to know actual black children, they would *really* hate them!

Sumner was appalled at the court's decision. Unlike Justice Shaw, he was convinced that school integration was the necessary first step to racial equality . . . a goal, by the way, that he – one of few at the time — thought was desirable. He favored a law that would ban segregated schools and he worked for passage of legislation that would accomplish just that. Six years after the Roberts case, the Massachusetts State Legislature passed the "Act Concerning Public Schools." The law said, "In determining the qualifications of scholars to be admitted to any public school or any district school in this commonwealth, no distinction shall be made on account of the race, color or religious opinions of the applicant or scholar." Thus, forced segregation of public schools was outlawed in Massachusetts one hundred years before it was struck down nationwide.

In 1855, of course, integration in Boston meant only a few African-American children going to the local school along with the hundreds of white children in the area. It remained to be seen what would happen when large numbers of black children who lived in distinct areas of the city needed to be integrated. That did not happen until 1974 when Federal District Judge Arthur Garrity ordered integration to occur through the use of mandatory school busing. The result was anti-black rioting in South Boston, rioting so severe that Boston, for a time, deserved the reputation as the most racist northern city in the country.

From 1851 to 1874 Sumner served as United States Senator from Massachusetts. He gained such a reputation for his hatred of slavery – and the southern slave owners – that he was almost beaten to death with a cane in the Senate chamber by an angry Southerner. When war finally came, he pestered President Lincoln almost daily to make emancipation a war aim. Lincoln finally did so in late 1862.

As the Civil War ended Sumner knew, perhaps more than Lincoln did, that emancipation would be a cruel hoax if it were not supported by guarantees of black civil rights. He favored a policy of denying re-admission to the Union of southern states until they had granted citizenship, the right to vote, and legal equality to the freedmen. When Lincoln was assassinated, and Sumner and his congressional colleagues took control of reconstruction from President Johnson, they required the southern states to ratify the Fourteenth and Fifteenth Amendments to the constitution before they would be readmitted to the Union. The 14th Amendment declared that all people who are born or naturalized in the United States are citizens of the United States and of the states wherein they reside and are entitled to "equal protection of the laws." The 15th Amendment asserted that no state may deprive a person of the right to vote on account of "race, color, or previous condition of servitude."

However, as the southern states returned to the Union and white Southerners began regaining control of their state governments, Sumner believed that the segregation laws were circumventing the Fourteenth Amendment. Reconstruction should not end, he decided, until segregation was stopped. Otherwise, the African-American would forever be a second-class citizen.

In May of 1870, he proposed a civil rights bill under which the federal government would guarantee to all citizens, regardless of color, "equal and impartial enjoyment" of all public and private facilities, including "common schools and other public institutions of learning." Very significantly, it stated that cases arising under the law would be tried in federal rather than state courts.

For three years Sumner brought up his bill again and again, but he was fighting a tough battle against senators who were tired of the problems of "the Negro" and eager to move on to other things such as building railroads. His fight went poorly and, in the midst of it, he fell critically ill with "angina pectoris." His heart was weakening by the day, but he struggled on, sometimes doubling over with pain as he spoke on the senate floor. Finally, in March, 1874, he was dying.

As he lay on his deathbed a crowd of African-Americans gathered outside the house to mourn the passing of their greatest white spokesman. To Senator George Frisbie Hoar, standing by the bed, Sumner moaned, "You must take care of the Civil Rights Bill. The Civil Rights Bill, don't let it fail."

On March 1, 1875, nearly a year after Sumner's death, the Civil Rights Act became law. But, Congress had seen fit to eliminate the section dealing with education. Thus, there was to be no federal requirement for the integration of schools until the Supreme Court's *Brown v Board of Education of Topeka* decision in 1954. That ruling, which asserted that segregated schools are "inherently unequal" was a clear echo of Charles Sumner.

In 1883 the United States Supreme Court declared Sumner's Civil Rights Act of 1875 unconstitutional. Equal access to public and private accommodations was going to have to wait for the Civil Rights Act of 1964. Thus, every step towards complete integration of the races that Sumner had achieved was wiped out by the end of the 19th century.

Clearly Charles Sumner was way ahead of his time on the subject of racial integration. The statue of Charles Sumner needs to have a plaque that says more than merely "Sumner." It should at least say:

CHARLES SUMNER, HUMANITARIAN
UNITED STATES SENATOR, 1851-1874
FOUGHT FOR THE INTEGRATION OF BOSTON SCHOOLS
FOUGHT FOR THE ABOLITION OF SLAVERY
FOUGHT FOR THE EQUALITY OF ALL RACES

A PLAN TO SAVE THE STATUES

WHEN IT COMES TO MONUMENTS, THE TRUTH
SHALL SET US FREE.

In my book *American History: It's More than the Crap You Learned in High School*, I relegated Robert E. Lee to the chapter on "Rogues and Cautionary Tales." I did this because Lee violated the oath he took when he joined the United States Army. He led a rebellion of southern slave states against the government and tried to create a nation that guaranteed slavery. To me he was a racist slaveholder and a traitor. At the end of the Civil War, the country he made war against freed all of his slaves and took his plantation in Virginia – Arlington – to use as a cemetery for those Union soldiers who were killed in the fight against his army. That was the fate he deserved. Some would say he deserved imprisonment or even execution, but I think Lincoln got it right (as he usually did) when he called for "malice toward none, with charity for all."

Clearly, I see no valid reason to erect a memorial statue to Robert E. Lee. And yet, there are many people who have felt compelled to cover him with great honors. They have added his name to that of Washington to give a university the name "Washington and Lee"; they have cast him in bronze sitting nobly on his horse in Charlottesville, Virginia.

It took a while, but a confrontation finally came between those who feel as I do about Lee and those who honor him as a man who fought effectively for the cause of states' rights – and, white supremacy, we might presume. The ugly street fighting in Charlottesville, and the debate over the President's response to the fighting, has brought the issue of memorials front and center very rapidly. Now, the propriety of statues all over the land is being questioned and the President has asked, quite rightly I think, where do we stop building statues when it comes to slave-owners. Many of the founding fathers owned slaves; if we disown Washington and Jefferson for owning slaves, an awful lot of changes will have to be made! Will we have to dynamite the two faces on the left side of Mount Rushmore?

Before any more drastic events occur, I think there is a way most people on all sides of the statues debate can be satisfied. I propose that we leave all statues in place and be fairly liberal about the creation of new ones, but also require that all statues bear an inscription, prominently placed, that tell the stories of the people being honored in historically accurate ways – ways that do not sanitize their records. There should be full disclosure. For example, the statue of Lee could have at its base a plaque that says:

ROBERT E. LEE

Lee served his country honorably as a colonel in the United States Army during the Mexican War (1846-

1848). In 1861, he chose to follow his home state, Virginia, when it seceded from the Union and attempted to create the "Confederate States of America" and preserve the institution of African slavery. He fought bravely and effectively for the cause of southern independence and slavery but was ultimately defeated in 1865. The war resulted in the preservation of the Union and the emancipation of all of the slaves in the United States. As punishment for his actions, which were regarded as treasonous by many people, Lee lost not only his slaves but also his plantation which was confiscated by the U.S. government and became Arlington National Cemetery.

Clearly, what I have proposed for Lee's statue would not appeal to many Southerners. In almost every instance in which a statue's plaque would be considered there would be great debate over what these plaques would say. But the process of having the debate would increase everyone's understanding of American History – always a good thing! – and the resulting inscriptions would forever give viewers a better appreciation for the contribution the person depicted in the statue actually made to our history. My proposed inscription would certainly be better than a simple ROBERT E. LEE, which allows the viewer to conjure up all kinds of false heroics about the ten-foot tall man on horseback.

The same treatment would be given to all statues and memorials in the country. I say, "Let the truth be told!" The Washington Monument would declare, at its base, that besides leading the American colonists to victory in the revolution, presiding over the constitutional convention, and serving for eight years as the first President of the United States, Washington owned slaves. Two days before he died he was riding his horse around his plantation estate, Mount Vernon, checking on the work his chattel slaves were doing.

There could be a plaque in the Jefferson Memorial, right next to his Declaration of Independence, that tells the tourists that he also owned slaves and fathered several illegitimate children with one of them.

Even the Lincoln Memorial would have full disclosure: He hoped to ship all the freed slaves out of the country and tried throughout the Civil War to find a way to do it. He issued the Emancipation Proclamation as a military necessity – a war measure to disrupt the South and defeat the Confederacy.

By the time all of the debates over the statues and memorials are over and all of the plaques are in place, the people of this country will be much better informed about our history and the people of future generations will at least have a chance to get the story straight when they view the inscriptions.

LITTLE KNOWN CONSEQUENTIAL PEOPLE

Some People Never Achieved Fame, but They Had an Impact on History

INTRODUCTION

I have always had a soft spot in my heart for the drummer in a band. The singer is up front getting all the attention and acclaim. Meanwhile, the drummer is back in the dark pounding out the beat and, in many important ways, making the music happen. This struck me once many years ago when I watched Gloria Estefan singing the catchy "Rhythm is Gonna Get You." As she sang and danced around the stage to the heavy beat, she had the good grace at one point to stop and sing next to the drummer as he worked the bongo drums. He was nameless, of course, but smiling away, happy to be a part of a great show as he beat the skins and gave life to her song. No one says it, but we all know the song would be pretty flat without him.

Likewise, in history there were many people who "performed" in the shadows, never getting much attention, and yet whose contribution was vital to the success of the person who got all the acclaim. I am not talking about sidekicks such as "The Lone Ranger's faithful Indian companion, Tonto," or Butch and Sundance, or Superman and Lois Lane. I'm talking about totally obscure people who are *completely* unknown but who, nonetheless, were vital to the success of a great enterprise or were important actors — not always in a good way — in a major event. What follows are the stories of ten people who made major contributions to our history and yet have been lost in the mists of time.

JOHN WITHERSPOON

THE AMERICAN REVOLUTION HAD RELIGIOUS MOTIVES. WHO KNEW?

Everyone has heard of George Washington, Benjamin Franklin, and all the other luminaries of the American Revolution, but who has ever heard of John Witherspoon? This man never led armies or held a lofty government position, but he made major contributions to the theoretical bases of the revolutionary era and bequeathed a legacy of thought from which we have all benefitted. Witherspoon is one of those consequential people whom history has ignored.

In 1767, Witherspoon was the preacher and spiritual leader of a fast-growing and vibrant church in Paisley, Scotland, just outside Glasgow. He was devoted to his congregation, and they to him, but he had become convinced that his destiny as a servant of the Lord lay in America, and so he decided to accept a position that had been offered to him a year before – the presidency of Princeton College in New Jersey. With many tears, he left his beloved Scotland and made the arduous sail to America. In New

Jersey, he presided over Princeton College for the next twenty-six years and brought fundamental changes to the school – changes that would profoundly affect the future of America, particularly the revolution and the creation of a new government.

Although Witherspoon himself was theologically an evangelical, he introduced a broad range of study at Princeton and required all students at Princeton to immerse themselves in the writings not only of prominent theologians, but also the great humanists and even atheists of the day. He organized discussion and debating clubs at Princeton and encouraged all his students to improve their public speaking and persuasion skills. Under his leadership, Princeton was not to be an institution of theocratic indoctrination but rather a place where freethinking and inquiry were encouraged.

One of the most significant concepts Witherspoon fostered at Princeton was the idea that disagreement and even confrontation honed people's thinking and enabled people to achieve clarity, if not solutions. As Arthur Herman says in his fascinating book, *How the Scots Invented the Modern World*, "Witherspoon's attitude was that even if you disagreed with a philosopher or thinker, you still needed to read him in order to appreciate his arguments and refute them." If only John Witherspoon were alive today he would have much to say to the 'snowflakes" on today's college campuses who claim to be threatened and unsafe when exposed to ideas that do not conform to their own views of the world. He would certainly tell them to attend the lectures or the speeches that offend them, hear the speakers out, and, if they still disagree with them, formulate opposing arguments and counter punch. They should not just cry, drown the speaker out with screams, or demand that the offending person be silenced and dragged from the room.

Among John Witherspoon's students at Princeton in the early 1770s were James Madison and Aaron Burr, two men destined to play major parts in the coming revolution and creation of a new government. Madison was so enthralled with Witherspoon's teachings that he spent an extra year at Princeton to further his studies and participate in the discussions. In the coming years, as we all know, he played a major role in the debates and compromises that made the Constitution of the United States possible. Aaron Burr went on to have a promising career in politics, as well, until he killed Alexander Hamilton in a duel and then schemed to create an empire for himself in Louisiana Territory. Fortunately, Witherspoon had died before either of those things happened, so he did not have to witness the fall of one of his prize pupils – a pupil who followed his own primal urges rather than God.

Meanwhile, in the summer of 1776, Witherspoon himself became a delegate to the Continental Congress. In that august body he became a prominent speaker, extolling the idea that they were creating a government that would be God's great hope on earth. He introduced the viewpoint of a theologian to the discussions. Most people assume that the fundamental driving forces for the independence movement were the secular concepts of "no taxation without representation," "Give me liberty or give me death," and "unalienable rights." What few realize is that the American Revolution had a theological component as well. The "Great Awakening," the religious revival movement that swept the colonies in the 1730s and 40s had unified the colonies as never before and had sparked a broad religious fervor that centered on the individual's relationship with God and not the church – particularly not the Church of England (the Episcopalian Church in America). Many of the members of the Continental Congress who voted for independence did so for the political principles stated in Jefferson's Declaration, but many others supported independence for the *theological* reasons that Witherspoon espoused. He was such an anathema to the British that when the

British army invaded New Jersey in 1777, their soldiers burned to the ground Witherspoon's cherished library at Princeton that he had built over a period of ten years with many of his own books.

The British government, and even King George III himself, all believed that the revolutionists in the colonies were inspired by religious doctrine – the doctrine of "Presbyterianism," a derivative of Puritanism which stood against the Church of England (the Anglican Church) headed by the King. "Are they not Presbyterians?" the King asked, and he was told, on several occasions, that the revolutionary war was a "Presbyterian war from the beginning."

It would be absurd to claim that "Deists" such as Thomas Paine, Thomas Jefferson and Benjamin Franklin were motivated by religious doctrine, even if Jefferson did conclude the Declaration of Independence with an appeal to "Divine providence." But it would also be incomplete to ignore the religious component of the independence cause. For this, John Witherspoon, pastor and president of Princeton, was the driving force.

At Princeton University today, there is a larger than life bronze statue of John Witherspoon. There is an identical one in Paisley, Scotland. As we see monuments and statues being challenged and torn down all across the country, most of us would agree that the statue of John Witherspoon at Princeton should remain. Atheists will have to accept the fact that many revolutionists in 1776 were motivated by religion. John Witherspoon believed that people who ignore the religious principles involved in a movement do so at their peril. Therefore, though he is "little known," let us not forget he was very "consequential."

ROBERT MORRIS AND HAYM SALOMON

EVEN A REALLY GREAT CAUSE NEEDS CASH.

We all know about the heroes of the American Revolution: Thomas Jefferson, author of the eloquent Declaration of Independence, Patrick Henry, the "Give me liberty or give me death" orator, George Washington, the charismatic general, and several more. What few people know about the American Revolution is that without the work of a wealthy Philadelphia financier and a recently arrived Jewish immigrant from Poland, those famous revolutionists would have been nothing but a lot of hot air, and the famous military leader would have had to fight with rocks and sticks. The financier was the bon vivant Robert Morris; the Polish immigrant was the entrepreneurial Haym Salomon. Together these two men kept the new American army, such as it was, on its feet long enough to win the Revolutionary War against the greatest military force in the world at that time. It is doubtful that any of the heroics we eulogize when we speak of the American Revolution would have been possible without them.

Robert Morris was a large man – tall, rotund, affable and friendly. He was a "hail fellow, well met" and he and his wife, Mary, were the epicenter of Philadelphia's elite social scene in the early 1770s. As a self-made entrepreneur, he owned merchant vessels plying the seas all over the world; as a popular figure in Philadelphia society he was a member of the Pennsylvania Assembly and, in 1774, was elected to represent Pennsylvania in the Continental Congress. In that assemblage of luminaries he stood out among the lawyers and plantation owners as the only man who dealt directly with finance and trade. That distinction would soon make him the most valuable, albeit least famous, member.

In the early days of the Congress, Morris took a moderate position on the issues concerning Britain's treatment of her American colonies. His role, in some ways, seemed to be as the social chairman, hosting dinners and parties at his comfortable home. When events heated up after the battles of Lexington and Concord, Morris stood firm in his opposition to the idea that a complete break with the mother country was inevitable or desirable. He did not attend the meeting when the delegates voted to declare independence on July 2, 1776. However, two days later, when the time came to sign the Declaration of Independence, he had a change of heart and scrawled his name to the right of the flowing script of John Hancock and took his place as a revolutionary – in line to be hanged as a traitor if their efforts failed.

The early months of the Americans' fight to win the independence they had just declared were discouraging to say the least. Within days after the vote for a break with the crown, an enormous British force drove George Washington's army of volunteers out of New York. The great American general barely got his men across the Hudson River in a thick fog and came within a few minutes of being captured himself. The situation was ominous, especially because many of the men in the Continental Army were ready to go home when their enlistments were up, and because even providing basics such as food for the troops was always problematic. The usual story that is told about how Washington kept the army going is that he pulled off a daring crossing of the frozen Delaware River on Christmas night, caught the sleeping and hung-over Hessians off guard in Trenton, and won a stirring victory that inspired his men to stay with him. What is not usually told is that the soldiers had to be clothed and supplied or they would have given up in disgust, even after a stirring victory.

This was where Robert Morris came in. He was able to use his global connections to secure loans and procure food, clothing and weapons for Washington's men. A very generous and public-spirited man, he also used his own personal credit and put himself into debt for considerable amounts in order to keep the army in the field. The Congress appointed Morris to be the head of the Office of Finance, and in that role he was tireless in his efforts to secure the weaponry and provisions necessary to fight a war. The estimates vary on how much of his own money Morris put into the cause, but it could have been as much as twenty million dollars in today's money.

As the war years dragged on, Morris realized that a more formal structure for procuring loans and provisions had to be made, so he induced Congress, with great difficulty, to create a Bank of North America, an institution that could issue bills of credit and be a secure place to house any hard money that came in from foreign powers. After the victory at Saratoga, New York, in the fall of 1777, Benjamin Franklin in Paris was able to secure French assistance for the American cause. Part of this aid was in the form of silver which arrived in Boston on a French vessel in 1781. The hard coinage was arriving just in time because Washington's army was on the verge of disintegrating (yet again!) if the men were not paid . . . and they would only accept hard currency, no bank notes. The silver was crated in re-enforced barrels and placed on wagons, one thousand pounds per wagon, which were pulled by oxen from Boston to Philadelphia. It is doubtful that any of the farmers who saw the wagons rumble along the road had any idea what was in them. As an example of Morris's attention to detail, when the coinage arrived in Philadelphia, he saw to it that the Continental Congress recouped the expense of the trip by selling the beasts that had pulled the carts to local buyers.

Haym Salomon was Robert Morris's exact opposite; he was a small, withered and sickly figure who arrived in North America in 1775. He joined the "Sons of Liberty" in New York but was captured by the British and held as a traitor. His likely fate was execution but, miraculously, he was able to escape (the details of this are unknown) and in 1778 he arrived in Philadelphia ragged and worn out. Soon, however, he had set himself up in an office on Front Street as a broker. He was fluent in several languages and Philadelphians could go to him with bank notes and other forms of commercial paper and he would arrange to convert their assets into hard currency – for a fee, of course. At the local coffee house Salomon bought and sold bills of exchange and arranged for the disposal of prizes that men who owned vessels that attacked British shipping ("privateers") had captured on the high seas. These prizes might be kegs of molasses, barrels of rum, bales of cotton – anything the British ships might be carrying.

As different physically and in background as Robert Morris and Haym Salomon were, they were a natural team when it came to working for the revolutionary cause. Morris could secure foreign loans in the form of bonds, and Salomon could sell them and convert them into hard cash.

The climax of the efforts of this financial team came when that load of French silver arrived in Philadelphia. At that very moment Washington was trying to move his army to Yorktown, Virginia, where he had a golden opportunity to trap General Cornwallis on the Yorktown Peninsula and win a huge victory that might very well end the war. The problem was that Washington's men, as usual, were threatening to go home if they were not paid in hard currency. Morris and Salomon came through for the general, and even put up some of their own cash and credit. The soldiers were paid, and off they went to Virginia to win the war. Most of us have often heard the story that Washington heroically marched his army from New York to Virginia, trapped Cornwallis, and won the great victory that caused Britain to quit and give the United States its independence. We never stopped to think that the army had to be fed and supplied and that *someone* had to come through with the cash to make that happen.

After the Revolutionary War ended, Haym Salomon's life fell apart. The bonds he held decreased in value and he went into debtor's prison. There in 1785 he fell ill with tuberculosis and died, basically a pauper, at the age of forty-four. In a very real sense this Jewish man from Poland gave his life for American independence.

Robert Morris signed the Articles of Confederation creating a new American government in 1781 (the same year as he financed Washington's Yorktown campaign), and he went on to play a major role in the drafting of the new United States Constitution in 1787. He is one of only two people – the other was Roger Sherman – who signed all three founding documents: *The Declaration of Independence*, *The Articles of Confederation*, and the *Constitution of the United States of America*. In the new government he served for six years in the United States Senate as Senator from Pennsylvania. President Washington asked him to continue his work in finance and become the first Secretary of the Treasury, but he declined, telling Washington to appoint Alexander Hamilton instead. If Morris had accepted, who knows? We might have a Broadway musical today called "Morris!"

Ironically, and tragically, just like his friend Haym Salomon, Robert Morris also died in poverty. In the late 1790s, he speculated heavily in land and, very strangely, made very poor choices. By 1798 he occupied a cell in debtor's prison. There was a very sad reunion when George Washington visited his old financial savior in prison. The two men must have wondered how it had all come to this! Morris was freed in 1800 but lived very modestly – a far cry from the lavish, high society life he had led in Philadelphia in the "old days." He died nearly penniless in 1806.

Robert Morris's name is fairly well known in Philadelphia, but across the country and around the world hardly anyone has heard of him. Poor Haym Salomon is known even less. It is unfortunate that George Washington never wrote his memoirs. He could have told the world that without Robert Morris and Haym Salomon he could never have kept his army going, would never have been able to force Cornwallis to surrender at Yorktown, and might very well have had to take a place next to Thomas Jefferson, Patrick Henry, Benjamin Franklin and all the other traitors standing on the gallows waiting to be hanged.

NICHOLAS TRIST

IT'S NOT ALWAYS BAD TO DISOBEY ORDERS!

The territorial results of the Mexican War (1846-1848) were very important, but they might have been quite different if Nicholas Trist had not taken bold action and ignored the wishes of his boss, President James K. Polk. Polk was a difficult man to deal with, but he was, after all, the President of the United States and Trist took a huge risk when he followed his own counsel rather than the President's orders. Fortunately for Trist and the country, it all worked out very well because he had a friend in a high place.

In the early years of the nineteenth century Nicholas Trist was like Forrest Gump; he seemed to be everywhere that important things were happening. Because his grandmother ran a rooming house in Philadelphia in the 1780s where Thomas Jefferson and James Madison liked to stay, young Nicholas met and became attached to these two men. (Think Forrest meeting the young Elvis.) By the 1820s he was personal secretary to Jefferson and he married Jefferson's granddaughter, Virginia Jefferson Randolph. When Jefferson died on July 4, 1826, it was Nicholas Trist who was by his bedside keeping the old man apprised as to whether he had lived to the fiftieth anniversary of his great document. Trist went on to serve as the personal secretary of Andrew Jackson and, in that capacity, would stay up nights telling the President stories about their hero, Thomas Jefferson. Had there been photography in those days there would be pictures of Jefferson, James Madison, John Quincy Adams, and Andrew Jackson with Nicholas Trist appearing somewhere in the background – without the trickery of photo shopping.

In the mid-1830s, Jackson appointed Trist to be the American consul in Havana, Cuba. His ability to speak fluent Spanish made him well suited to the job, but his somewhat arrogant demeanor made him unpopular and when the Whig President, William Henry Harrison, took office, Trist was quickly removed. He stayed in Cuba, however, and he took up running a boarding house just as his grandmother had in Philadelphia. He was, in a sense, back to square one, but he was about to take a step that would change his life and the future of his country.

When Andrew Jackson, now old and dying, heard of Trist's poverty in Cuba, he prevailed upon his protégé, James K. Polk, who was just taking office as President of the United States, to bring Trist back to Washington as the chief clerk of the State Department. It was in that role that Nicholas Trist was to get his chance to be more than just one of the people in the background.

In May of 1846, the United States went to war with Mexico. After several brilliant victories by General Zachary Taylor in northern Mexico in 1847 it seemed as if the Mexican army was on the ropes. However, the Mexicans fought on, so Polk ordered General Winfield Scott to land at Vera Cruz and advance overland to Mexico City. Polk wanted Scott rather than Taylor to lead a victorious march into the enemy capital because, while Taylor and Scott were both Whigs (Polk was a Democrat), Taylor, nicknamed "Old Rough and Ready," was becoming very popular in the U.S. and might be a very formidable candidate for President. Scott was much more regal and austere. At 6'5", he cut an imposing figure wearing a snappy uniform and riding a huge white horse, but he would not win many votes from the average voters. His nickname was "Old Fuss and Feathers," hardly the tag of a "man of the people!" If there were going to be military glory doled out at the conclusion of the Mexican War, Polk wanted it to be doled to Scott who could not do much with it politically rather than to Taylor who could.

(Polk's judgment of these two men proved correct. In 1848 Taylor, "Old Rough and Ready," won the presidency. In 1852 "Old Fuss and Feathers" Scott ran for President but lost to the colorless Franklin Pierce of New Hampshire. Scott just did not have any popular appeal. By the way, he was the tallest man ever to seek the presidency, beating Lincoln by an inch.)

After choosing Scott to lead the military advance on Mexico City, Polk made an extraordinary move. He decided to send a peace negotiator to join Scott's army and be ready to negotiate a peace settlement whenever the moment seemed propitious. For this delicate job the President reached down into the State Department and plucked Nicholas Trist. In a White House meeting the President said, "Mr. Trist, if you can succeed in restoring peace, you will render a great service to your country and acquire great distinction for yourself." From that moment on, motivated either by the first half or the second half of that sentence, Trist took his mission very seriously.

When Trist arrived in Vera Cruz, "Old Fuss and Feathers" was not at all happy to see him. He thought the new man sent out from Washington was going to undercut his authority. It did not help matters that Trist was just as arrogant and self-aggrandizing as the general was. However, just when it seemed that relations between the two imperious men might reach the breaking point, Trist came down with a severe illness that totally incapacitated him. Taking pity, General Scott reached into his stores at army headquarters and found a jar of guava marmalade that he sent to Trist along with a get-well note. As it happened, guava marmalade was Trist's favorite delicacy in the whole world. He dated his improvement in health from the moment he received that delightful jar. The two men became fast friends, and Scott was very much in Trist's corner when the ambassador made a very controversial decision. (How a very small thing such as a jar of marmalade sometimes has a significant effect on history is the subject of another essay, "The Bowl of Cherries Theory of History.")

In September, 1847, Scott's army entered Mexico City with Scott astride his enormous white horse in regal triumph. In October, President Polk decided that having an ambassador for peace in Mexico City was an embarrassment; it made the United States appear overly eager for peace. Furthermore, he had concluded that Nicholas Trist was arrogant and untrustworthy. He ordered Trist to return to Washington at once.

In a singular move that has never been duplicated in high level diplomacy, Trist decided to ignore the President and continue doing what he had already started – negotiating with "moderate Mexicans" to reach a peace agreement. Trist believed that these men, as opposed to the "Puros" – the "Pure Ones" who would fight to the death for Mexican honor – were the men the United States needed to make peace with immediately before they lost whatever power they had.

Part of Trist's bold and insubordinate decision stemmed from the word he was hearing from newspaper reporters that a movement was growing in the United States Congress to demand *all of Mexico!* Southerners, in particular, were ranting that now that we had destroyed the Mexican army and had occupied the capital, we should annex the entire country! As preposterous as that may seem today, it was a very real demand in 1848 espoused by men drunk with the sweet wine of "Manifest Destiny," and by hardheaded Southerners who saw the possibility of several slave states carved out of Mexican land.

Trist sent a message to President Polk informing him of his intention to continue negotiating. In effect, he was telling the President to get lost! When Polk received Trist's message he was beyond outrage; he was apoplectic. "I have never in my life felt so indignant," he wrote in his diary. "If there was any legal pro-vision for his punishment," he went on, "he ought to be severely handled. He has acted worse than any man in the public employ whom I have ever known." Polk stomped about the White House vowing to put his insubordinate ambassador in prison.

While Polk raged and readied a new appointee to send to Mexico City, Trist's negotiations went on. By early February, in the Mexico City suburb of Guadalupe-Hidalgo, Trist and his Mexican friends signed a treaty that gave the United States the Rio Grande River as the southern boundary of Texas. The U.S. would also acquire California all the way south to the northern border of the Baja Peninsula, and all of the Mexican land between California and Texas. The territory constituted a million square miles and increased the size of the United States by one third. In return, the United States agreed to pay Mexico compensation of fifteen million dollars – the same amount Jefferson had paid France for the Louisiana Territory.

When President Polk received the "Treaty of Guadalupe-Hidalgo," he had to admit the terms were pretty good even though it was negotiated by an agent whom he hated and had fired, and who had dealt with a group of Mexicans who had no recognized authority. Seizing the moment, Polk sent the treaty to the Senate where it was approved 38 to 14, only one vote over the two-thirds required by the constitution.

Those who believe the United States has been divinely blessed note that in the month preceding Trist's finalizing his rogue treaty with Mexico, a saw mill operator near Sacramento, California, discovered tiny flecks of gold in the stream near his mill. Within a year, prospectors from all over the world were flocking to California and the great gold rush of '49 was on. During the first five years of prospecting, California produced twelve million ounces of gold – worth seventeen billion dollars at today's rates. The gold rush set the United States up for a prosperous industrial revolution. Can there be any doubt, many newspapers across the country asked, that God has destined the United States not only to rule from sea to sea, but also to dominate the world economically?

Despite the satisfaction President Polk took in the terms of the Treaty of Guadalupe-Hidalgo, he only partially cooled off in his opinion of Nicholas Trist. Although he did not order him arrested and imprisoned as he had once threatened, he docked his salary for the final six months of his tenure in Mexico. Trist and his wife – Jefferson's granddaughter, as you recall – settled in Pennsylvania, started a private girls' boarding school, and lived in virtual poverty for the next twenty years. Finally, at the behest of Senator Charles Sumner of Massachusetts, Congress voted to pay Trist back salary amounting to $14,599. A short time later, President Grant appointed him postmaster of the small Virginia hamlet of Alexandria. It was in that role that Nicholas Trist died in 1874, twenty-six years after he had negotiated the treaty that ended the Mexican War. Just like several of our "unknown consequential people," Nicholas Trist died obscure and poor.

It is not possible to say with certainty what would have happened if Nicholas Trist had not taken bold action but, instead, had compliantly returned to Washington when he was recalled. A few things are certain. His completion of a treaty giving the United States California removed any chance that there would be a dispute over which country had claim to the gold resources of California. His swift conclusion of a treaty also ensured that the "all of Mexico" politicians in Washington would not gain traction. If their movement had gained more momentum, they probably would not have been able to annex the entire country, but they would at least have been able to push the southern border of the United States much further south toward Mexico City.

For all his pomposity and arrogance, Nicholas Trist was a moderating influence in the Mexican War peace process. In truth, he thought the war was an aggressive and terrible act by the United States. Several years after the war he wrote, "(The Mexican War) was a thing for every right-minded American to be ashamed of." He said he tried to make the treaty "as little exacting as possible from Mexico." And yet, there are those who condemn Trist for being the man who forced the Mexicans to turn over half their country to the United States. In an historical evaluation of him, Nicholas Trist suffers the fate of all moderates. They do a little of what both sides want and thereby satisfy neither.

Last spring, when I was part of a mission trip in Juarez, Mexico – a poverty-stricken city just across the Rio Grande from El Paso, Texas – I thought of Nicholas Trist. Everyone with me was thinking "Where can we get a good burrito?" and I was thinking of Nicholas Trist. Anyway, I was thinking that because of him – a man practically no one has ever heard of – we were in Mexico and not the United States.

"PRINCE OF FIRE-EATERS"

THE MAN LOVED THE SOUTH AND DID ALL HE COULD TO DESTROY IT.

The American Civil War was by far the bloodiest war in American History if not in the history of the world. Any evaluation of the causes of the war that tries to identify the major people responsible for that horrific tragedy would have to include politicians who have been referred to as "fire-eaters." These were southern men who advocated the secession of the slaveholding states from the Union and the creation of a Confederate States of America, even if it meant civil war. The leading "fire-eater," and the man I would pick as the one most responsible for the Civil War, was William Lowndes Yancey of Alabama. A spellbinding orator, a silk-tongued charmer, a skilled organizer, and a fervent believer that slavery was a "positive good" for both races, he almost singlehandedly brought about a north-south split in the Democratic Party that led inevitably to a Republican victory in the 1860 presidential election and the subsequent secession of the southern states. Secession led to war, as everyone knew it would. Yancey was fortunate not to live long enough to see how that war obliterated everything he held dear.

William Lowndes Yancey was born in South Carolina and lived there until he was five when his father died. His widowed mother married a Presbyterian minister. An irony in Yancey's life was that much of his youth, after his mother's remarriage, was spent in the North – Troy, New York – where his stepfather was called to preach. His stepfather was strongly anti-slavery and William spent his formative years in the company of some very notable abolitionists including Charles Grandison Finney and Lyman Beecher, father of Harriet Beecher Stowe. But, his stepfather was a cruel man who beat his mother and eventually left her. Thus, William's contact with abolitionism took on an obnoxious smell that probably drove him to hate abolitionists and, by extension, all Northerners.

By the way, if you believe that history can be determined by chance events – what I've referred to in another essay as the "Bowl of Cherries Theory of History" because of the food poisoning caused by tainted cherries that killed President Taylor and paved the way for passage of the Compromise of 1850 – then you might believe that a yellow fever virus caused the Civil War. You see – it was yellow fever that killed William Lowndes Yancey's birth father, which paved the way for his stepfather who was a tyrannical abolitionist who abused his mother. That led to William's hatred of the North and his subsequent actions to bring about secession and civil war. Thus, a microscopic virus caused a war that killed 650,000 people.

Anyway, in 1834 Yancey was in his final year at Williams College in Massachusetts, just six weeks away from graduation, when he suddenly decided – for unknown reasons – to leave. He seceded from the school, so to speak, and went to live with a slave-holding uncle in South Carolina. Shortly thereafter he married Sarah Caroline Earl who brought to their marriage a dowry of thirty-five slaves. Thus, in less than two years, he took the long step from being a Yankee college student who had been raised by abolitionists to a southern slave owner. Will the ironies ever cease?

By the 1840s, Yancey had become a full-throated supporter of slavery and southern rights. He was elected to the U.S. House of Representatives in 1844 where he quickly earned a reputation as a silver-tongued orator. He also became known for his temper, his highly developed sense of honor, and his adherence to the "code duello." He challenged two men to duels and he killed one of them.

In 1846, Yancey resigned from the House because he was disgusted with the northern Democrats' lack of willingness to recognize southern rights. He moved to Montgomery, Alabama, purchased a dairy farm, and began to play a leading role in Alabama politics. In 1848, he and his colleagues developed what they called the "Alabama Platform" which stated:

The federal government cannot restrict slavery from the federal territories.

Alabama delegates to the national convention of the Democratic Party must oppose any candidate who favors banning slavery from the territories or the concept of "popular sovereignty" under which the people in a territory could vote to exclude it.

At the Democratic Convention of 1848, Yancey walked out when the delegates refused to adopt the Alabama Platform. Shortly thereafter he and his followers began to organize "Southern Rights Associations" to protect southern rights, particularly the right to bring slave property into the western territories. In his *Address to the People of Alabama* he wrote: "(Southerners are treated) as inferiors in the Union – as degraded by our contact with slaves, and as unworthy of an association with the northern man in the great work of expanding the institution of slavery over the vast plains of the west." Yancey began to believe that the only salvation for the South was secession from the Union, and that the only way secession would happen was if a "black Republican" – a man who favored laws banning Southerners from bringing their slave property into the territories – were elected President in 1860. Only then would Southerners finally realize the peril they were in.

To that end, he began to focus all his energies on *weakening* his own party!

Yancey's first step was to knock down the only leading Democrat who stood a chance of winning states in the South as well as the North – Senator Stephen Douglas of Illinois. In April of 1860, when the Democrats met in Charleston to nominate their candidates for President and Vice President, Yancey and the Alabama delegation made it very clear that the platform and the candidates must be true to the "Alabama Platform." When the "Alabama Platform" was voted down, 165-138, Yancey led the Alabama delegation out of the hall. They were followed by the men from Mississippi, Louisiana, South Carolina, Florida and Texas. The next day, the Georgia and Arkansas delegations left as well. The Democratic Party was in ruins, and that was exactly what Yancey wanted. His own party was doomed to be defeated by the scurrilous Republicans and that would cause Southerners to realize that their only route to salvation was secession.

Two months later the two factions of the Democratic Party met again in Baltimore. One member of the northern faction offered Yancey the nomination for Vice President on a Douglas ticket and he flatly rejected it. Such a ticket might win . . . and that would ruin his plan. The northern Democrats, left with little choice but to proceed, nominated Douglas for President and adopted a platform of "popular sovereignty" on the issue of slavery in the territories. A week later the southern Democrats met and nominated John C. Breckinridge of Kentucky and adopted the Yancey platform – the right to bring slaves into the territories must be strictly guaranteed.

Left with a rump of his party, Stephen Douglas made a heroic effort to win votes across the entire nation. He campaigned in northern and southern states trying to convince voters that his plan of popular sovereignty – letting the people in each territory decide the issue of slavery – was the most democratic and peaceful way of resolving the issue. But Abraham Lincoln and the Republicans had great appeal across the North when they called for banning slavery so that the territories would be free and open to settlement by "free white people." Breckinridge and the southern Democrats won nearly every southern state with their declaration that their right to bring their property into the territories was constitutionally guaranteed. The Supreme Court had said so in the *Dred Scott* decision. A fourth candidate, John Bell of Tennessee, stood for ignoring the slavery issue entirely and won a few border states. Douglas did win votes across the nation but only won the electors of Missouri and a couple of electors in New Jersey. Abe Lincoln won only northern states — his name was not even on the ballot in most southern states — but that was enough to give him the majority of electors and the White House. Yancey had been right: destroying Douglas was tantamount to giving the presidency to the Republicans and that horrendous result would soon cause the southern states to secede from the Union.

Yancey's native state, South Carolina, led the way out of the Union on December 20, 1860. In Alabama Yancey wrote: "Shall we (the people of Alabama) remain in the Union and all be slaves? God forbid!" When the Alabama secession convention met on January 7th, there were some who wanted to wait and see what the other southern states would do. Yancey called them "misguided, deluded, wicked men in our midst." Immediate secession passed, 61-39. Georgia, Mississippi, Florida, Louisiana and Texas soon followed, and the Confederate States of America was a reality by February.

When Jefferson Davis came to Montgomery to take the oath as the Confederacy's first President, Yancey gave the welcoming address. "The man and the hour have met," he proclaimed. "We now hope that prosperity, honor and victory await this administration."

On April 12, 1861, Confederate guns fired on Fort Sumter in Charleston harbor. Two days later Lincoln called for volunteers to "put down the southern rebellion" and four more slave states, Tennessee, North Carolina, Arkansas, and Virginia joined the Confederacy. The "War for Southern Independence," as Yancey and his fellow Southerners called it, was under way.

President Davis appointed Yancey to lead a delegation to Europe to try to secure recognition for the Confederate States of America as an independent nation. Yancey was a terrible diplomat because everywhere he went in Europe he extolled the benefits of slavery. This did not appeal in Great Britain where slavery had been outlawed in the empire for over thirty years. After a few months, Yancey admitted his mission had flopped. "*Uncle Tom's Cabin* has been read and believed," he complained. "I ought never to have come here."

Back home, Yancey's health, never very good, began to decline. In July of 1863 he knew he was dying. He must also have known the cause he had fought for so eagerly had begun to die as well. During the first week of July, Lee's Army of Northern Virginia suffered a terrible defeat at Gettysburg and the town of Vicksburg, the last Confederate stronghold on the Mississippi

River, surrendered after a six-month siege. The South was going down and Yancey must have known it.

Death came to Yancey later in the month. He was spared the sight of his beloved South in ruins and the knowledge that his traitorous scheme for breaking up the Union had killed or maimed ten percent of the men in the South, reduced almost every southern city to rubble, destroyed the South's economy, and set free four million souls he had hoped to keep enslaved forever.

The historian Bruce Catton wrote an excellent account of the origins of the Civil War entitled *The Coming Fury*. Fittingly, the first two words in the book are, "Mr. Yancey." The first chapter describes how Yancey engineered the plot to destroy Stephen Douglas in the Democratic Party and thus ensure a Republican victory. William Lowndes Yancey bore more responsibility for the start of the Civil War than any other single individual.

In Montgomery, Alabama, Yancey's law office still stands and has been designated a National Historic Landmark. In light of the recent controversies over statues and monuments, and in keeping with a proposal I made in another essay, I suggest that Yancey's old office should remain a "landmark," but there should be a plaque on the front of the building that reads:

> *In this building William Lowndes Yancey maintained his law offices from 1848 until 1863. An avid proponent of slavery, Mr. Yancey was dubbed the "Prince of Fire-Eaters" and was instrumental in splitting the Democratic Party into northern and southern components. That split led to the election of Abraham Lincoln as President, the secession of eleven southern states, and the Civil War. The war's casualties numbered 650,000 young men killed. Mr. Yancey died in 1863 as his beloved South was collapsing into total ruin.*

HANNIBAL HAMLIN

TWO OF HISTORY'S "WHAT IF" QUESTIONS CENTER ON THIS MAN.

On April 14, 1865, John Wilkes Booth murdered Abraham Lincoln, and Andrew Johnson became President. The Republican Party had chosen Andrew Johnson to be Lincoln's running mate for a second term because they wanted a Southerner who had been a Democrat and a Union man in the war. Johnson, who had remained staunchly loyal to the Union throughout the war and had served as the military governor of Tennessee after the Confederacy lost control of the state, fit the bill perfectly.

Johnson, a surly, stubborn man, soon ran into trouble with the "Radical Republicans" in Congress. He vetoed twenty-five major bills and the Radicals overrode his veto every time. Ultimately, the Radicals impeached him and tried unsuccessfully to remove him from office. By the time he left the White House in 1869, Johnson had compiled such a terrible record that many historians rate him as the worst President of all time.

Yet, it could have been very different if Lincoln had stayed with his first Vice President, Hannibal Hamlin, an abolitionist from Maine. In many ways Hamlin was much like Abraham Lincoln. They were both born in 1809; they both grew up on farms and prepared for the legal profession largely through their own study; they were both sturdy and athletic as young men and gained positions of leadership among their peers by taking down challengers in wrestling matches; they were both popular as story tellers and they were both trustworthy and honest friends, much admired by everyone who knew them.

In their political careers, Lincoln and Hamlin both began in their respective state legislatures – Hamlin in Maine, Lincoln in Illinois – and both became known as men who opposed slavery but felt it was a state issue and the national government should only act to restrict slavery from spreading into the federal territories. They differed in that Hamlin became more ardent in his opposition to slavery and, by the early 1850s, was very close to being an outright abolitionist. Lincoln kept his distance from abolitionism until almost a year into his presidency.

In the mid-1850s, the Republican Party was born. Its platform opposed the Kansas-Nebraska Act which had repealed the Missouri Compromise line (36-30) that had restricted slavery to the areas south of the line. The party further advocated the banning of slavery from all the federal territories, including the lands of the southwest that had recently been acquired from Mexico. Although he was a Democrat, Hannibal Hamlin eagerly joined this new party in Maine. Lincoln, as a Whig who had always admired Henry Clay, the man who had crafted the compromises that allowed slavery to expand, was more reluctant to join the Republicans lest people would think he was too radical. It took him almost a year in 1854 to give up his Whig loyalty and join the Republican Party of Illinois.

By 1855, both men were thoroughgoing Republicans adamantly opposed to the spread of slavery. Many of their friends in their respective states felt they were of presidential timber and urged them to seek the office. Hamlin was in the United States Senate after 1847 and could have worked hard to pursue the presidency as many senators do, but he harbored no presidential ambitions and never did a thing to advance his prospects. Lincoln, by contrast, failed twice in runs for the Senate – in 1854 and again in 1858 when he held the famous debates with Douglas – yet still yearned to achieve the highest office in the land. "His ambition," his law partner William Herndon later wrote, "was a little engine that knew no rest." When Lincoln impressed everyone with his speech at Cooper Union in February, 1860, Hamlin became a Lincoln disciple and began to work in New England to recruit delegates for the candidacy of the man from Illinois.

Lincoln's nomination by the Republican Party at its convention in Chicago in 1860 was a case study in political maneuvering at its best. Lincoln's men used every possible political ploy to get their man over the top. After nominating him, the party turned its attention to his running mate. As usual, the major considerations were balancing the ticket geographically and appealing to factions of the party that might not be philosophically in tune with the presidential nominee. Thus, the focus became to find a man from the east who might be a little more of an abolitionist than Lincoln and thus appeal to the more radical branch of the party. To many at the convention, Hannibal Hamlin fulfilled all these requirements: He was popular in Maine, he was adamantly opposed to slavery, he was a solid speaker, and he was an experienced parliamentarian who could preside over the Senate competently. Thus, without any input from Lincoln (It was not customary for the nominee to choose his running mate in those days), Hamlin was selected, and the convention adjourned.

Hamlin himself was shocked. He wrote to his wife back home in Maine, "Nell, dear, I presume you were as much astonished as myself at my nomination for Vice President. I was amazed at it. I neither expected it nor desired it. But, it has been made, and as a man faithful to the cause, it leaves me no alternative but to accept it."

As soon as the Republican platform of opposition to the extension of slavery and its ticket of Lincoln and Hamlin were made public, there was outrage across the South. One of the most egregious reactions came from Robert Barnwell Rhett, Senator from South Carolina and a leader in the secessionist movement. Because Hamlin had a dark complexion, Rhett and many Southerners assumed he was part African-American and Rhett indignantly shouted, ". . . They (the Republicans) design to place over the South a man who has Negro blood in his veins!" For strongly pro-slavery Southerners the Republican Party was too much to endure and they made plans to take their states out of the Union if Lincoln and Hamlin were elected.

At this point I will pause to throw out an idea that might have some merit: In view of the outrage many Southern political leaders harbored about the Republican Party, would it have been wiser *not* to nominate a known abolitionist for Vice-President and instead chosen a more moderate Republican politician from a border state? There were Republicans from border states where slavery was legal – Maryland, Missouri, Kentucky and Delaware – who might have made the party slightly less obnoxious to the South and therefore might have made less difficult the struggle to keep those border states in the Union after the election. There were two notable Republicans, both of whom eventually became part of Lincoln's cabinet, who might have served as less offensive Republican Vice Presidential candidates without sacrificing Republican principles. There was Edward Bates of Missouri (later, Attorney General) who actually sought the presidential nomination himself, and Montgomery Blair (later, Postmaster General). Both of these were men of substance and ability; both might have brought their respective states into the Republican column, and each would have made the Republican ticket appear a little less radical and thus given support to the arguments of the unionists in the South – and there were a considerable number of those men, at least in the *upper* South – who did not want to overreact to the Republican Party. My choice would have been Bates because he was not as racist as Blair. Is it possible the Civil War would have been shorter and less severe – or, indeed, avoided altogether – if Edward Bates had been the Vice Presidential nominee?

It is possible that either Bates or Blair would have left the true abolitionists in the North cold, and they would not have turned out to vote for the Republican ticket. In today's political parlance, a moderate would not have helped the party "secure its base." But I believe the abolitionists in 1860 had nowhere else to go than the Republican Party, and while a few of them might have stayed home on election day if a moderate were on the ticket (staying home was not done very often at that time; election day was a big social event) enough would have turned out to give Lincoln the northern states he needed. Meanwhile, a few border states – such as Maryland – might have actually gone Republican. At the very least, when South Carolina started the secession ball rolling after the election by screaming "abolitionism is now in power," Unionists would have had more evidence to support their view that cooler heads needed to prevail, and the South should wait to see what the new President might actually do.

The idea that a less radical nominee for Vice President might have weakened the call for secession is one of two major "what ifs" about Hannibal Hamlin. The other appears at the end of the war.

It surprised me to learn that Lincoln had never met Hamlin – in fact, barely knew who he was – and the two men did not see each other face-to-face until Lincoln asked his new Vice President to meet him at the Tremont House in Chicago two weeks after the election. Their meeting was very cordial, and Lincoln asked Hamlin for advice on appointments to the cabinet. The two very similar men seemed to like each other and, from that point on, Lincoln did consult his Vice President somewhat more than most chief executives did at that time. It should be remembered that in those days the Vice President was not considered to be in the executive branch. His job was to be in the legislative branch presiding over the Senate; he did not attend cabinet meetings or have an office in the White House.

In later years Hamlin described his conversations with Lincoln this way: "I was more radical than he. I was urging him; he was holding back on his problems and he was wiser, probably, as events prove." There was one moment, however, when the two were in total agreement. In July of 1862, Lincoln asked Hamlin to ride with him out to the "Soldiers' Home," his summer residence outside the city, to see something very important. (Let us pause for a moment here and consider the President and Vice President of the United States, riding on horseback ten miles along a dusty road outside Washington with no military escort or bodyguards!) Of course, they did make it without incident and, after supper, Lincoln showed Hamlin a document he had been working on. It was an emancipation proclamation. Naturally, Hamlin was delighted, as Lincoln knew he would be, and I'm sure they shared a moment as they absorbed the significance of Hamlin's righteous impatience and Lincoln's strategic caution coming together at last to achieve an enormous moral victory!

Throughout the war Hamlin served the Union cause in any way he could. He helped recruit soldiers, especially in Maine, and, after the Emancipation Proclamation was announced, he strongly urged Lincoln to form black regiments, which the President did. In June of 1864 Hamlin, at age 55, reported for duty when his National Guard unit was called up. "I am the Vice President of the United States," he explained to the commanding officer, "but

I am also a private citizen and, as an enlisted member of your company, I am bound to do my duty." He served through the summer, even doing guard duty, and did not return home until his unit was dismissed.

That same summer the Republicans held their nominating convention in Baltimore. There, the foundation for the second "what if" question about Hannibal Hamlin was laid. The Republicans, looking ahead to the expected successful conclusion of the war, decided to call themselves the "National Union Party". The delegates took pains not only to extol the success in the war, but also to prepare for the reuniting of the Union. With that in mind, it now seemed wise – four years after they might have thought along those lines but did not – to nominate a candidate with some appeal in the South. Hamlin did get forty percent of the votes, but, in the end, they pushed him to the side and gave the nomination to Andrew Johnson.

President Lincoln claimed to have played no part in all of this. In fact, some sources portray him as being disgusted with the Johnson nomination. There is no doubt that there was considerable political intrigue at the convention and it is very likely that Hamlin was stabbed in the back by at least a few Republicans who – perhaps taking a cue from Lincoln himself – thought the ticket would be strengthened by the presence of a "War Democrat" on it. The President was already looking ahead to reconstruction; he wanted to signal his conciliatory intentions to the South, and there was no better way to do that than to get his party to nominate a Southerner as his running mate.

It all went as planned. Hamlin loyally campaigned for the Lincoln-Johnson ticket and the President was overwhelmingly re-elected.

When inauguration day came the following March, Andrew Johnson, the Vice President-elect, came into Hamlin's office to prepare for the nomination ceremony. It was certainly an awkward moment when the two met. Hamlin had to have been at least a little annoyed that it was not he who was about to be sworn in as Vice President for the next four years. When he had first taken office, Hamlin had ordered all liquor removed from the Senate – to the dismay of many – but Johnson said he wasn't feeling well and asked if he could get a glass of bourbon. Hamlin accommodated, a bottle was sent for, and Johnson proceeded to slug down two or three straight shots (the exact number was later debated). Shortly after that he was sworn in before the Senate and gave a drunken speech in which he forgot peoples' names, slurred his words, and generally made a terrible impression. Hamlin, and Lincoln who was also in the Senate chamber, were thoroughly disgusted.

An hour later Lincoln stood outside on the Capitol steps and delivered his second inaugural address, one of the finest speeches ever made. It was so magnificent that it has been engraved in marble on the walls inside the Lincoln Memorial. Following the speech, Hamlin boarded a train for the trip back home. Johnson, presumably, adjourned to his new office to finish the bottle.

Six weeks later came the assassination and Johnson's ascendancy to the presidency. Johnson was an illiterate tailor in Tennessee before he elevated himself. As a young man he got married, learned to read with his wife's help, and went into politics. As a poor southern white man he had only supported emancipation as a way of striking a blow at the southern aristocrats, people he hated almost as much as he hated the African-Americans. Now that the "n - - - - - s" were free, Johnson had no interest in helping them. As a result of these attitudes, every time the "Radical Republicans" in Congress passed legislation to help the "freedmen," Johnson vetoed the bill and, after Congress overrode his veto, obstructed the enforcement of the law. He vetoed a bill to extend the life of the Freedmen's Bureau, an agency run by the army to help the freedmen get educated, find jobs or go into farming. He vetoed the Civil Rights Bill that would give equal citizenship to everyone regardless of race. He opposed the Fourteenth Amendment which would guarantee equal citizenship for the freedmen for all time. Finally, he vetoed the Reconstruction Acts which kept Union soldiers in the South to protect the freedmen from terrorist groups such as the Ku Klux Klan. Ultimately the radicals in Congress got so fed up with Johnson's obstructionist tactics that they devised impeachment charges against him and came within one vote in the Senate of removing him from office. A few months later the Republican Party nominated and elected Ulysses S. Grant as President — a man who shared most of the Radicals' views on race – and the freedmen received another few years of support from the federal government.

Clearly, the "what if" question here is: What if the Republicans had nominated Hamlin for a second term and *he* had moved into the White House on April 15, 1865? First of all, because he shared most of their views on race, he would have had much better relations with the Radical Republicans in Congress. The freedmen would have enjoyed a much longer period of equality under President Hamlin. It might even have been possible for them to have gotten off to such a strong start in their new lives that they would not have been beaten down by Jim Crow laws and intimidation in the years that followed. Given the level of racism that existed at that time, even among Northerners, that is very much wishful thinking, but at least there would have been a better chance of it.

Part of what might have made a better life for the freedmen possible under President Hamlin is the way he would have treated the former Confederate leaders. Johnson pardoned most of them in 1865 because it delighted him to watch those men, who once lorded over him, have to come before him, hat in hand, begging for pardons. He benignly bestowed pardons on them, restored them to power, and watched approvingly as they took steps to "put the Negro race in its place."

Hamlin, by contrast, was even inclined to try many of the Confederate political leaders and military officers for treason. As a forgiving man, he would not likely have favored executions – although he occasionally spoke of hanging the top rebels – but there would have been prison sentences and extended periods of political disenfranchisement for all those who were leaders of the rebellion.

For decades after the Civil War Southerners complained about "Radical Reconstruction," about how unfairly they were treated by the military and how obnoxious it was to have the ignorant, uncivilized black man "shoved down their throats." During those years, Southerners got many Northerners to agree with their interpretation of reconstruction. Modern "revisionist" historians, however, contend that the Radical Republicans merely wanted to ensure equal treatment for the African-American race, and these historians believe the so-called "radical" policies did not go far enough. Disenfranchisement of the rebel leaders should have lasted longer; military rule in the South should have lasted longer. Perhaps the freedom the black race achieved would have had real meaning if the "Radical Republicans" had had a sympathetic President to work with.

I believe Hannibal Hamlin of Maine could have been that man. Throughout the war he showed he was not only in favor of emancipation but also favored arming the African-Americans, creating black regiments, and even taking land from rebels and distributing it to the freedmen to get them started in farming. As landowners, they would have been far less vulnerable to exploitation by unscrupulous whites. Thus, it was a great tragedy for the black race that it was not Hannibal Hamlin rather than Andrew Johnson who took the presidential oath on that sad

April morning when Abraham Lincoln died. So much would have been different!

Ironically, Hannibal Hamlin was the only Vice President to return to the Senate in the years after leaving office and Andrew Johnson was the only President to enter the Senate after leaving the White House. In the mid 1870s, they were both in the Senate and must have frequently crossed paths in the hallways of the Capitol building and, perhaps, even debated each other on the Senate floor. I don't know of any encounters having been recorded, but it must have been very tempting for Hamlin to look at his rival and think of how much would have been different if the Republicans had chosen *him* in the summer of 1864 instead of the racist, stubborn man from Tennessee on the other side of the aisle.

I am not usually a practitioner of "what if" history. It is usually useless to hypothesize about what might have happened if something had been different. In this story, however, analyzing how the choices made by the Republican conventions of 1860 and 1864 affected the Civil War and its aftermath helps us understand how truly consequential in the war the practically unknown Hannibal Hamlin was and how consequential the decision to replace him was in 1864. In the first instance, selecting him may have made secession and war a little more likely; in the second instance, passing over him may have made life for African-Americans a little bit worse.

THE KLAN BUSTER

HE PRESERVED THE REULTS OF THE CIVIL WAR ...
AT LEAST FOR A WHILE.

For many years, most American History textbooks and most teachers, myself included, relegated Ulysses S. Grant to the cellar of our Presidents. He was one of the worst, we proclaimed. Yet, I always wondered: if Grant was so incompetent, how was the Ku Klux Klan destroyed and how were the rights of newly freed African-Americans protected as they were when he was President? Apparently, the general was able to accomplish *something* while he sat in a drunken stupor in the White House. Recently, some historians are writing revisionist versions of the Grant Administration and now Ron Chernow has weighed in with a fresh look at Grant, highlighted by a glowing account of his racial policies, most notably his crushing of the Ku Klux Klan. For this achievement Grant owed a great deal to the man he appointed as Attorney General, Amos T. Akerman. Indeed, the unknown Akerman emerges in Chernow's book as the hero of the fight for African-American rights.

When Grant took office in March of 1869, the Civil War had been over for four years. The "Radical Republicans" in Congress had passed three amendments to the constitution – the 13th, which freed the slaves, the 14th which bestowed citizenship and "equal protection of the laws" on the freedmen, and the 15th which proclaimed that no person could be denied the right to vote on account of "race, color or previous condition of servitude." Southerners were begrudgingly accepting their defeat and the crushing of secession, but they were not going to live with equality for African-Americans if they could avoid it. Many Southerners were determined to restore the freedmen to slavery in everything but name . . . the amendments be damned!

In many areas of the South the method used to prevent black people from enjoying equality and voting rights was outright intimidation. The Ku Klux Klan, organized in 1865 to restore the supremacy of the white race, terrified the freedmen and their white friends. Those white friends of the freedmen, strange as it may seem today, were Republicans. The Klan, riding at night and disguised as ghosts of dead Confederate soldiers with their white sheets, brutalized and often murdered blacks who were "uppity" enough to attempt to go into "whites only" establishments or to vote. Republican governors of southern states and former abolitionists wrote letters to Grant telling him that for all practical purposes the Civil War was still being fought. Having watched men by the thousands die hideously in the war, Grant was not about to let the cause they died for be crushed by bands of lawless thugs.

Chernow tells us that Grant had the confidence of most of the northern abolitionists. Wendell Phillips of Boston spoke for them. "There is still a state of war with the South," he said." "Let General Grant lay his hands on the leaders in the South, and you will never hear of the Ku Klux Klan again." His words were to prove prophetic.

In 1870, and again in 1871, Congress passed enforcement acts that established greater federal oversight of elections in order to enforce the 15th Amendment. But those laws were limited to the election procedures; they did little to counter the extreme intimidation before election day that the Klan was able to exercise. To remedy this deficiency, Grant proposed yet a third enforcement act, called Congress into special session to consider it, brought his entire cabinet to Capitol Hill to lobby for it, and on April 21, 1871, returned to the Capitol to sign it. Known forthrightly as The Ku Klux Klan Act, the law made it a federal offense to deprive any person of the "equal protection of the law" guaranteed by the 14th Amendment. Lest there be any doubt about what behavior was outlawed, the act made it a crime to "conspire together or go in disguise on the public highway" to deprive any person of his rights. In simple terms, there could be no more riding at night wearing bed sheets to terrorize freedmen or their white friends.

All of this would have been only cosmetic without Grant's iron determination to make it happen. This is where Amos T. Akerman came in. In June of 1870, Congress had created the Department of Justice. Headed by the Attorney General, this department would make enforcement of federal law much more effective, especially in areas in which local authorities were unable or unwilling to enforce it. Grant appointed Akerman to be the new Attorney General. Akerman's major responsibility was to be the enforcement of the 14th and 15th Amendments and, after April of 1871, the Ku Klux Klan Act. He was just the person to do it.

Amos Akerman was one of those men who looks and behaves like he has an I-beam for a backbone. Tall, slim, a native of New Hampshire (the "Granite State") and a graduate of Dartmouth College, he had spent much of his life practicing law in the

South. During the war he had served as a quartermaster in the Confederate Army. After the war, he had one of those conversions I admire: He became a Republican and supported voting rights and equality for the newly freed African-Americans. He was one of those people who, having decided on the right course of action, proceeds to fulfill the mission with an iron will. He was just the right man – a man like Grant himself — whom the President needed to crush the life out of the Ku Klux Klan.

Akerman acted swiftly and effectively. He sent into the South an army of federal marshals and attorneys to prosecute every law-breaker they could get their hands on. They found that they were confronting not just random, crazed individuals who rode at night, but a gigantic movement of "never-say-die sons of the Confederacy." In some jurisdictions, hundreds of criminal acts were being committed every week. Grant sent federal troops and, in South Carolina, suspended "habeas corpus" so individuals could be arrested and held without charges long enough to assemble witnesses and get convictions in court. On September 12th, 1871, Akerman went south to take personal charge of the entire campaign.

In his pursuit of justice, Akerman was relentless. Grant had issued "General Order Number 48" which allowed federal troops to arrest violators of the Ku Klux Klan Act. Under Akerman's supervision, arrest them they did. Akerman was convinced that what he was doing was going to benefit the South in the long run so, for now, the bands of outlaw brigands were going to have to be dealt with severely. The Klan's actions amount to war, he proclaimed, and they cannot be "effectively crushed on any theory."

By the end of 1871, Akerman had issued 3,384 indictments, out of which he secured 1143 convictions for violating the Ku Klux Klan Acts. In South Carolina, he announced he had taken two thousand prisoners. Black people in the state "can sleep at home, now," he said with justifiable satisfaction. "The most atrocious organization that the civilized part of the world has ever known" had been crushed. Even the outspoken black leader Frederick Douglass was impressed. "Peace has come to many places as never before," he wrote.

By the end of 1871, the back of the Klan was broken. At this point, unfortunately, Grant did the kind of thing that prevents him from getting high marks for his presidency. He gave in to the special interests. The railroad plutocrats were unhappy with Akerman who, along with his anti-Klan prosecutions, was resisting railroad efforts to bribe him and was actually enforcing regulations against the railroads. The big money men pressured Grant to get rid of his iron-willed Attorney General, and the President supinely obliged. To spare Grant embarrassment, Akerman quietly resigned, and the two men parted ways with no acrimony. Fortunately, the Klan prosecutions were well under way and the new Attorney General secured even more convictions during the next two years.

Akerman returned to Georgia to resume his law practice. He had been Attorney General for less than two years, yet he had accomplished so much during those months that, as Chernow says, he has to be regarded as one of the great Attorneys General of all time. Some top Justice Department officials have earned titles such as "trust buster" or "crime buster." Amos Akerman accomplished something even more important – putting out of business the organization that threatened to undo the achievements of the Civil War. He was the "Klan buster."

FRANCES, WITH AN "E"

FRANCES PERKINS: THE FIRST FEMALE MEMBER OF A PRESIDENT'S CABINET

On March 25, 1911, Frances Perkins was part of a genteel group of public-spirited young women attending an afternoon tea at a luxurious townhouse on North Washington Square in New York City. As they sat down to begin their discussions on poverty and factory conditions, they heard noises in the street and rushed to the windows to see what was happening. Across the square they saw flames shooting out of a twelve-story building that they all knew housed the Triangle Shirt Waist Company.

As Frances rushed out of the house and began running down the sidewalk towards the fire she thought about the recent history of the Triangle Company. Workers in New York textile factories had been complaining for years about the dangerous and un-healthy conditions in their buildings, but the Triangle Company had been notorious as one company that refused to make any improvements. As a result, hundreds of workers, mostly young Jewish and Italian women, worked twelve-hour days sitting before sewing machines crammed into tight quarters. There was very little ventilation and the doors were locked to prevent workers from sneaking out for breaks.

What Frances saw as she arrived at the scene of the fire horrified her and everyone else who was standing there watching helplessly. The firefighters did not have ladders long enough to reach the tenth floor windows where the girls were leaning out screaming for help. One after another, they jumped or fell to their deaths on the pavement below. By the time the horror was over, 146 workers, most of them young immigrant women, had died. Their bodies lay scattered on the street or pathetically heaped by the windows and doors in the building.

After witnessing this incredible tragedy Frances Perkins could no longer go to afternoon teas to discuss ways to improve factory conditions. "It was without doubt that the Triangle fire was a turning point," a close friend said. "What Frances Perkins saw that day started her on her career." That career was to serve as a crusader for workers' rights in the halls of the New York State government. She would carry her message to the men in her world who had the power to change things: Governor Al Smith of New York, and Franklin D. Roosevelt, as Governor of New York and then as President of the United States. She never let her gender prevent her from standing up to anyone who neglected the rights of the working poor.

She was born Fannie Coralie Perkins in 1880 in Boston near Beacon Hill. When she was young her family moved to Worcester, but the home she remembered most while growing up was her grandmother's house in Newcastle, Maine, where she spent her summers. Her family descended from pioneers who arrived in America from Scotland in the mid-17th century. From that background she acquired her New England accent and her firm belief in hard work and self-reliance. By the time she was a young woman heading off to Holyoke College in the late 1890s, she was developing a mind of her own and was already thinking independently.

At Mount Holyoke, where she earned a degree in Chemistry and Physics, and then at Columbia, where she earned a Master's Degree in Political Science, she became interested in the problems of poor people and began to appreciate the fact that not all the people in the lower classes were simply too lazy to improve their condition as she had been taught to believe in her younger years. She began volunteering at settlement houses and, in 1910, became head of the "Consumers' League," an organization that lobbied for better working conditions in factories.

After the Triangle fire, newly energized and committed to the cause of worker safety, Frances became the executive director of the New York City "Committee on Safety." She directed the group's actions beyond fire safety and into all things that affected workers' health and well-being. Frances became committed to the notion that government did have a role to play in protecting workers; that laissez-faire capitalism must be made an outdated concept.

When Al Smith became governor in 1919, he appointed Frances to the New York State Industrial Commission. This body investigated safety conditions in factories, enforced existing safety laws, and recommended new ones. Through most of the 1920s, Frances Perkins was New York state government's expert on labor issues and chief champion of workers' rights. In 1928, when Smith went off to wage his unsuccessful bid for the presidency, the new Governor, Franklin Roosevelt, entrusted Frances with even more responsibility. He appointed her Industrial Commissioner of the state and she, along with FDR, began battling the unemployment that began sweeping the state after the stock market crash of 1929. One of her primary goals was to establish a program of "unemployment insurance," whereby workers who became unemployed through no fault of their own could receive weekly income while they searched for a new job.

By the summer of 1932, the nation was mired in the Great Depression and Roosevelt was running for President on the promise to provide a "New Deal" for the American people. Once he was elected, no one knew what this "New Deal" would be – even FDR himself – so the President needed knowledgeable people around him to figure it out. With that in mind, he decided he needed to take the unheard-of step of naming a woman to be part of his cabinet. To get her into the office of Secretary of Labor he had to overcome several obstacles: the men who led the major labor unions in the country who felt that one of *them* should be Labor Secretary, the members of the Senate who could hardly imagine a woman – impractical as "they" are – being the head of a major executive department, and Frances herself who had a husband and a teenaged daughter living in New York whose lives would be totally disrupted. FDR almost always got what he wanted, so the men involved had to "get over it," and Frances had to figure out how to make it work – and set an example for the thousands of women who were to follow her into responsible positions of authority. It was difficult, but she managed, and in March of 1933 she was sworn in as Secretary of Labor, a position she was to hold for the next twelve years (FDR's entire presidency).

FDR's major challenge in 1933 was, as he put it, "to put people to work." Right off the line, the first program to accomplish that was the Civilian Conservation Corps. The "CCC" offered young men ages 18-25 the chance to leave the streets where they were unemployed and go to camps where they would do conservation work and be paid a dollar a day. FDR asked Frances to administer this unwieldy enterprise and it was she who envisioned the idea of bringing in the U.S. Army to run the camps – after all, that's what the army did – and the program got off to a smooth and rapid start.

My father-in-law was an immediate beneficiary of the CCC. He was unemployed in Cleveland and, as the oldest in the family at age 22, he felt the responsibility of providing for his two siblings and his mother. So he signed up for the CCC, went to a camp in Oregon, and was soon sending home money for his family to survive. By the end of 1933, there were 300,000 men in the program; by 1936, there were 2,158 camps around the nation; by 1942 when it disbanded during World War II, 3.5 million Americans had been part of the CCC. Franklin Roosevelt gets all the credit for this imaginative and highly successful program, but it was really Frances Perkins who made it happen.

Frances and FDR believed that, as he put it, "to dole out relief . . . is to administer a narcotic, a subtle destroyer of the human spirit." Thus, the emphasis was to be on public works, projects that paid a wage and accomplished useful things such as building schools and playgrounds, repairing bridges and roads, and even writing and producing theater productions.

Undoubtedly the most significant contribution Frances Perkins made to the New Deal was the Social Security System. Basing her ideas on what she had read, what she had seen in her years in New York government, and what she had seen and heard during a trip to Great Britain, Frances crafted a program of unemployment insurance, old age pensions, and disability insurance paid for by a system of combined employee and employer contributions. It took considerable lobbying to get the bill through Congress, but it finally emerged in the summer of 1935 and FDR signed it. In the photos of the signing we see Frances standing, somewhat lost in the crowd of men, behind him. The picture does not really tell the story. Frances was the one who wanted the program and did all of the grunt work to get it passed. FDR, as one member of Congress put it, merely went along to keep her happy. Nevertheless, there it was: a system that has become part of the fabric of the country. On the day it was signed Frances put out a statement calling it "one of the most forward pieces of legislation in the interest of wage earners" in history.

During her tenure as Labor Secretary, Frances was a consistent advocate of workers' right to organize and bargain collectively. The union movement reached its peak in 1935 when the disparate craft unions of the automobile industry banded together into an industry-wide union called the United Auto Workers. In 1937, this new, much more potent union, staged the country's first sit-down strike at the General Motors plant in Flint, Michigan. Secretary Perkins supported the strikers and, in spite of court injunctions against the strike and calls from people as influential as Vice President John Nance Garner for federal intervention to break up the strike, the union prevailed. General Motors recognized the U.A.W. as the sole bargaining agent for its workers, and UAW membership mushroomed from 30,000 members in 1936 to 500,000 members by 1938.

When President Roosevelt broke precedent with history and ran for a third term in 1940, Frances stayed loyal and continued at her post. He needed her to manage the labor side of the enormous war production schedule that was necessary to fight two major powers on a global scale. Taking her cue from Eleanor Roosevelt who traveled all over the world during the war to visit the troops, Perkins traveled around the country to visit factories and encourage all the "Rosie the Riveters" who were on the job. She was not a gifted speaker, but her quiet presence and obvious enthusiasm for their work was important, and the information she brought back to the President was very useful. A case can easily be made that the major reason the United States defeated Nazi Germany and Imperial Japan was the enormous industrial output the country was able to generate. In the deserts of North Africa, when Rommel ran low on tanks, Eisenhower was still bringing many more into the fight. And so it went all over the world all through the war. In no small way, Frances Perkins was responsible for making that happen.

Frances Perkins remained at her post until April of 1945 when Roosevelt died. She had been Secretary of Labor for over twelve years; she and Harold Ickes, Secretary of the Interior, were the only two cabinet members who had been with the President for his entire tenure. When she left office she was proud of the fact that she had achieved most of the goals she had set for herself and for the new Roosevelt Administration in early 1933: drastically reduce unemployment, establish a system of unemployment insurance, institute a minimum wage system, abolish child labor, set up a system of social security, and introduce federal safety standards for factories and other places of employment. The only goal she failed to reach was the establishment of a national system of health care that would provide medical services for the poor as well as the wealthy.

Some historians regard Frances Perkins as the person most responsible for the "New Deal." FDR thought up the name, but she gave the name meaning by putting new laws and new programs into action. When she stood outside the Triangle Company building in 1911 and saw those poor girls fall to their deaths because of inadequate safety standards, Frances knew the government needed to do more to help the workers. She also knew that she, personally, was going to have to make a greater commitment to the cause. On the day of the fire, the "New Deal" was born. Frances put it plainly: "I came to Washington to work for God, FDR, and the millions of forgotten, plain common workingmen."

GEORGE KENNEY

THIS "CAN DO" MAN MADE
"ISLAND HOPPING" POSSIBLE.

In early 1942, the military situation in the Pacific was bleak. The Japanese attack on Pearl Harbor had left four battleships in smoldering ruins, many other warships crippled, and almost the entire air squadron of the eastern Pacific destroyed. A month after Pearl Harbor, the Japanese invasion of the Philippines drove General MacArthur's forces into a desperate defensive position on the Bataan Peninsula across the bay from Manila. From there, under orders from Washington, MacArthur escaped in a PT boat with his family and miraculously made it to Australia where he hoped to organize an American and Australian force to counter-attack and liberate the Philippines. "We came through," MacArthur proclaimed in a statement to the press that has become famous, "and I shall return!"

MacArthur did, indeed, return to liberate the Philippines in 1944. For the brilliant "island hopping" campaign he has been quite rightly acclaimed. But an important unknown factor in

MacArthur's success – indeed, it could be argued, the sine qua non of his success – was the steady and resourceful leadership of his air commander, George Kenney.

George Kenney was short, solid and breezy, with a dark crew cut and an engaging demeanor. He was also a hard-driving task-master imbued with a "can do" spirit, a man who did not suffer fools gladly. From the summer of 1942 when he reported to MacArthur at his hotel in Brisbane, to the summer of 1945 when Japan surrendered, Kenney was MacArthur's indispensable man, the man who made "island hopping" possible.

The first job Kenney realized he had to take care of was to assert his control over the air corps, and that meant putting a stop to the meddling of MacArthur's chief of staff, Richard Sutherland. Sutherland, arrogant and insufferable, had no combat air experience, but he had assumed the authority to order air strikes and select targets. As soon as Kenney found out about this, he stormed into Sutherland's office, grabbed a sheet of paper and a pencil, and drew a tiny black dot in the middle of the page. "That," he said, pointing to the dot, "is what *you* know about air power. The rest of the sheet is what I know about it!" When Sutherland tried to assert himself, Kenney said, "Let's go into the next room, see General MacArthur, and get this thing straight. I want to find out who is to run this air force." From that day forward, Kenney made all the air force decisions and Sutherland kept his distance.

Immediately, Kenney proved his worth to MacArthur when he undertook a complete inventory of all the aircraft they had at their disposal and established a ground maintenance system that would be the envy of any airline today. To put it simply, he kept the planes flying. MacArthur, in his memoirs, comments that when the war was over and he was able to assess the Japanese military capabilities more closely, he found that they had hundreds of fighter planes that were not flyable only because they

were missing a part or two. If they had had the system of maintenance that Kenney had organized, they would have been a much
more formidable opponent.

MacArthur was rarely willing to share the limelight with
anyone. One of his officers once commented he would rather put
a rattlesnake in his pocket than have a news story hit the papers
that credited him and not the general for even a minor success.
Yet, in his memoirs MacArthur heaps praise on his air commander, George Kenney, as the man who gave him control of the
skies for every island landing he made in the Pacific.

Strategically, Kenney's biggest contribution was the means he
proposed to get MacArthur and his forces out of the defensive
box they were in down in Australia in mid-1942. The Japanese
had captured all of the Pacific islands down to, and including,
the northern coast of New Guinea. Their next target was certainly Port Moresby on New Guinea's south coast, and from there
they would likely invade Australia. MacArthur had wisely decided to defend Port Moresby rather than draw a defensive line
in Australia. The Australians were planning to draw such a line,
and he called that the worst form of defeatism. He would not only
defend Moresby, he would use it as a base for an island-hopping
strategy to return to the Philippines. But, how could he get a force
of 26,000 men and all the food and equipment they would need
across the six hundred mile "moat" that separated his Australian
supply depots from New Guinea? That "moat" was the Coral Sea,
and it was infested with Japanese war ships.

General Kenney provided the answer. "We can *fly* 26,000 men
up and keep them supplied," he asserted. That, alone, seemed an
overwhelming task; and what about the trucks, he was asked. His
answer: "We can cut the chassis frames in half with acetylene
torches, stuff the halves into C-47's, and weld the frames back
together when we get them there. Give me five days and I'll ship

the whole damn U.S. Army to New Guinea by air." This bit of confidence – indeed, bravado – convinced MacArthur that his decision to break out of Australia immediately was the right one. The U.S. Navy lent a hand when they fought the Japanese to a standstill in the Battle of the Coral Sea, and MacArthur was able to get his whole force and all the equipment they would need to Port Moresby without cutting trucks in half, but Kenney's confidence and resourcefulness exemplified the "can do" attitude that was a major factor in the U.S. war effort.

After my father was drafted into the Navy in 1943, he was shipped to New Guinea and spent most of the final two years of the war unloading ships at Port Moresby and sending supplies to MacArthur's army as it advanced up the Pacific towards the Philippines. Dad just did his job and, after the war, talked only about MacArthur, no other commanders. I doubt that he knew about the key role played by George Kenney in keeping Port Moresby in American hands.

MacArthur's confidence in Kenney was illustrated clearly when a group of war correspondents who were covering his campaign in the Pacific asked him, "What is the air force doing today?" MacArthur replied, "I don't know. Go ask Kenney." The correspondents persisted, "General, do you mean to say you do not know where the bombs are falling?" MacArthur's response: "Of course I do. I know where they are falling. They are falling in the right place. Go ask Kenney where it is."

For two years, MacArthur led his forces past heavily defended Japanese islands, landed on lightly defended ones that would serve as good air bases, and then used his new runways to advance to the next island. He preferred to call his strategy "leap frogging" rather than "island hopping" because he wanted to emphasize the way he jumped from one good air base to another, bypassing the heavily defended ones and using the islands he occupied as unsinkable aircraft carriers. For every landing, Kenney's pilots gained control of the skies and made the fighting much easier for the marines going ashore. It was George Kenney who made it possible for General MacArthur to wade dramatically onto the beach at Leyte in the Philippines and have a picture of that event published in every newspaper, magazine, and history book in the world. He did, indeed, return; he was a national hero.

Meanwhile George Kenney was just one of the other guys in the photograph at Leyte getting his pants wet wading behind the general.

THE FIRST COLD WARRIOR

THE CONCEPT WAS SIMPLE. THE EXECUTION WAS THE TRICKY PART.

In appearance, George Kennan was a very unremarkable man. Good looking, balding, of average height, he could be just one of thousands of bureaucrats in gray double-breasted suits carrying briefcases around Washington in the late 1940s. Indeed, when he made the enormous contribution to the foreign policy of the United States for which he should be famous, he was an unknown functionary in the U.S. Embassy in Moscow. In 1946, he was the deputy chief of the State Department's Moscow mission, a position so obscure even President Truman probably had only a vague idea who he was.

In February, the Treasury Department cabled the embassy in Moscow asking for an explanation for the Soviet Union's recent strange behavior, specifically its refusal to join the International Monetary Fund. Kennan responded with a 5,600-word telegram, often referred to (for obvious reasons) as the "long telegram." Kennan's central point in all those words was that Russia had always feared the outside world. At the "bottom of the Kremlin's neurotic view of world affairs," Kennan wrote, "is the traditional instinctive sense of Russian insecurity." When this insecurity became leavened by communist ideology after the revolution of 1917, the Soviets saw an inherent conflict between the communist and capitalist worlds. Despite its neuroses, the Soviet Union is a formidable adversary, he warned. "With many of the world's traditional power centers devastated and the Soviet leadership controlling vast natural resources and the energies of one of the world's greatest peoples," a contest about the nature of the world order was inevitable.

The following year Kennan published an article in *Foreign Affairs* magazine in which he argued that the way to deal with Moscow was by "a policy of firm *containment* designed to confront the Russians at every point where they show signs of encroaching upon the interests of a peaceful and stable world."

This article, entitled *The Sources of Soviet Conduct*, featured a memorable sentence that became the guiding light for American foreign policy for the next fifty years. "It is clear that the main element of any United States policy toward the Soviet Union must be that of a long term, patient but firm and vigilant *containment* of Russian expansive tendencies." Kennan was convinced that the communist system was so inherently flawed that if it were held in check and not allowed to expand, it would ultimately collapse under the weight of its own contradictions. The word "containment" caught on as the one-word description of our foreign policy toward the Soviet Union – and, after 1949, China.

In 1947, the same year his *Foreign Affairs* article appeared, Kennan became part of Secretary of State George Marshall's "Policy Planning Staff." In that capacity he guided the formulation of the "European Recovery Program," a plan of massive economic aid to Western Europe that became known to history as the Marshall Plan. This policy of building the economic health of capitalist democracies so they could resist the lure of communism was exactly what Kennan meant when he spoke of "containment."

Also in 1947, President Truman delivered a groundbreaking speech to Congress requesting $400 million for military aid to Greece and Turkey who were threatened by communist takeovers. "It must be the policy of the United States," Truman proclaimed, "to support free peoples who are resisting attempted subjugation by armed minorities or by outside pressures." For most Americans at that time, and for almost every student of American History since then, this "Truman Doctrine" was the essence of Kennan's containment concept. But, for Kennan himself, Truman's doctrine was not exactly what he had in mind when he wrote the "long telegram" and *The Sources of Soviet Conduct.* He wanted U.S. support for non-communist governments to be selective; he wanted to focus on *Soviet* expansion, not internal communist movements; and he greatly preferred to use economic or diplomatic rather than military means to resist Soviet aggression.

For the next forty years, most of the foreign policy actions regarding the Soviet Union, China or local insurgencies that were made by a succession of American presidents were undertaken under the umbrella of "containment." For Kennan, some of what was done in the name of his policy was abominable. He was particularly appalled by the arms race and the inexorable buildup of nuclear weapons. The "Cold War" should never have become an arms race, he asserted.

And then came the war in Vietnam. Kennan admired John Quincy Adams who once wrote, "Nations should not go abroad in search of monsters to destroy." In Southeast Asia, Kennan was convinced that the United States was doing just that. When

President Lyndon Johnson invited foreign policy "wise men" to the White House in 1965 to advise him on what to do in Vietnam, he did not, for reasons unknown, invite George Kennan. Perhaps he should have. In 1966, in testimony before the Senate Foreign Relations Committee, Kennan spoke out against the administration's Vietnam policy. "We have no strategic interests at stake there," he asserted. The originator of the "containment concept" was telling the committee and the world that containment did not apply to Vietnam, that the Southeast Asian countries would not fall to communism like a row of dominoes if South Vietnam fell. Supporters of the war argued that if we did not stop the communists in Vietnam we would some day be fighting them on our west coast. George Kennan scoffed at that notion.

Kennan's 1966 testimony on Vietnam was like an echo of General Omar Bradley's assertion in 1951 that expanding the war in Korea to China would be "the wrong war, at the wrong time, in the wrong place and with the wrong enemy." Vietnam, in Kennan's view, was a burden that the United States did not need to carry – certainly not alone.

Of course, the United States stayed in Vietnam for nine more years, casualties mounted, the anti-war movement became intense, and ultimately President Nixon gradually withdrew our forces and the communists took over. When that happened, Cambodia and Laos did, indeed, fall to communists. But the remainder of Southeast Asia avoided the contagion and no Vietnamese communist ever came ashore in California except, perhaps, as a surfer.

Ultimately, in spite of the Vietnam debacle, the United States and our allies – who helped a little bit — won the "Cold War." We won because in the 1980s, in the face of President Reagan's military build-up, the weaknesses of the communist system became apparent. Concurrently, the people of the Soviet Union and Eastern Europe, inspired by what they could now see in the media and the music of the West, became thoroughly disenchanted with their oppressive governments. Communism collapsed of its own inherent rot, just as George Kennan said it would.

Kennan lived to see the collapse of communism in the late 1980s and early 1990s. His policy of containment appeared to have worked! But Kennan was anything but exultant. He believed the United States had meddled too often in the affairs of other nations. This was not what he had meant by "containment." He was also concerned that we would take the success of containment the way it was implemented as justification for future incursions into regions where we would stir up hornets' nests because of our ignorance of the cultures. The invasion of Iraq in 2003 appalled him.

George Kennan lived to be 101. When he died in 2005 he was heralded as the father of the policy that won the Cold War. But, he was never comfortable with that role. If he had ever been Secretary of State, he would have applied containment very differently. In interviews before he died he said we did not need to build enough bombs to blow up the world six times, and we did not need to sacrifice 58,000 of our young men in a futile effort to keep a popular communist from becoming the leader of Vietnam. Containment was the wise alternative to appeasement, of course, but it needed to be applied more judiciously than it was. Exactly how it should be applied in various circumstances he never fully explained, probably because, since he was not in power, he didn't need to.

I have often thought over the years that George Kennan had a very clear-headed view of the world, that he would have carried out a containment policy that would have been effective but less reckless and destructive, and that it was unfortunate that he was never Secretary of State. But, as is often the case, there would have been a few sour notes in that symphony. In my research for this piece I found him to be quite unpredictable — indeed, rather mercurial. It was never very clear to me just exactly where he thought his containment line ought to be drawn. He was even a little fuzzy about whether he even thought the 38th parallel in Korea was worth defending.

Kennan was also quite racist. For example, he had no use for Latin Americans. On a plane trip to California, as he looked down on the border between the United States and Mexico, he wrote in his diary: "Before us stretches the whole great Pacific coast and my only thought as we approach it is: throughout the length and breadth of it (the Mexican border) not one single thing of any importance is being said or done." Wow!

Perhaps we should remember George Kennan as the originator of the "containment concept" that policy makers used as a guiding principle for over forty years and let it go at that.

WHAT THEY COULDA, SHOULDA SAID

Ideas on How Certain Things Might
Have Gone Better if Certain People Said
Things Other Than What They *Did* Say

DAN QUAYLE: OCTOBER 5, 1988

BEING COMPARED TO JOHN F. KENNEDY COULD
HAVE BEEN A GOOD THING FOR DAN QUAYLE.

After an embarrassing put-down or a heated argument from
which you emerged the loser, it's easy to think of a pithy thing you
could have said to perform a verbal jujitsu and win the encounter.
In American history there have been many circumstances when
one of the protagonists, in a tight situation, said something lame
or said nothing at all and, most likely, felt annoyed later that he
or she hadn't thought of a good response. One of the most famous instances of this sort in modern times occurred during a
presidential election. I'm not claiming I could have thought of the
response I'm going to suggest here if I were in the same situation,
but it is amusing to think of what might have happened if the
person involved had had the presence of mind to get off a zinger.

Dan Quayle suffered one of history's most humiliating put-
downs and I'm sure, to this day, he has gone over in his mind a

thousand things he could have said but didn't. I am here to suggest a response that would have quite possibly been a winner.

It is 1988 and the Republican candidate for president, Vice President George H.W. Bush, has surprised the world by selecting as his running mate a young and somewhat inexperienced senator from Indiana, Dan Quayle. With his choirboy looks Quayle does not look presidential. The Democratic Party candidate, Massachusetts Governor Michael Dukakis, has chosen as his running mate the stately senator from Texas, Lloyd Bentsen. On October 5th, in Omaha, Nebraska, the two vice-presidential candidates square off for a debate before a large audience. Sixty-seven-year-old Bentsen is nervous about the encounter because he feels his opponent, a forty-one-year-old photogenic man, is much better equipped to appear on television. In his insecure moments he wonders if he is about to suffer the same death by television that Richard Nixon did when he faced John F. Kennedy in 1960. Ironically, JFK *is* about to figure in this debate, but in a way very different from what Bentsen fears.

One of the newscasters asking questions of the debaters is NBC's Tom Brokaw. In the newsman's opinion Quayle has avoided the issue of how well he thinks he could handle the responsibilities of the presidency if the President were to die or become incapacitated. Since Quayle is young and has limited experience, Brokaw thinks the question deserves a complete and honest answer, so he asks the candidate how he would handle being suddenly thrust into the Oval Office. Looking a bit testy because he is having to answer this question yet again, Quayle describes what he would do if the worst happened and concludes by saying he has had as much experience as John F. Kennedy did when he sought the presidency.

As he says that, the camera catches Bentsen looking like a lion who sees a timid gazelle crossing his path. Hmmm, he's thinking;

won't you be a tasty dinner. When the camera turns to him for his response, he pounces.

"Senator, I served with Jack Kennedy," he says condescendingly, "Jack Kennedy was a friend of mine. Senator, you're no John F. Kennedy."

For a brief second Bentsen's words hang in the air as the audience absorbs their impact. Then, the entire crowd bursts into a cacophony of laughter, cheers and applause. The raucous noise goes on for nearly a full minute. Quayle can only stand at the podium and look shell-shocked. When the audience finally settles down he lamely says, "That was really uncalled for, senator." Bentsen easily parries that by commenting that Quayle was the one who brought up the comparison between himself and Kennedy.

Of course, thirty years later, it is so easy to sit back and compose what could have been a perfect response for Quayle. But it would have flipped the duel completely if Quayle had done this:

After waiting for total quiet so the audience can hear his every word, Dan Quayle speaks in a level and composed voice: "Senator, when I come home to my *own* wife each day after work . . . she is very *glad* that I am no John F. Kennedy."

I bet that response would have triggered a response equally as loud as the one Bentsen received as the people in the audience recalled JFK's reputation for sexual licentiousness and marveled at Quayle's ability to think on his feet. There might have been some in the crowd who loved JFK and resented Quayle's reference to all those old rumors about his infidelities, but Kennedy had been dead for twenty-five years, so I don't think most people in the audience would have had a negative reaction.

The Bush-Quayle ticket survived this debate. It went on to win the election quite handily even though Bentsen was widely acclaimed for his body slam of Quayle. Quayle's reputation as a lightweight has followed him to this day. If he had come back with a great zinger in 1988 such as the one I've suggested, possibly he would have immediately increased his stature and have been seen as a quick-witted man who could handle tough negotiations.

Quayle later made a bit of a name for himself as a champion of public morality. When he criticized the TV show "Murphy Brown" for seeming to glamorize unwed motherhood he became a mini-hero to conservatives across the country. The response I've suggested for that Bentsen debate would have been a good kick-off for a political career centered on moral issues.

Dan Quayle is seventy-years-old by now, and his political career has been over for a long time. In the 2000 presidential race he tried to mount his own campaign but couldn't get any traction. The image of the way Senator Bentsen humiliated him in 1988 follows him wherever he goes. If he had been able to come up with my one-liner – or something similar – he might have been able to build a following based on the need for a return to old-fashioned morals.

Today, amidst a galaxy of immoral scoundrels – Harvey Weinstein, Anthony Weiner, Kevin Spacey – not to mention Bill Clinton, Donald Trump and hundreds of others – a political leader such as Dan Quayle, who had once thought fast on his feet and called out the unseemly realities of JFK might be a huge breath of fresh air and have renewed relevance.

RICHARD NIXON: JUNE 26, 1972

THIS WOULD BE A MUCH EASIER SPEECH THAN THE ONE HE GAVE LATER!

On June 17, 1972, five burglars were caught trying to bug the telephones in the Democratic Party headquarters at the Watergate Office Complex in Washington, D.C. In discussions with his top advisors, H.R. Haldeman and John Ehrlichman, President Nixon learned that the break-in was ordered by men who were working for his "Committee to Re-elect the President." – men who had offices right in the White House. Nixon feared that the news of this criminal act would cause the American people to turn against him in the coming election and vote for his Democratic opponent who was likely to be South Dakota Senator George McGovern.

This could happen, Nixon believed, in spite of the fact that he had achieved important things during his first term. Just five months earlier he had opened diplomatic relations with China by making a dramatic and historic trip to Beijing. Just two months earlier he had signed an historic arms treaty with the Soviets. And, during his three and a half years in office he had wound down the unpopular war in Vietnam. What a shame it would be, he thought, if a stupid burglary prevented him from accomplishing the great things he intended to do in his second term.

In a meeting with Haldeman on June 23rd, Nixon was steamed, to put it mildly. "What asshole ordered that stupid break-in?!" he asked in exasperation. Finally, after cooling off, Nixon asked, "What should we do now?" Haldeman suggested having the C.I.A. intervene to call off the F.B.I. investigation into the break-in so that the White House ties would not come out. He proposed a classic cover-up.

At this moment, Nixon had a turning point decision to make. After a conversation that took all of six minutes he finally agreed with Haldeman that they should play hardball with the F.B.I. and hunker down and wait for the storm to pass. "Good. Good deal!" Nixon enthused. "Play it tough. That's the way *they* (the Democrats? The FBI?) play it, and that's the way *we* are going to play it." And thus began the cover-up that would bring down many of the men who worked for Nixon and ultimately the President himself. It was the tape of this June 23rd conversation in the Oval Office that was the final nail in Nixon's political coffin.

This is the well-known story of the beginning of the Watergate scandal. Yet, it did not have to be the beginning of Richard Nixon's fall. On June 23, 1972, he could have decided on a different course of action. He could have said, "Well, Bob, I hate to say it, but everyone involved in this hair-brained scheme will have to resign and face the music. We cannot run the risk of a cover-up being exposed. That would open me to obstruction of justice charges and probably impeachment and removal from office. I have too many important things I want to do in my second term to allow that kind of stupidity to bring me down."

A few days later, after E. Howard Hunt, G. Gordon Liddy, John Mitchell, and all the other clowns who had been involved in the break-in had been given their notice, Nixon could have gone on national television and made the following speech:

My Fellow Americans:

I speak to you tonight with sadness in my soul, but with full confidence that the actions I am taking are morally and ethically correct. As you know, on June 17th five men were arrested in the offices of the Democratic National Committee in the Watergate Office Complex. They were trying to attach listening devices to the telephones. Subsequent investigations have led to certain individuals in the Committee to Re-Elect the President who allegedly gave orders to those five men to execute the break-in.

During the last six months, I have left the details of running my campaign for re-election to subordinates while I attend to the awesome responsibilities of improving relations with our long-standing adversaries, China and the Soviet Union, and achieving peace with honor in Southeast Asia. As a result, I was unaware of some of the things that were being done on my behalf. Had I been apprised of some of the plans that were being made, I would never have allowed them to go forward.

When people are in the heat of a political campaign – especially one in which, they believe, the future security of their country, and indeed the world, are at stake – they are likely to be extremely zealous. Sometimes their zeal exceeds their good judgment. I believe that is what happened in this case. The people who ordered this break-in and the men who carried it out were determined to see to it that this administration be given another four years to complete its work of achieving peace and prosperity at home and abroad. With that noble motivation, they were even willing to break the law to get the desired result. Of course, this kind of thinking is unacceptable and to me, personally, it is abhorrent.

Accordingly, I have asked several of my top advisors and campaign officials to resign and face any criminal charges that may be filed by federal authorities or the District of Columbia.

These last four days have been very painful for me, personally, as I have had to say good-bye to several old friends who have been with me over the years and through many difficult times as we have strived to serve this nation to the very best of our abilities. I know that they are decent, honorable men and that the source of their misdeeds was an excess of loyalty to me.

If Richard Nixon had acted in this way and spoken to the nation in this fashion he almost certainly would have avoided the ignominy of the Watergate Scandal. Voters may have even given him an even wider margin of victory in the election because of their appreciation for his refreshing candor.

Nixon himself said, in August of 1973 – over a year *after* his fateful meeting with Haldeman — that the worst thing you can do if you have done something wrong is try to cover it up. So, why did he try to cover up and get into the mess that Watergate became? Why didn't he give a speech such as the one I've composed for him? Thousands of pages have been written on just that question and many of them center on Richard Nixon's extreme insecurity. He never could believe that people would like him, let alone forgive him for a mistake. Also, he always felt he had to "fight like hell" for everything he ever achieved – often against popular people who seemed to have it easy, people such as John F. Kennedy. He had been a fighter – a scrappy fighter – his whole life; he had always been the underdog who had to scratch and claw his way to victory.

Ironically, the fact was that in the summer of 1972, Richard Nixon was not at all the underdog. He was riding a wave of popularity generated by his trips to Beijing and Moscow. Furthermore, his opponent was far too liberal to carry very many states, and polls showed Nixon gliding to an easy victory. In the election, he won sixty percent of the vote and carried forty-nine states. But, he was unaccustomed to this situation; he still thought the slightest glitch would take him down. He had seen victory slip away from his grasp before and he was not going to let it happen this time.

The speech I've written for Nixon to deliver in late June of 1972 was easy to write because I simply paraphrased parts of Nixon's first actual speech on Watergate – a speech he delivered on television the night of April 23, 1973. By then, the cover-up had been going on for ten months. By then, many people, including Nixon himself, had told many lies. By then, he was wide open to charges of obstruction of justice, and events were spiraling out of control. His only hope by then was to keep the ever-weakening cover-up alive. After the existence of the Oval Office tapes became known, that became increasingly impossible.

In the years after he "resigned in disgrace" (as it is almost always put), Nixon was often asked why he did not simply burn the tapes – especially the one of that June 23rd meeting. He never had a clear answer to that, except to agree that he probably should have. But, I think a better question would have been: Why didn't you simply throw a few people – those who had committed crimes — to the wolves (secretly promise them a pardon after the election, if necessary) and move on? Certainly, as an experienced lawyer, you knew what thin ice you were walking out onto when you began the cover-up.

Politicians – indeed, all people – should learn from Nixon's Watergate debacle. Sadly, many have not, and they continue to try the cover-up tactic. It may even be going on in Washington today. Defending oneself with whatever means are available is a natural human response. But, as Nixon's Watergate experience showed, it is crucial to think beyond the immediate and very temporary safety that beginning a cover-up provides. The long view will reveal consequences that are far more severe than admission of the original offense would be.

If you are old enough to recall the agony of Nixon's farewell speech to his White House staff on August 9, 1974, you know how gut-wrenching that scene was. All but the most rabid Nixon haters had to feel sorry for him at that moment. If you are ever about to embark on a cover-up of a misdeed, conjure up the image of Richard Nixon and his family dying a thousand deaths on world-wide television and you will decide to come clean and face the consequences. For Nixon, delivering my speech on June 26, 1972 would have been much easier than delivering the one he had to give on August 9, 1974.

LYNDON JOHNSON: APRIL 7, 1965

WAS THERE STILL TIME TO STEP BACK AND
AVOID THE QUICKSAND?

While preparing to write this I have time-traveled in my mind back to the mid-1960s when most of us were fixated on the war in Vietnam. It was a very dreary time, and it has not been pleasant to be mentally back there. Back then, we were increasingly divided between people who passionately believed we needed to put more troops into the region and use more bombs ("hawks") and people who passionately believed we needed to get out of Vietnam as quickly as possible ("doves"). The division between those two camps grew increasingly vicious and it continues to this day. Virtually no one thinks the American military effort in Vietnam reached a satisfactory conclusion in the mid-70s.

President Lyndon Johnson was at the center of the controversy since he was the man who made the decision to send American combat troops to Vietnam in 1965. Once he did that, it became increasingly difficult to leave Southeast Asia without seeming to have been defeated. On the other hand, no one, including President Johnson, was interested in slaughtering hundreds of thousands of people with nuclear weapons in order to "win." With an eye to avoiding similar foreign policy mistakes in the future, it is instructive to consider the alternatives Johnson had, and what he could have said to the nation in 1965 that would have put us on a better path.

Johnson sent combat troops to South Vietnam and began bombing the North in 1965 because he believed in the "containment policy" which President Eisenhower had applied to Southeast Asia with the so-called "domino theory:" The fall of South Vietnam to communism would inevitably lead to the fall of the other countries in Southeast Asia like the toppling of a row of dominoes. With containment in mind, we could not allow those dominoes to fall. Johnson was also a very political animal and he remembered very well what had happened to the popularity of President Truman when China fell to the communists in 1949. He was accused of "losing China." Lyndon Johnson did not want the stigma of "losing Southeast Asia" hung on him.

I think it is fair to say that LBJ believed in containing communism but not so much in waging war. In 1964, he had run for President as the "peace candidate" against the far more militant Barry Goldwater. Who can forget the "Daisy" TV commercial that showed a little girl picking flowers, a nuclear blast filling the screen, and President Johnson's voice saying, "We must love each other, or we shall die"? This President, who had been a young congressman from Texas back in the 1930s when Franklin Roosevelt was creating the New Deal, deeply desired to complete the federal government's help for the weak and disadvantaged by providing medical care for the poor and the elderly, guaranteeing civil rights for African-Americans, and removing prejudicial restraints on immigration. He had wrangled Kennedy's Civil Rights Act through congress and now, in 1965, he wanted to tackle voting rights, health care, and immigration. He did not want a war to interfere with those very worthy aims.

In the spring of 1965, I was taking an economics course in college and I remember the professor telling us that a government cannot manage "guns" and "butter" at the same time. In other words, if the country is going to fight a war, the economy has to be placed on a war footing with the great majority of the resources going to the war effort (guns) and very little going to luxuries (butter). Then, with a bit of a cynical laugh as college professors are wont to use, he commented that LBJ was going to defy economic logic and try to have guns and butter at the same time.

The arrogant professor was right. President Johnson put the "Great Society" in place at the same time as he escalated our commitment to South Vietnam. He did, indeed, get his landmark legislation passed: Medicare and Medicaid, the Voting Rights Act, and an immigration reform act all passed in 1965. Meanwhile, he escalated our troop commitment to over 180,000 soldiers by the end of the year. Every advisor he had, from Secretary of State Dean Rusk, to Defense Secretary Robert McNamara, to his military men in the field, repeatedly told him that we could win there if we just put in enough troops. One officer who was interviewed on the evening news took a drag on his cigarette and told the reporter we could defeat the Vietcong even though the French had not been able to because the French "didn't kill enuff 'Cong."

One man outside the administration whose advice Johnson frequently sought was former president and five-star General Dwight D. Eisenhower. Ike applauded Johnson's decision to support South Vietnam and urged him to use "overwhelming force" to get the job done. Ike's only criticism of Johnson's handling of the Vietnam situation was that he was not being aggressive enough and he needed to give General Westmoreland, the commanding general, more leeway and possibly threaten the use of nuclear weapons . . . or even use them. The man who sent 1,000 soldiers into Little Rock Arkansas in 1957 to escort nine black students into Central High School always believed that once you have decided force is necessary, use so much of it that the result is never in doubt. People who knew him joked that Ike carved the Thanksgiving turkey with a chain saw.

Two men whom Johnson could have consulted but did not were five-star General Douglas MacArthur, hero of the Second World War in the Pacific, and George Kennan, the originator of the "containment policy" that was at the core of our Vietnam intervention. In his last year of life, MacArthur told President Kennedy that the "domino theory" was nonsense and that the real crisis was not in the teeming jungles of Southeast Asia but in the concrete jungles of American cities. Kennan, now in academia and out of government, believed that Vietnam was not a vital interest of the United States. In a major speech at Harvard he said, "Following the logic of our present policy in Vietnam, it is difficult to conceive . . . of an outcome that would be less than disastrous."

In early 1965, Johnson made his decision. On April 7th, he gave a major policy speech at Johns Hopkins University. The address was televised and watched by sixty million people. Viewing it today, decades after my draft eligibility has ended and his words mean NOTHING to me personally, I am struck by how articulate and reasonable he seems. The students and faculty in the hall had the same reaction; at the end they gave him a standing ovation.

He began by explaining "Why we are there." We have made a promise to the people of South Vietnam to protect the freedom and independence of their country, he said, and we cannot abandon this nation to the terror that will surely follow. We learned in the years before the Second World War that the appetite of aggressors is never satisfied, so we will follow the words of the Bible, "Hitherto shalt thou come, but no further." We will not grow tired, he went on, and we will not withdraw under some artificial agreement (which, of course, in the end is exactly what we did do).

Then, after explaining why we needed to use the stick and how we would use it, he went on to offer North Vietnam a carrot. He offered to work with the Secretary General of the United Nations who was familiar with Southeast Asia (U Thant, of Burma) on programs of economic development to rebuild North Vietnam and bring a measure of prosperity to the long-suffering people. For this effort, the United States would pledge at least one billion dollars.

President Johnson may have thought this would be a clincher. Long before "The Art of the Deal", Johnson was the consummate dealmaker as a congressman and as President. In his world, no congressman would say "no" to him after he promised the guy a bridge in his district. Surely Ho Chi Minh would negotiate a peace with big money in the offing. When Ho did not respond, LBJ was baffled.

So, the war went on, escalated, and then escalated more until, by 1968, we had over 500,000 American troops in Vietnam, and we were suffering casualties as high as one thousand a week. The war had become a giant millstone around Johnson's neck and he decided not to seek re-election.

So, what should Johnson have decided in 1965, and what should he have said in his speech at Johns Hopkins on April 7th? When I suggest what a person in history should have done, I always try not to use my advantage of hindsight too much; I at least try to put myself in the person's shoes at that time. In this case, there was a factor in play that few people knew about or considered: Lyndon Johnson's health was very poor. In 1957, when he was majority leader in the Senate, he had suffered a near fatal heart attack. He knew that none of the men in his family lived long lives. Back in 1964, after he had led the country out of the horrid post-Kennedy assassination doldrums and had worked the Civil Rights Act through Congress, he almost decided he had made his mark on history and would not run for a term of his own. After all, he might not live through it. He did run, of course, and won a huge majority of sixty percent of the vote. But, when he took the oath of office in January of 1965, he *could* have made a private decision that he would not seek yet another term in 1968 – that four more years in the weightiest job on earth in his physical condition would be enough. Of course, he would not have wanted to weaken his political position by *announcing* his intentions, but if he had had that *private* view, he would have felt free to do exactly what he thought best without worrying about whether it would weaken his chances for re-election. This would have made it possible for him to – at least partially – ignore the "he lost Vietnam" charge. I say "partially" because a man such as Johnson – or probably anyone who becomes President – will always worry about the "verdict of history."

With his mind free of re-election nightmares, LBJ could have felt more free to follow his heart (so to speak). He *could* have said . . . and I think he *should* have said in his April 7 1965 speech:

> *We are in Vietnam to ensure that the people of South Vietnam are free to live under a government of their own choosing. Unfortunately, the government of South Vietnam has been nearly as oppressive as the communist regime in North Vietnam. Our young men are fighting and dying in that faraway land to achieve a result that would be a hollow victory at best. The South Vietnamese people deserve a choice that is better than deciding between an autocrat-*

ic, communist regime and a corrupt so-called democratic regime.

What I am about to put in place is a policy that is free of ambiguity, pretense, and lies. I am, today, issuing the following orders for a new American policy in Vietnam:

1. The bombing of North Vietnam is hereby suspended. American bombers will remain stationed in the Gulf of Tonkin to respond, if needed.

2. An additional one hundred thousand American troops will be sent to Vietnam in the next three months to bolster the force of seventy thousand that is already there.

I call upon our allies in the S.E.A.T.O. alliance to send troops to support this effort.

3. United States forces, along with forces from South Vietnam and our SEATO allies, will establish bases to supplement those already in existence to secure the safety of the populations in each province.

4. I call on the United Nations to work with the government of South Vietnam and the United States to conduct free and unfettered elections in that country at a date to be determined, but no later than January 1, 1967. In these elections the voters will determine who the people will be to write a new constitution for a united Vietnam and establish procedures for the election of a government for the country – a united Vietnam.

5. I ask the United Nations to join the United States in inviting the government of North Vietnam to participate in those elections in order to create a united, independent and democratic republic of Vietnam. Should North Vietnam refuse to take part, the Republic of South Vietnam will proceed with its elections on its own.

6. I pledge that, once elections have been successfully conducted, I will ask the Congress of the United States for two billion dollars in economic assistance for the Nation of Vietnam, or the Republic of South Vietnam, whichever has been the result of the election process.

7. I further pledge that once the new government of South Vietnam – or a united Vietnam – has been in place for three years, American troops will begin a phased withdrawal to be completed within two years.

8. Finally, I pledge that if the government of North Vietnam or its Vietcong allies violently interfere with the election process I have just described or renew their attacks on the Army of the Republic of Vietnam or United States forces, the bombing of North Vietnam will resume without any of the limitations that have thus far been in place.

The United States seeks no territory or dominion in Southeast Asia. We do not seek to impose our political or economic systems on anyone. We simply seek to protect the freedom of the peoples of the world to live in peace and prosperity under governments of their own choosing. I pray that what I have proposed here tonight will bring the people of Vietnam one step closer to the fulfillment of that dream.

I pray that fifty years from now people will look back at us and say, "They did the right thing."

I think a speech such as this would have shown continued resolve on the President's part to hold the line against militant communist expansion, but also shown the world that we truly do believe in democracy. If the people in a country, in free and democratic elections, wished to elect a communist such as Ho Chi Minh, it should not have been the role of the United States to go in and kill them for making the wrong choice. My plan would also highlight the lack of help we were getting from our SEATO allies by asking them to live up to the promises they made in 1954 when they signed the agreement. Finally, it would involve the United Nations and thus make that hitherto rather feckless organization become effective or rip the shroud off its *ineffectiveness.* The first result would be preferable; the other result would be acceptable. Also, a speech such as this would send a clear signal to the government of South Vietnam that it had better shape up because the United States' support for it was not open-ended. They would have two years to get results at the polls. After that, they could expect no further help from us if they continued in their corrupt ways.

President Johnson's overwhelming victory over Barry Goldwater in 1964 showed clearly that the American people would not support the use of nuclear weapons in Vietnam, tactical or otherwise, and wanted to keep the war in Southeast Asia as limited as possible. Yet, it was also true, that the forty percent of the people who voted for Goldwater, plus a pretty sizable number who voted for Johnson, would be enraged if Johnson simply abandoned South Vietnam and let the communists waltz right in. In the speech he made at John's Hopkins, he *tried* to steer a moderate middle course. I believe the speech I have written here would have worked better because it has clear time limits, it involves more power centers, it does more to justify the use of force if it comes to that, and puts the United States in a better light in the eyes of the world – and of our own people. The anti-war movement would have had a hard time convincing people we were warmongers if we followed this policy. By 1968, we would have had a clear result – possibly one we would have liked – without anywhere near the number of casualties or financial expense. At that point, LBJ might have decided he *would* seek another term after all.

LBJ died at his ranch on January 22, 1973 at age 64. It was two days after his second full term would have ended.

HISTORY AND PRESIDENT TRUMP

The Ways History Helps Us See Our Current President

A BUSINESSMAN PRESIDENT

BEFORE DONALD TRUMP THERE WERE OTHER BUSINESSMEN CANDIDATES WHO DIDN'T MAKE IT.

Donald Trump's election to the Presidency in 2016 came as a shocker to many people, and it has been widely discussed that this is the first time the American people have elevated a businessman who has had no political or at least military experience to the White House. What has been discussed very little, however, is the fact that in two twentieth century elections very capable businessmen ran for President and showed in their campaigns that they might have been very successful had they won.

The most recent businessman to have a legitimate chance of moving into 1600 Pennsylvania Avenue was Texas billionaire H. Ross Perot in 1992. Perot had built a financial empire based on the sale of his company, Electronic Data Systems (E.D.S.) to General Motors in 1982 for $2.4 billion. By 1990 he had an estimated fortune of $4 billion and was listed as one of the 150 wealthiest people in the world.

Beyond accumulating wealth, Perot had earned a measure of fame by organizing flights to North Vietnam in 1969 to bring food and supplies to Americans being held as prisoners there. A decade later, he organized a successful rescue mission to bring two E.D.S. employees, who had been jailed by the Iranian Revolutionary Guards, back to the United States. By the 1990s, Perot was known nationwide as a "doer" and a compassionate human being. He had never held or sought any political office, but that was about to change.

In 1992, Perot announced that he would run as an independent candidate for President on a platform of balancing the federal budget and establishing "direct democracy" in the country through a system of electronic voting. With his folksy demeanor and slow Texas drawl he captured the attention of many people who were tired of the old politics. In June of '92, polls showed him leading the two major candidates by a healthy margin: Perot: 39%, Bush (the incumbent): 31%, Bill Clinton: 25%.

As the 1992 campaign wore on, however, Perot had to give some of the details about how he would balance the budget and those details, of course, were where the devil was. He was going to increase the federal gas tax by fifty cents a gallon and cut Social Security. His poll numbers slipped to 20% and, in August, he dropped out of the race.

However, he was not finished yet. In September his supporters completed the mammoth task of getting enough signatures on petitions in all fifty states to get his name on the ballots. In October, Perot re-entered the race and participated in the debates. He spent over $12 million dollars of his own money for half hour television "infomercials" in which, using charts and speaking in his folksy style, he explained to the people how he would bring economic stability back to the country. It was estimated that over ten million people watched these presentations and it was clear that Perot was an important factor in the race once again.

For his running mate, Perot chose retired Vice-Admiral James Stockdale. No one knew much about the man when he appeared in the vice-presidential debate with Clinton's running mate, Al Gore, and Bush's Vice President, Dan Quayle. Stockdale began his opening statement by asking, "Who am I, and why am I here?" Of course, this was his way of beginning an introduction of himself to the 95% of the viewers who had never heard of him, but it made him the object of much ridicule. He appeared to be an addled old man who didn't know who he was or where he was. The fact was that he was a hero of the Vietnam War who had spent years in a North Vietnamese prison after being shot down. In 1984, he had co-authored a book with his wife, Sybil, titled *In Love and War,* which received much acclaim, and he went on to publish *Courage Under Fire* and *Thoughts of a Philosophical Fighter Pilot.* He was an intelligent and compassionate man – very much in the John McCain mold – and certainly had as much right to be on that stage as a vice presidential aspirant as the other two men up there.

In the election the Perot-Stockdale ticket received 18.9% of the popular vote (19,741,065 votes). That was the largest percentage of the popular vote received by a third party candidate since Theodore Roosevelt ran as a Progressive in 1912. However, since the Perot votes were spread evenly around the country and not concentrated in a few states, he did not win any electors. Some analysts say that Perot's presence on the ballot deprived President George H. W. Bush of votes and threw the election to Bill Clinton but, of course, that kind of conjecture can never be proved.

Perot might have made a very good President. His financial expertise was genuine; he had built his fortune on solid foundations. Moreover, he had a compassionate world-view that was based on true international experience. He was a bit quirky and eccentric, and his folksy southern drawl might have worn a bit thin for people, especially in the North, but it is possible we missed the chance to have a very competent businessman as President in 1992. As an independent candidate, of course, Perot's chances had always been very slim.

There was another businessman in the twentieth century who actually won the nomination of a major party and would have stood a good chance if he had not been up against the greatest campaigner in history. His name was Wendell Willkie and, in 1940, he became the Republican candidate for President.

Willkie was a big, rumpled, gregarious and energetic lawyer from Indiana who had earned his fortune as corporate President of Commonwealth and Southern Corporation (C&S), a utility holding company. In 1933, when Franklin Roosevelt created the Tennessee Valley Authority (T.V.A.), Willkie saw the enormous project as a severe threat to his private electric power business and he spent several years battling the T.V.A. in courtrooms and in the "court of public opinion." Ultimately, he sold C&S for $78.6 million.

For most of his life Willkie was a Democrat. In fact, in 1896 when William Jennings Bryan came to Indiana, Willkie's parents hosted the famous "Great Commoner" and Willkie, a young boy at the time, had been infatuated with the Democratic Party hero.

However, by 1939, after battling the T.V.A. and observing all the other huge New Deal programs in action, Willkie began to see the Democratic concept of big government programs and federal regulations as hostile to the growth and success of business. Without a great deal of fanfare, he switched parties.

As the presidential election of 1940 approached, Willkie, a newly minted Republican, began to get attention around the country for his lucid ideas and his energetic style. In April, he wrote an article for *Fortune* magazine titled, "We the People: A Foundation For a Political Platform For Recovery." He urged both parties to be pro-business in their platforms, to oppose foreign aggression, and support world trade.

When the Republican Party met in June to nominate their candidate for President, the country was in turmoil. Europe was embroiled in a new world war and Hitler's Germany was winning. In fact, Hitler completed his shocking conquest of France the very week the Republicans were holding their convention. In response to that, many Americans were following the lead of the aviation hero Charles Lindbergh and his "America First Committee" by advocating American neutrality. We should stay out of the European conflict at all costs, the "America First" people were saying. What Europe does is none of our business, they proclaimed. All the major contenders for the Republican nomination – Senator Robert Taft of Ohio, Governor Thomas Dewey of New York, and Senator Arthur Vandenburg of Michigan – were isolationists who agreed with the "America First" position. Wendell Willkie was the only major figure at the Republican conclave who believed the United States had a moral duty to assist Great Britain, the only democracy still standing, in her hour of need.

As the balloting began none of the leaders was able to secure the majority of votes necessary to be nominated, and so the delegates began casting about for alternatives. The gallery of spectators was packed with Willkie supporters who kept up a raucous chant: "We Want Willkie!" That show of support may have had an effect on the delegates on the floor. Willkie began to pick up votes and he ultimately went over the top to secure the party's nomination. This was the first time any major party had ever nominated a candidate with no political or military experience, let alone one who had only been a member of the party for a year. One disgruntled Taft delegate muttered, "I don't mind the local whore joining the church, but should she be leading the choir the next day?"

In 1940, the Democrats nominated Franklin Roosevelt to run for a third term, a move that, if successful, would break a 150-year-old tradition of Presidents serving only two terms. A war was on in Europe; FDR and his party thought the country needed his experienced leadership. Besides, he liked being President! He expected to run against an isolationist – either Taft or Dewey — and he was gratified that Willkie, who also favored sending aid to Great Britain, was virtually taking that issue out of the race because they both held the same position. To appease the isolationist voters, however, they both had to promise they would not get the country into the war, FDR going so far as to pledge that he would not send American boys to fight in any foreign wars.

In the election, FDR won 55% of the vote to Willkie's 45%. Willkie carried only ten states, mostly in the Midwest. Nevertheless, Roosevelt thought Willkie had been his toughest opponent yet and he admired his skills. He admired them so much, in fact, that he asked Willkie to travel to Great Britain as his personal emissary. Willkie gladly accepted and, in early 1941 traveled to London where he met with Churchill and other British leaders to assure them of American support as they stood alone against the Nazi tide. Churchill was impressed with Willkie and later referred to him as an "able and forceful man."

Two years later, after the U.S. had entered the war, Willkie traveled again, this time to the Middle East, the Soviet Union, and China. He came home convinced that the answer to world peace was a world peacekeeping organization that the United States should take the lead in organizing. He described his travels and his vision for the future in his book *One World* which came out in April, 1943, and sold one million copies in its first month.

In April, 1941, a Gallup poll showed that sixty percent of the American people thought that Wendell Willkie would have been a good President. African-Americans were particularly impressed with him. In the 1940 election Willkie had repeatedly spoken for civil rights and had seen to it, much to the dismay of many in the party, that a strong civil rights plank was included in the Republican platform. After Willkie died the NAACP named its headquarters "The Wendell Willkie Memorial Building."

Wendell Willkie was a large man who lived large and paid very little attention to his personal health. In 1944, as another presidential election loomed in which he was sure to play some sort of key role, he ignored warning signs and, at age 53, died suddenly of multiple heart attacks. Shortly before his death Willkie wrote, "If I could write my own epitaph and if I had to choose between saying 'Here lies an important President,' or 'Here lies one who contributed to saving freedom at a moment of great peril,' I would prefer the latter."

Because of his experience and competence in financial affairs, his world vision, and his sturdy reliance on solid principles, Wendell Willkie would very likely have been a great President. A lifetime before the advent of Donald Trump, he would have proved that a man with solid business experience and no political credentials can effectively lead the United states as its President.

NOT *MY* PRESIDENT!

WHAT HAS HAPPENED IN THE PAST WHEN MORE THAN HALF THE COUNTRY OPPOSED THE MAN WHO TOOK OVER THE WHITE HOUSE?

In the presidential election of 2016, Hillary Clinton won the popular vote, 48% to 46%, but Donald Trump won a majority in the only vote that really counts, the Electoral College. Nevertheless, the President cannot get over that loss in the popular vote. He has even gone so far as to point out that if California were removed from the vote total – being, as it is, a weird state that should actually be a separate country – then he would have won the popular vote! On this issue, "The Donald" should calm down and examine the record of past presidential elections. If he does so he will see that – as he would say – "some very fine people" have been "fantastic, beautiful" Presidents in spite of the fact that more than half the country was against them.

Allow me to present two Presidents who succeeded very well, even though they won an even smaller percentage of the popular vote than Donald Trump did:

President #1: Abraham Lincoln

Abraham Lincoln is the man rated by most historians as our greatest leader. His accomplishments in office were . . . "HUGE!"

In 1860, four men were seeking the White House: Abraham Lincoln, the Republican candidate whose position on slavery was to keep it from spreading into the western territories; Stephen Douglas, the candidate of the "Northern Democrats" who proposed "popular sovereignty" for the territories – letting the people who settled there decide for themselves whether or not to have slavery; John C. Breckinridge, the candidate of the "Southern Democrats" who demanded that slavery be allowed into all the territories without restrictions because slaves were "property;" and John Bell, the candidate of the new "Constitutional Union Party" who wanted slavery left as a local matter not to be legislated on at the national level at all. When the votes were tallied, Lincoln had the most, but his support was only 39.65% of the total. More than 60% of the American people did not want Abraham Lincoln to be the President! *But,* the 39% of the people who *did* want him to be President all lived in the North and, as a result, he won almost all of the northern states and enough electoral votes to have a majority and the presidency.

In 1860, just as in 2016, there was a HUGE number of people who shouted, "Not *my* President!" Unfortunately, *all* of those people lived in one section of the country – the South. Eleven southern states voted to leave the Union and the stage was set for the worst civil war in the history of the world.

For his adept handling of the secession issue and the slavery issue, historians have given Lincoln high praise. There has also been almost universal acclaim for several major pieces of legislation that Lincoln saw through Congress even though there was a war going on: The "Pacific Railway Act," which created the first transcontinental railroad; The Homestead Act, that gave 160 acres of land to any settler willing to farm them for five years; and the Morrill Land Grant Act, which set aside land for several colleges in the west such as Michigan State University.

Of course, Lincoln had a big advantage in his presidency that President Trump does not have. Many of the people who shouted "Not MY President!" in 1860 left the Union and left Lincoln alone with a supportive Congress that could do whatever it wanted without those annoying Southerners around to block things. President Trump has no similar prospects – unless the states on each coast secede from the Union, which they might be tempted to do if secession hadn't gone so poorly the last time it was tried!

Anyway, let's take a look at another famous President who won a smaller percentage of the popular voter than President Trump did. His situation might be a little more instructive for the President because, in his case, no one left the Union.

#2: Woodrow Wilson

The 1912 Presidential race was also between four candidates: Governor of New Jersey Woodrow Wilson, Democrat; President William Howard Taft (seeking re-election), Republican; former President Theodore Roosevelt, Progressive; and Eugene V. Debs, Socialist. Wilson won 41.8% of the votes; Roosevelt garnered 27.4%; Taft won 23.2%, and Debs, surprisingly, took 6%. Wilson dominated the electoral votes: 435 to TR's 88, Taft's 8, and Debs's 0. So Wilson entered the White House in 1913 with 58% of the voters wishing another man had been elected.

Wilson, of course, did not rant about the popular vote or calculate how he would have won the popular vote if only New

York, South Dakota and Wyoming weren't counted. He simply expressed his gratitude to the American people for electing him. During his presidency he prevailed upon Congress to pass an impressive list of progressive legislation including the creation of the Federal Reserve System, child labor laws, and the Clayton Anti-Trust Act, which specifically protected labor unions from its anti-monopoly provisions. When the "Great War" broke out in Europe, he successfully kept the United States neutral until the German government made such a policy impossible with its "unrestricted submarine warfare." Once in the fighting, Wilson led a dynamic war effort and inspired people with his calls to "make the world safe for democracy," and to make the conflict the "war to end all wars." His Fourteen Points Peace Plan contained several important concepts that might have, if adopted, indeed made the Great War the "war to end all wars." Until late 1918, through almost six years as president, Woodrow Wilson was tremendously successful and well-liked, if not adored, even though he had entered the White House with only 42% of the peoples' votes.

In November, 1918, however, Wilson's fortunes headed south. His Democratic Party lost control of the Senate that year and, at this point, the President *did* need to pay attention to the numbers because he would need two-thirds of the Senate to approve the treaty he was about to negotiate with our allies in Europe. Unfortunately, he ignored the numbers and paid a great price. The Republicans now controlled the Senate, but he did not take any significant Republicans to the Paris peace negotiations with him. When he returned with the Treaty of Versailles that contained his beloved League of Nations, he stubbornly would not accept any Republican amendments to the ratification and insisted on a straight "up or down" vote on the treaty as he had negotiated it. As a result, the Senate did not ratify the Treaty of Versailles, the United States did not join the League of Nations, and Wilson left office in 1921 a sick and broken man.

Wilson's story has two cautionary messages for President Trump:

Be like Wilson in his first term. Do not rant about the popular vote that you didn't win. Just get on with the job that you were *legitimately* elected to do. BUT:

Don't be like Wilson and be insensitive to the fact that many people – perhaps more than half the country – oppose your views. You will have to work with the other party and you will certainly have to compromise a bit. Otherwise, you will end up being the worst of all possible things in *your* world . . . a loser!

So, we have two men who received a smaller percentage of the popular vote for President of the United States than Donald Trump did who were, nonetheless, very consequential – and in most ways, successful – Presidents.

There were two other Presidents who won a smaller percentage of the popular vote than Donald Trump did. Richard Nixon received only 43.4% of the popular vote in 1968, pulling out a razor thin victory over Hubert Humphrey (42.7%) and George Wallace (13.5%). Nixon had a very successful first term – opening diplomatic relations with China, achieving détente with the Soviet Union, gradually withdrawing from Vietnam. It was in his second term, after he had been re-elected with 60% of the vote, that he hit the skids.

William Jefferson Clinton won the White House with 43% of the vote to incumbent George H.W. Bush's 37% and third party candidate Ross Perot's 19%. It didn't bother Bill that over half the country did not want him to be President. He felt perfectly at home in the Oval Office. He felt free to do anything he wanted there. Indeed.

So, Donald Trump is not alone in being the President when over half the country is against him. Besides the four I have just listed who got even less percentage than he did, there were five others who got less that 50% of the nation's popular vote:

John Quincy Adams (1825-1829): 31%. Adams not only did not win the popular vote, he did not win the electoral vote, either. It was a four-man race and the first finisher, Andrew Jackson, had even more electoral votes than the others . . . but, not a majority. So, the race went into the House of Representatives where the Speaker, Henry Clay, threw his support to Adams and Adams consequently won the vote. When Adams then appointed Clay to be Secretary of State, the Jackson supporters screamed that a "corrupt bargain" had been made and they spent Adams's entire term campaigning against him and obstructing everything he tried to do. In 1828, Jackson defeated Adams in the dirtiest campaign in American electoral history.

James K Polk (1845-1849): 49.5%. Undeterred by his minority status, Polk took drastic steps to double the size of the country. He threatened war with Great Britain to secure half of the Oregon territory. He provoked war with Mexico and, after our armies won it, his negotiator in Mexico City signed a treaty in which Mexico turned over half of its land to the United States.

Rutherford B. Hayes (1877-1881): 47.9%. Hayes ended Reconstruction by withdrawing federal troops from the South. He did this because the Democrats, enraged that their candidate, Samuel Tilden, who won 50.9% of the vote, lost three states under suspicious circumstances, demanded it as payback for their acceptance of Hayes's "victory."

Benjamin Harrison (1889-1893) 47.8%. Harrison signed the Sherman Anti-Trust Act that attempted to outlaw monopolies, but never enforced it. Other than that he did nothing except watch business plutocrats such as Carnegie, Vanderbilt, Morgan and Rockefeller accumulate their fortunes.

George W. Bush (2001-2009): 47.9%. Once in office Bush never said a word about the bizarre circumstances that ushered him into the White house, which was certainly wise. He did show a willingness to work with Democrats – as in the "No Child Left Behind Act" on which he worked with Ted Kennedy – and he truly had the country behind him (80% approval!) after 9/11 and the start of the Afghanistan invasion. Thus, the circumstances that brought him into office did not really affect his ability to accomplish things or his popularity. He was re-elected in 2004 with 51.2% of the popular vote, but that is when his popularity started to go down, largely because of the war in Iraq, reaching as low as 29% before he left office in 2009.

It should be noted that minority status is not at all a "kiss of death" for a President or his administration. It is after they are *re-elected* – especially if it is by a large margin – that they run into trouble.

And now it is Donald Trump (2017-?): 46%. We shall see if the ninth President to enter the White House with less than fifty percent of the popular vote can make the most of the opportunity to lead the nation. So far, over a year in, he has not followed the example of the successful "minority presidents" before him. He has not carried on without complaining about the vote, and he has not worked assiduously with the other party. If he can stop seeing politics as a game – with scores and winners and losers — if he can stop being hypersensitive about coming up short in the popular vote, and if he can start seeing governance as a cooperative effort rather than a confrontational joust, he will be much more successful.

"THE DONALD" AND "OLD HICKORY"

HOW DOES THE 45ᵀᴴ PRESIDENT COMPARE WITH THE 7ᵀᴴ?

President Trump admires Andrew Jackson and has ordered Jackson's portrait hung in the Oval Office. Aside from Jackson's abrasive, no-nonsense personality, just what is it about our seventh President that so captures the imagination of our current leader? Is Donald Trump at all like "Old Hickory?" Let's visit some of the key periods in Jackson's life and think about what Donald Trump would have done had he been in the shoes of "The Hero of New Orleans".

Period 1: In the early 1800s, Andrew Jackson gained a national reputation as the general who led the successful defense of New Orleans against the British in the War of 1812. Following that, he gained further fame by leading several brutal campaigns against the Native American tribes in the South, at one point far exceeding his orders by chasing the Seminoles into Florida and creating a diplomatic crisis with Spain, the country that owned Florida at that time. During all of this, Jackson acquired land outside of Nashville, Tennessee, and a small number of slaves. He called his estate "The Hermitage," and it was modestly grand, although not as great as the huge plantations owned by the "great planters."

Would – or could – Donald Trump have done this? It is easy to imagine him fighting Indians and there is no doubt that he would have been disdainful enough of "proper diplomacy" and the sensitivities of the Spanish government that he would have, just like Jackson, exceeded his orders and chased the Indians into Florida. But, Donald Trump never would have done any of this because he never would have gone into the military in the first place. He would have claimed flat feet or some other infirmity to avoid military service and busied himself making money on slave trading and acquiring large quantities of land in Tennessee. He never would have been a hero of New Orleans or a famed Indian fighter. Instead, he would have been a planter aristocrat. Typical of the planters of the day, he would have owned hundreds of slaves and thousands of acres of land. And, he would have been deeply in debt. Later, he would have joked that "*his* Battle of New Orleans" was avoiding getting "the clap" from the prostitutes in the Crescent City.

Period 2: In 1824 Jackson ranted that his loss of the presidency to John Quincy Adams was the result of a "corrupt bargain." In essence, he said the election had been rigged. Jackson had some justification for his outrage. He had, after all, won the popular vote and the electoral vote. But, he had not garnered a majority of the electors and so he had to watch his fate decided by the House of Representatives. In the House, the Speaker, Henry Clay, threw his support to Adams and swayed enough votes to win the election for the crusty old New Englander. When Adams appointed Clay to be his Secretary of State, Jackson screamed "corrupt bargain!"

Trump most certainly would have done just what Jackson did and gone into a public rage against the corrupt system that had denied him high office. He is still enraged at the fraud he claims took place at the polling places that cost him the popular vote. Imagine what he would be saying if he *won* the popular vote, but lost in the Electoral College, or, if he had won the popular and electoral votes and had lost in a "rigged" vote in the House!

Period 3: Jackson won the election of 1828 by claiming to be the champion of the "common man." All over the country, backwoodsmen, farmers, "mechanics," and factory workers flocked to Jackson's banner. As a wealthy plantation owner Jackson had very little in common with these folks but, having grown up in poverty, he spoke their language. He asserted that even the most common of them could handle a government job and he became their hero.

Donald Trump would have played the same role very easily. Perhaps this is the major reason why he admires Jackson. The 7th President spoke in plain terms to the average people and he expressed their fears and aspirations in ways that made them feel he understood them. Jackson even gave voice to the peoples' prejudices. Donald Trump is the twenty-first century incarnation of that kind of political leader, so it is no wonder that he hangs the man's picture in his office.

Period 4: Jackson was very protective of women. In 1806, he fought a duel to protect the honor of his wife, Rachel. His opponent, Charles Dickinson, had spoken of the fact that Rachel's divorce from her first husband had not been finalized when she married Jackson, so she was, technically, a bigamist. Jackson vowed to kill Dickinson no matter what and, in a very dramatic way, he was true to his word. In the duel, Dickinson shot first and the bullet lodged in Jackson's chest less than an inch from his heart. Jackson flinched, but remained standing and then proceeded to shoot Dickinson dead. The near fatal bullet remained painfully in Jackson's body for the rest of his life.

When Jackson became President he was enraged that Peggy Eaton, the wife of John Eaton, his Secretary of War, was excluded from social functions by cabinet wives because she had once been a bar maid. His rage caused a rift between himself and his Vice President, John C. Calhoun, whose wife was the leader of the anti-Peggy cabal.

Donald Trump would have defended those women as well . . . or, at least he would have if they were "10s" or at least "9s." Peggy, apparently, had looks that would have caught "the Donald's" eye and, just like Jackson, he would have insisted she be included in Washington social functions. However, unlike Jackson, he would have made a play for her, won her over with his charm – and power and money – and booted her hapless husband out of the cabinet.

Period 5: Jackson presided over the wildest inauguration day the country had ever seen. After his swearing in at the Capitol Building, a monstrous crowd of muddy-booted frontiersmen crowded into the White House for an enormous celebration party. It got so out of control that the punch bowls, laden with heavily spiked brew, had to be brought out onto the lawn to draw the crowd outside and spare the President's house.

Eager as he is for public adoration, Donald Trump probably would have hosted a similar event. The difference would have come after it was over. He would have wanted to know how many people were at the party and how that number compared with the crowds that had assembled for each of his predecessors. He would be particularly focused on how his numbers stacked up against Washington's, so he could crow about how had had whipped "Little Georgie Porgy" in crowd size.

Period 6: Andrew Jackson despised the National Bank of the United States and its president, Nicholas Biddle. In 1832, Jackson vetoed a bill to re-charter the bank and, after he won re-election in a campaign centered on the bank issue, he proceeded to remove all the federal government's funds from the bank and distribute them to state banks in states that had supported him in the election. The net result was a severe economic dislocation and a collapse of the economy resulting in the deepest depression the country had ever experienced.

It is a tough call on how Trump would have handled this. With his obvious preference for big businessmen for cabinet posts, he might have appointed Nicholas Biddle to be Secretary of the Treasury. More likely, he would have invited Biddle to a fancy dinner, led him to believe he was going to get the post, and then publicly humiliate him by not even considering him.

As for the Bank itself, his penchant for destroying institutions he detests without anything substantial to replace them (such as the Affordable Care Act) would probably cause him to do the same thing Jackson did . . . and, with similar consequences.

Period 7: As a slave owner, Jackson loathed the abolitionists in the North who were publishing newspapers and printing broadsides to send through the mail. When he took office, Jackson ordered his Postmaster General to confiscate all abolitionist material that appeared in mail destined for the South on the grounds that those materials were "incendiary," designed to incite slave rebellions, and were therefore a threat to the public safety.

President Trump most likely would have done the same thing. He would have hated the abolitionists – particularly Angelina and Sarah Grimke, sisters from South Carolina who forsook their parents' slave-owning values and went north to join the abolitionist crusade. He would have taken one look at their pictures and judged them to be merely women – and "3's" at best – who were not entitled to any respect or anyone paying them a bit of attention. Besides, they and all their abolitionist friends were peddling "fake news" about how bad things were for the slaves when everyone knew the slaves were all well-fed, happy "Sambos."

With his chief advisor telling the media it needs to "shut up," and his press secretary putting out "alternative facts," President Trump has shown the same kind of disdain for a free press that Jackson did. Had Trump held power in the 1830s, he, too, would have gagged the abolitionists.

Period 8: Jackson's policy toward the Native Americans was simply to get rid of them. He signed the "Indian Removal Act," defied the Supreme Court which ruled that the Indians were entitled to their ancestral lands, and ordered the tribes of Georgia and Tennessee to trek a thousand miles west so white men could move in. Trump probably admires Jackson's disregard for the Court and his racist attitude toward the Native Americans.

So, there we have it. Donald Trump *is*, in many ways, just like Andrew Jackson. He shares all of Jackson's negative qualities – his racism, his petulance, his rash behavior, his egotism, his disregard for consequences — and very few of his good ones – his unquestioned courage, to name one.

Jackson's face may soon disappear from the twenty-dollar bill and be replaced by a picture of Harriet Tubman, the runaway slave who led over three hundred slaves to freedom on the "Underground Railroad." Fortunately, the decision to remove Jackson from the twenty was made before Donald Trump took office. He most certainly would have opposed removing Old Hickory's face, unless it was to replace it with his own.

TRICKLE DOWN
OR SPURT UP?

IN ECONOMICS, THIS IS THE ESSENTIAL
DIFFERENCE BETWEEN REPUBLICANS AND
DEMOCRATS.

In his great "Cross of Gold" speech of 1896, William Jennings
Bryan gave a succinct lesson in political economics: "There are
two ideas of government. There are those who believe that if you
only legislate to make the well-to-do prosperous, their prosperity
will leak through on those below. The Democratic idea, however,
has been that if you legislate to make the masses prosperous, their
prosperity will find its way up through every class that rests upon
them." Bryan thus became one of the first politicians to put forth
the concept of "trickle down economics" — in order to attack it.
His idea at that time for making the masses prosperous was to
expand the currency by coining silver as well as gold, the theory
being that with more money in circulation, the farmers and laborers would earn more and have an easier time paying off their
debts, the economy would burgeon because of their purchases,
and everyone would prosper.

The problem with Bryan's speech was that he never explained – and no one ever really has – how the newly coined silver would first find its way into the pockets of the farmers and laborers. The government couldn't send everyone in the country a check redeemable in silver, and it couldn't hand out silver coins on the street corners. So, just how would the inflated money supply get into the people's hands?

The answer is that the inflated money could only make its way into the economy in two ways: 1. The government could spend it on the military, public works projects, and other government operations such as the postal system and send the money into the economy that way. 2. The government could lend the money to banks (There was no Federal Reserve System in 1896.) who would then have more money available to lend to farmers, laborers and business people, presumably at low interest rates.

Regardless of *how* the inflated money was introduced into the economy, the fact was that within very little time, the people who would have ended up with most of it would have been the wealthy people – those who owned businesses such as construction companies, railroads, oil refineries, and department stores. They would then have been able to hire more workers. Thus, in an ironic way, Bryan's free silver plan would have ultimately resulted in the very "trickle down" paradigm that he despised.

The inescapable fact is that only rich people and wealthy companies can give average people jobs or raise their wages. I have never worked for any person or any entity that was poorer than I was, and I'll wager most people haven't. Thus, it makes sense, that the more rich people there are, and the more wealth rich people get, the greater will be the number of people who will have employment and well-paying jobs.

We see how this works all around us. A few blocks away from where I sit right now a wealthy man – a *very* wealthy man – is building his house. It is a twelve-room mansion with over four thousand square feet of living space, a four-car garage, a swimming pool, and extensive landscaping that makes liberal use of expensive granite and labor-intensive stonewalls. In its ostentatiousness the house is, I must say, obscene. BUT! Every day there are dozens of workers busily plying their trades on the site. Carpenters, masons, landscapers, painters, etc., all have work because the rich man is building a big house.

So, clearly, there is a trickle down effect at work here. And yet, hundreds of economists and almost every Democratic Party politician living today and all who came before from Bryan to FDR have proclaimed that "trickle down economics" has been tried several times and it has always failed. They point to the enormous businesses of the "Gilded Age" built by the "Robber Barons" in the totally "laissez-faire" economy of the late 19th century. Those industries created great wealth at the top and abject poverty on the bottom and then plummeted the nation into an enormous economic depression in 1893 that lasted for six years. They point to how history repeated itself in the 1920s with more business growth spurred on by lax government controls and low tax rates and the crushing economic depression that followed in the 1930s. They point to President Reagan's big tax cuts for the wealthy and relaxed government regulations of business – "Reaganomics" – in the 1980s which made the country prosperous for a while but created a huge budget deficit, a stock market crash in 1987, and a recession that brought Bill Clinton, a Democrat, into the White House in 1992. Finally, they point to George W. Bush's tax cuts for the wealthy in 2002 that resulted in an economic surge followed by a devastating crash in 2008 that left over 10% of the people unemployed and brought another Democrat, Barack Obama, into the presidency. With that kind of "track record," the Democrats argue, how could any sane person believe that "trickle down" would work if we tried it again? The definition of insanity, they argue, is doing the same thing over and over again expecting a different result.

I think the trickle down concept was working in all of those periods – remember, there were five to ten years of great prosperity in each of them – but there was a "pill in all that jam," as the old British saying goes. The "pill" was this: All the rich people were greedy and were eager to take more than full advantage of the tax cuts and reduced government regulations. Thus, there were wage increases, but not nearly as large as there could have been, and, perhaps worse, there were risky mortgages and fraudulent investment schemes that created huge bubbles that were, naturally, destined to burst and cause havoc.

Democrats argue that if the country had had Carter as President in 1980 and Gore as President in 2002, there would have been tax cuts and more liberal welfare benefits for the *poorest* people in society. The increased purchasing power of the middle and lower classes would have stimulated the economy in a more durable way. There would have been additional stimulation by increasing taxes on the wealthy and using the increased revenue for government projects such as improved infrastructure and schools. This would have been the ideal model for a "spurt up" stimulation to the economy as a way of bringing prosperity to everyone.

The fact is that each approach – "trickle down" and "spurt up" – has problems. "Trickle down" does work – rich people create jobs – until the rich get greedy and reckless. If the wealthy people would behave themselves, share their wealth with good wages, and not get so caught up in maximizing profits that they forget about the environment and other societal issues such as child care and the health of the families in their employ, then the trickle down theory works well. "Spurt up" works if the people who get tax cuts and welfare benefits are responsible with their "new" money and spend it wisely. "Spurt up" also requires government to be a little restrained in its regulations so that entrepreneurs are able to start up new businesses or expand older ones without having to cut their way through miles of "red tape."

I was a child in the 1950s and, ever since I wrote *Leaders in Dangerous Times* I have admired Dwight D. Eisenhower. I think the 1950s were the golden age of American economics. Wealthy people were taxed pretty heavily in the 1950s, but the government mostly stayed off their backs and they were able to expand their businesses. That same government was creating many jobs by building new schools and the interstate highway system. Suburbs were growing dramatically, so builders and their suppliers were prospering, and people were buying new cars and appliances. In general, the economy was booming. It was a time of "trickle down economics" as it was supposed to work.

Today, with the new tax cut act, we are about to give "trickle down" another go. The early signs are good: large corporations are making plans to expand, they are giving their workers bonuses and even some wage increases. If wealthy people and employers – usually, the same people, of course – react to their new wealth and freedom in a responsible way, we may see the beginning of a golden age of "trickle down" and "spurt up" working together to produce the most prosperous nation on earth. I would be more optimistic if the tax bill had included some sort of wealth tax – inheritance tax perhaps – to fund major infrastructure improvements. Good roads, bridges, railways and airports are essential to a burgeoning economy and we could have them if we put together a good amalgam of private enterprise and government support. That means both Republicans and Democrats – lately stuck like glue to their "trickle down" and "spurt up" concepts – need to relax their ideologies a bit and come together for the good of the country.

NUKE THE NORTH?

DROPPING AN ATOMIC BOMB ON NORTH KOREA IS NOT A NEW IDEA.

In 1972, as the United States slogged through yet another year of war in Vietnam, there were some, perhaps many, who advocated we end the war quickly with a resounding and total "victory" by dropping a few nuclear bombs on North Vietnam. Annihilate Hanoi, the cry went, and those commies will surrender soon enough! "Nuke the North!"

For most of us, this "strategy" was simplistic, to put it mildly, and simply outrageous. Innocent civilians would be killed by the tens of thousands and the reputation of the United States around the world would be irreparably destroyed. President Eisenhower had rejected the idea back in 1956 by stating categorically that he would not be the President who dropped atomic bombs on yet another Asian country.

In this context, and with our current President implying he might use his huge button to launch nuclear weapons against

North Korea, it might surprise most Americans to know that President Eisenhower threatened to do just that in 1953. In his memoir *Mandate For Change,* Ike tells us that when he was President-elect in December of 1952, he visited the Korean front as he had promised to do during the campaign and became convinced that the only way to break the stalemate along the 38th parallel was to counterattack with more force than was currently in place. "To keep the attack from becoming overly costly," he went on, "it was clear that we would have to use atomic weapons." Then, perhaps to give his former boss credit where credit was due, he added, "This necessity was suggested to me by General MacArthur while I was President-elect."

Without seeming to blink, Eisenhower went on to contend that because of the underground tunnels and other fortifications that the Chinese communists in Korea had been able to construct, it would probably be necessary to use atomic weapons against targets in North Korea, Manchuria and along the Chinese coast. His biggest fear, if he adopted this strategy, was that the Soviet Union, with atomic weapons, would jump into the conflict and bomb the "unprotected cities of Japan." I'm sure that if the American people had known about this strategy as it was being discussed it would have scared the daylights out of them.

President Eisenhower was playing high stakes poker. His administration let it be known through emissaries in India and other people who were known to have access to "Soviet and Chinese communist ears" that "we intended to move decisively without inhibition in our use of weapons, and we would no longer be responsible for confining hostilities to the Korean Peninsula." One does have to wonder just what Eisenhower would have done if the communists had called his bluff.

Fortunately, the enemy decided to negotiate. The death of Stalin and the resulting instability in Moscow probably had much to do with this, but in *Mandate For Change* Ike implies they were intimidated by U.S. atomic power and became much more responsive at the negotiating table. Within five months they signed an armistice agreement at Panmunjom – a cease-fire that has been in place to this day.

And so, despite his unwillingness to use nuclear weapons against North Vietnam in 1956, Dwight Eisenhower was an advocate of using our nuclear arsenal to intimidate. He did so in North Korea in 1953 and, again, in 1958 when the Chinese communists threatened to attack the Nationalist Chinese offshore islands, Quemoy and Matsu. Once again, in this instance, the communists backed down.

In the last year of his life, an ailing Eisenhower counseled President Johnson to use "overwhelming force" to end the war in Vietnam. You've chosen to engage militarily, he told Johnson, so now you have to do what is necessary to win. Did "overwhelming force" mean nuclear weapons? His grandson's father-in-law, Richard Nixon, bombed Hanoi on Christmas Eve in 1972, but he never used or threatened to use nuclear weapons. So, perhaps, when Ike advised Johnson he did not mean "use nukes," but his record shows that he was quite willing to make the threat and see how the enemy responded.

If President Trump, or those advising him, know the Eisenhower history they may be trying to take a page from his book. But, it should always be remembered, that Ike had a generous measure of what almost every great and successful leader seems to have had – incredibly good luck. He was lucky that the Soviets were going through a leadership crisis in 1953; he was lucky for his entire eight years that he was never forced to carry out a threat. We can only hope that President Trump will have similar good fortune.

My military friends assert that Eisenhower's success was not based on luck at all. He had credibility as a military leader, the whole world knew he was never lacking in courage, and his successes were simply what always happen when you stand up to aggressors from a position of strength. Does Donald Trump have the standing in the world that Eisenhower did? For better or worse, we may soon find out.

THE TWENTY PERCENT CHANCE

V.P. CHOICES ARE ALWAYS AN AFTERTHOUGHT, BUT THEY SHOULDN'T BE!

Twenty percent of the Presidents of the United States have left office before their terms were over and have been replaced by their Vice Presidents; one out of every five Presidents has either died in office or resigned. Thus, the odds that the current President will be replaced by his Vice President are fairly high and there are some people who are actually praying for that to happen. Let's look at the historical record and see how presidential turnovers have worked out in the past. Given the way vice presidential choices are made, it is startling that the changes have often been good for the country.

The first President to leave office early was William Henry Harrison in 1841. He left *very* early – one month after his term began. The seventy-year-old Harrison gave a three hour-long inauguration speech in a cold rain, caught pneumonia, and died.

Harrison had won his fame in 1811 at the Battle of Tippecanoe against the warriors of the great Indian chief, Tecumseh. In the 1840 Presidential campaign the Whig Party nominated Harrison for President and chose John Tyler, a former Democratic senator from Virginia, as his running mate. The Whig's slogan, as nearly everyone knows, was "Tippecanoe and Tyler, Too!" Now Tyler would be the President, not just the second half of the slogan.

Tyler knew the Whigs did not trust him since he was a former Democrat, so the first thing he did after hearing the old man had died was take the oath of office and move all his stuff into the White House. In that manner he made it clear that he viewed his succession as a constitutional mandate to *complete the Presidential term* rather than just hold the position until a new election could occur. There has never been any argument since then about whether the succession to the Presidency was for the completion of the term; for that measure of stability we owe a debt to John Tyler.

Tyler proved to be a competent but mostly unremarkable President. The major event of his term was the signing of the Webster-Ashburton Treaty which, as everyone knows, established the northern boundary of Maine. Just kidding – hardly anyone knows that, but it is important, especially if you are a hunter. After Tyler's (Harrison's) term was up, the Whigs ditched him and went back to nominating, yet again, Henry Clay who, of course, went down to defeat.

The next President to leave office early was Zachary Taylor in 1850. Taylor was also a military hero nominated by the Whig Party. The Whigs nominated two generals in the 1840s; they both won and then promptly died. (They did it again in 1852 when they nominated Winfield Scott. He lost the election, so he lived!) Taylor's malady was food poisoning contracted from something he ate at a Fourth of July celebration at the partially constructed

Washington Monument. Not long ago some historians became suspicious about Taylor's death because it was too advantageous to a certain member of Congress to have been purely accidental. So, they actually had the deceased President's remains exhumed (yuck!) and tested for the presence of poison. None was found, so foul play was ruled out.

The Congressman who stood to gain from Taylor's death was Senator Henry Clay. Taylor opposed Clay's compromise plan to save the Union, so his disappearance from the scene helped pave the way for the plan's passage because the new President, Millard Fillmore, approved of the compromise. Thus, in this case, the elevation of the Vice President helped save the Union, at least for the time being. Besides signing the compromise bills, Fillmore didn't do much as President. There is, however, a hospital in Buffalo named for him.

The next early departure from the White House sent an already grieving nation – or, at least, the northern part of it – into total shock. John Wilkes Booth murdered Abraham Lincoln only five days after the end of the horrible civil war the country had endured. Reconstruction was about to begin in earnest and there was a plethora of critical problems: the transition to freedom of four million African-Americans, the treatment of the ex-Confederates, the rebuilding of the South, and the trauma left by 650,000 deaths and a million severe injuries. Lincoln's brain might well have been contemplating those issues when Booth's bullet tore through it. The terrible responsibility of dealing with all those knotty problems now fell to Lincoln's Vice President, Andrew Johnson of Tennessee.

Like Lincoln, Johnson was born into humble circumstances and was largely self-educated. But, in every other way, he was completely different from the great man he was succeeding. Lincoln was articulate – probably the best writer ever to be

President; he was nuanced, capable of mixing humor with serious business, and increasingly non-racist in his outlook. Johnson was boorish, temperamental, humorless, and as racist as any southern white man could be. He very quickly came to be at odds with the Republicans in Congress who wanted to secure some level of civil rights for the newly freed African-Americans. Johnson vetoed every civil rights measure the Radicals passed and they overrode his veto every time. Finally, the Radical Republicans had had enough of his confrontational style and they trumped up impeachment charges against him. The House voted the impeachment, but the Senate fell one vote short of conviction, so Johnson remained in office. He served out the one year remaining in his term, but the Republicans had no intention of nominating him to run in 1868. Thus, as far as the Republicans were concerned, Andrew Johnson was a complete disaster. Historians rate him near or at the bottom of Presidents. The assassination was a tragedy on many levels, but mostly because Lincoln, as skilled as he was at dealing with Congress and public opinion, could have led the country through a reconstruction period much less full of rancor than the one it experienced under Andrew Johnson.

One would think that after the horrid Lincoln assassination the protection of the President would have been improved substantially, but clearly it was not because two more Presidents were shot in the thirty-six years after Lincoln's death. In August, 1881, six months into his term, James A. Garfield was walking through Union Station in Washington, D.C. when a man came up behind him and shot him in the back. The man was Charles Guiteau who was angry at Garfield because he had not rewarded him for his support in the election by giving him a government job. Garfield lingered for several weeks before dying, but die he did, becoming the second President in sixteen years to be assassinated. His death brought into the White House Chester A. Arthur, a man known by almost everyone in politics at the time as a political schemer and corrupt spoilsman of the highest order. One political wag, upon learning of the assassination, was said to have exclaimed, "My God! Chet Arthur in the White House!?" Arthur served the Presidency rather better than expected – no serious corruption – and, in a bit of irony, became the President who signed the Pendleton Act, a law requiring certain government jobs to be filled by competitive exams rather than as political rewards. Partly because of that, the Republicans chose not to nominate him as their candidate for President in the next election.

The third President to be taken off by gunshot was William McKinley, who took a bullet in the stomach in 1901. The assassin was Leon Gzolgosz, an anarchist who felt it was his duty to kill any leaders he could reach. He reached McKinley at the "Pan-American Exposition" in Buffalo where the President was holding a reception. Gzolgosz wrapped a pistol in a handkerchief and feigned an injured right hand as he waited in the reception line. When he reached the President, McKinley reached out to shake his left hand and Gzolgosz fired at point blank range.

The new President in 1901 was Theodore Roosevelt. The recent hero of the Battle of San Juan Hill in Cuba and governor of New York, Roosevelt was despised by Republican Party stalwarts for his reforming zeal; they had nominated him for Vice President as a way of getting rid of him. The Vice President has no real power and the party bosses figured "T.R." would never be heard of again. Clearly, they had not paid attention to history. In the previous sixty years, five Presidents had died in office. One party leader had recognized the danger. "Now only one life stands between that mad man and the White House!" he exclaimed.

T.R. was just as unmanageable in the Presidency as the party leaders feared he would be. He signed legislation regulating the railroads and the food and drug industry, he turned millions of acres of forest lands into national parks and monuments, and he went head-to-head with big business tycoons such as J.P. Morgan when he busted up huge, monopolistic trusts. McKinley had been slow and comfortable; Roosevelt was constantly on the move and a royal pain in the neck. The party leaders regretted they had ever put him into the job that launched him into the White House.

By the early twentieth century it seemed we were losing Presidents at the rate of approximately one every ten to twenty years: Harrison in 1841, Taylor in 1850, Lincoln in 1865, Garfield in 1881, and McKinley in 1901. The next presidential death occurred almost on schedule. In 1923, President Warren G. Harding died suddenly while on a trip to California. The cause was a bit mysterious – heart attack? stroke? food poisoning? Historians have even hypothesized that his wife poisoned him when she discovered he was having an affair. Perhaps we should dig him up, too! In any event, it was merciful for Harding that he departed the scene before the full extent of all the scandals engulfing his administration became known. It seemed as though every member of the cabinet was "on the take" in some way or another. Because his administration was so riddled with corruption, Harding is often listed as the worst President of them all – a tight contest between him and Andrew Johnson.

The new President in 1923 was Calvin Coolidge. Silent and taciturn, as exciting as oatmeal and just as zesty, Coolidge was the exact opposite of the gregarious, hard drinking, poker playing Harding. And, he was just what the country needed. As everyone knows, the country was going through a wild decade in the 20s – partying as if there were no tomorrow after the drudgery of the "Great War" – and people needed the assurance, as they careened though the streets, that there was a steady hand at the wheel. "Silent Cal" filled the bill. He was elected on his own in 1924 with the slogan "Keep cool with Coolidge," and the country went on its merry way. The party peaked in 1927 when Lindbergh flew non-stop to Paris, Babe Ruth hit sixty home runs, the first talking motion picture "The Jazz Singer" debuted, Henry Ford's "Model T's" sold over a million, the stock market went up daily, and it seemed as though everyone – in the cities, at least – was living "high, wide and handsome."

Of course, it all came crashing down two years later, but by then Coolidge had retired and the next guy, Herbert Hoover, got all the blame.

The seventh President to leave office unplanned was Franklin Roosevelt. When "F.D.R." died of a cerebral hemorrhage in April of 1945, he had been President for twelve years and was beginning his fourth term. Millions of Americans had never known any other President. He had been at the helm through the Great Depression and then through the Second World War. His jaunty style and wide grin were what kept many people going during the terrible times of economic collapse and a war that seemed, for a while at least, to be unwinnable. Now it seemed to everyone that their father figure was suddenly and without warning stolen from their lives.

In reality, of course, FDR's death was very predictable. He was a very sick man during his last two years in office. He had heart disease and blood pressure so high it is truly a wonder he did not have a stroke long before the one that killed him. The Democrats – at least the ones who were realists in 1944 – knew they were probably picking the next President when they nominated FDR's running mate. That is why it was a little surprising that they picked an obscure senator from Missouri for the job. When FDR died many people – probably *most* people – were very skeptical that Harry Truman would be able to fill the great man's shoes.

But, Harry Truman handled the job pretty well and most historians rate him in at least the top fifteen of American presidents. Some even place him in the top ten. He helped guide FDR's beloved United Nations into existence; he made the very difficult, but probably correct, decision to use the atomic bomb to end the war; he introduced the Marshall Plan to save the economies of Western Europe and got Congress to pass it; He used the Berlin Airlift to prevent the Soviet Union from taking over West Berlin; He organized N.A.T.O. to protect Western Europe from attack; He made the decision to defend South Korea and had the stature to fire General MacArthur for disobeying orders and talking about expanding the Korean War into China. In all, the Democrats were fortunate that Truman turned out to be as effective as he was. He even led the party to a dramatic come-from-behind victory in the 1948 presidential election.

After FDR's death, another eighteen years went by and then the country experienced another devastating and heart wrenching presidential assassination. We are still in an era when many people remember the assassination; everyone over sixty can remember where he or she was when the news came that President Kennedy had been shot as he rode in a motorcade through the streets of Dallas. For many of us the fact that the suave JFK was gone, and the new President was the grotesque pol from Texas was really hard to take. But, the job Lyndon Johnson did, at least on the domestic scene, was actually pretty solid. He engineered the passage of the Civil Rights Act that had stalled in Congress under Kennedy and went on to secure passage of the Voting Rights Act and several other major pieces of civil rights legislation.

The major controversy over Johnson's stewardship of JFK's policies centers on Vietnam. Kennedy apologists contend that he was planning to end U.S. involvement in Vietnam and would have avoided the horrors of the Vietnam War that ensued under Johnson. They point to Kennedy's statement at a press conference: "In the final analysis, it is their (the South Vietnamese) war. They're the ones who have to win it or lose it." Surely, the apologists say, that meant he intended to pull out. I tend to think he would have gotten into the quagmire just as deeply as Johnson did. In the sixties, we were at the height of the "Cold War." No President could politically afford to be the man who "lost Southeast Asia."

The Kennedy to Johnson succession illustrated very clearly the perils of choosing a Vice Presidential candidate purely on the basis of political advantage. The Kennedys did not like or respect Lyndon Johnson, and he felt the same way about them. But, as a Texan, he balanced the ticket and united the Democratic Party. This marriage of convenience may have been necessary to win the very tight electoral contest with the Republican, Richard Nixon. But the Democrats only thought about the election. They never imagined the forty-three-year-old Kennedy would die! Again, they should have given a little thought to the history of Vice Presidential nominations. The Republicans in 1900 had no idea McKinley would die and the firebrand T.R. would become President, either!

The last President – so far – to leave office early was Richard Nixon in 1974. For a year and a half, as evidence mounted that he knew of the efforts to cover up White House involvement in the break-in at the Democratic National Headquarters in the Watergate complex, Nixon had denied culpability and stonewalled attempts by the special prosecutor to get access to tape recordings of Oval Office conversations. Finally, after the Supreme Court ruled that he was legally required to obey a subpoena and a tape emerged that clearly demonstrated his involvement, he realized that impeachment and conviction were inevitable. To spare the country – and himself – that ordeal, he announced his resignation on August 8, 1974.

The new President, Gerald Ford, was a former congressman from Michigan whom Nixon had appointed to the Vice Presidency to replace Spiro Agnew, the Vice President who had resigned after admitting he had accepted bribes while Governor of Maryland. Washington was surely a swamp in those days! Ford was a solid and honest man. He was quite competent, and those of us who went to the University of Michigan, his alma mater, had always seen him as a superstar – All-American football player, big man on campus whose picture hung in every bar in Ann Arbor, great looking guy who would be the leader of anything he was part of. Unfortunately, some people did not see him that way at all. People joked that he had played too many football games without a helmet, that he was such a dufus, that, as Lyndon Johnson famously quipped, "he couldn't walk and chew gum at the same time." That image was totally unfair since he was clearly the greatest athlete ever to occupy the White House.

Ford did a very solid job in his two and a half years as President. He might well have been elected in his own right in 1976 if it were not for one very controversial decision. A month after he took office, he pardoned Richard Nixon. He wanted to spare the country the trauma of a civil trial, and he wanted to put "Watergate" behind us. But, many vindictive people were eager to see Nixon in a courtroom, convicted of crimes, and carted off to prison wearing an orange jumpsuit. Some people hated Ford for letting Nixon off the hook!

So, there's the record: nine Presidents out of forty-five – twenty percent – who did not serve their full terms. There has not been an early departure from the White House in forty-three years, so you might say we're overdue. As President Trump often says, "We'll see what happens."

But, one thing is clear. If President Trump does leave office early for whatever reason and Vice President Mike Pence takes office, the historical record on how that will go is very murky, indeed. If President Trump leaves office in some way, will Pence be a bland leader who simply completes the term in the tradition of John Tyler, Millard Fillmore, Chester A. Arthur, Calvin Coolidge and Gerald Ford? Will he be an utter disaster as Andrew Johnson was? Or, will he serve admirably and make a solid record of his own as Theodore Roosevelt, Harry Truman and Lyndon Johnson did? My guess is that Mike Pence, if he does move across town to the White House in the next two years, will look much like Calvin Coolidge. Re-read what I said above about the Harding-Coolidge transition and see if you agree.

THE SORRY HISTORY OF AMERICAN XENOPHOBIA AND RACISM

MOST AMERICANS ARE KIND AND WELCOMING TO EVERYONE. BUT NOT ALL ARE.

During the first one hundred and ninety years of immigration into North America (1607-1797), the people with the greatest amount of racism in their hearts were, ironically, the *immigrants.* White men coming ashore from England or a few other northern European countries looked with disdain at the native population and worked very hard and very effectively to push those people aside. By the time of the American Revolution, white Europeans controlled nearly all the land from the Atlantic Ocean to the Appalachian Mountains. The only non-white peoples east of the mountains were the Cherokees, Creeks, and Choctaw Indians who were still clinging to their lands in Georgia, and, of course, the African slaves who were being brought in ever-increasing numbers to work as forced labor for white people, mostly in the

South. The Native Americans had reason to be xenophobic, but they welcomed the white men who came in ships at first and did not grow hostile towards them until it was too late.

The first official xenophobia showed itself after the new American Government had been in place for ten years. In 1798, the Federalist Party, the party of "the rich, the well-born and the able" as John Adams so bluntly put it, were fearful that the newly arriving immigrants from impoverished areas of the British Isles and Western Europe were settling in the rural regions of the country and becoming citizens at an alarming rate. What was unnerving for Federalists was that these immigrants almost always supported the Democratic-Republican Party of Thomas Jefferson. As new states in the west came into the Union packed with these people as voters, the future of the Federalist Party looked bleak.

While they still had a majority in Congress, the Federalists passed a series of laws known as the Alien and Sedition Acts. These laws increased the time that was required to live in the United States before becoming a citizen from five years to fourteen. Clearly, the intent of these laws was to keep the "rabble" out of the polling places for as long as possible. Of course, howls of protest went up across the land. Thomas Jefferson and James Madison, leaders of the Democratic-Republican Party (today's Democrats) even argued that the states, if they deemed laws such as these to be unconstitutional, had the right to nullify those laws and refuse to enforce them within their own borders. That was a dangerous concept that would bear bitter fruit sixty years later – the Civil War. In 1800, the result was that the Federalists lost the Presidency and control of Congress for good. They never again won an election. In 1801, Congress repealed the Alien and Sedition Acts; by 1820, the Federalist Party had ceased to exist. Xenophobia was squelched. But, not for long.

In the 1840s, the potato famine in Ireland was driving large numbers of Irish immigrants to the United States where they hoped to become prosperous . . . or, at least find food! It only took a few years for a new political party to appear to oppose this stream of newcomers. Officially called the "American Party," this party instructed its members to maintain their anonymity by saying "I know nothing" when asked about its existence. Thus, the party came to be called the "Know Nothing Party." Its core belief was that the newly arriving Irish immigrants, with their dangerous Roman Catholic faith and out-of-control drinking habits, were stealing jobs from "real" Americans, dragging the country down and, if left unchecked, would make the United States into a drunken enclave of the Vatican. By the late 1850s, the party was gaining strength and attracting some noteworthy adherents such as former President Millard Fillmore. Some political leaders, such as Senator John J. Crittenden of Kentucky, were gravitating to it in a desperate effort to unite the country that was sliding ever closer toward civil war between the North and the South. Both Northerners and Southerners could agree on hating Catholic foreigners, these leaders reasoned. Of course, a shared hatred of foreigners was not enough to stave off civil war. The "Know Nothing Party" vanished even before the shooting started, but its putrid philosophy did not die. It only went into hibernation.

In the years following the Civil War, Americans briefly put their fear of foreigners on hold as they turned their attention to the vexing "Negro problem." Southerners passed Jim Crow laws, literacy test requirements for voting, and poll taxes designed to put the "black race in its proper place." They also donned bed sheet disguises and rode the countryside terrorizing and murdering "uppity" blacks. Northerners, after a brief period of attempting to help the "freedmen," finally acquiesced to the Southerners' solution to their "race problem." Northerners were equally as racist as Southerners, so that acquiescence came easily.

As white Americans were showing black Americans the limits of their new freedom, they were also busy exterminating a large portion of the Native American people and escorting the rest onto reservations. Chiefs Sitting Bull and Crazy Horse shocked Americans celebrating the centennial in 1876 with their victory over General Custer and his 7th Cavalry, but one-by-one the tribes succumbed to the starvation brought on by the slaughter of the buffalo and the overwhelming firepower of the U.S. Army led by men such as Phil Sheridan who famously said, "The only good Indian I ever saw was dead."

With the African-Americans and Native-Americans safely in place, Northerners and Southerners turned their attention, once again, to the damnable foreigners, this time the Roman Catholic immigrants from Southern and Eastern Europe, the Jews from Europe, and the Asians. Many Americans were convinced that these "new immigrants" were taking jobs away from Americans and, even worse, were "socialists" and "anarchists" – bomb throwers who would rend the constitution and destroy our great democracy. This notion was propelled by the fact that a Polish anarchist killed President McKinley.

In 1882, Congress passed the first-ever law to ban any immigrant group from entering the country. The Chinese Exclusion Act prohibited Chinese laborers from immigrating. We did not need these people any longer to build the transcontinental railroad (completed in 1869), it was reasoned, so it was time to turn them away.

In 1920, a bomb exploded on Wall Street killing several people. In 1921, two Italian anarchists, Nicola Sacco and Bartolomeo Vanzetti, were convicted of killing two men during a payroll robbery. By then the American people were ready for more anti-immigrant legislation – laws to keep out "certain types" of immigrants who came from "undesirable countries." The "Immigration Quota Laws" of 1921 and 1924 made it all but impossible for Southern Europeans and Asians to enter the United States because the annual "quotas" for peoples from southern Europe and Asia were exceedingly low. The Statue of Liberty's torch glowed considerably dimmer.

After 1924, Americans' racial intolerance, xenophobia and racism reached new heights. The Ku Klux Klan had a re-birth and even claimed many bed-sheeted adherents in the North. In the late 1930s, even liberal-minded Franklin Roosevelt would not relent and allow Jews fleeing Hitler's Germany to enter the United States. After the attack on Pearl Harbor, he issued an executive order that essentially incarcerated the entire Japanese population of three West Coast states into concentration camps.

The xenophobia did not abate even after the struggle in World War II revealed the horrors of the despicable Nazi ideology. Soldiers who put their lives on the line to defeat the Nazis came home with racial views very similar to those of the enemy they had fought. I recall neighborhood men at a barbeque in the early 50s talking about "japs" and "niggers" all afternoon, the racial slurs coming louder and more frequently as the empty beer bottles in the cases piled up. Even as a ten-year-old, I was shocked. That same summer two white men in Mississippi murdered a young black boy who had dared to speak "fresh" to a white woman. An all-white male jury took less than an hour to acquit the killers. Millions of white people around the country were horrified at the murder of Emmett Till, but millions more were not, or barely paid any attention to it.

It wasn't until 1964 that Congress finally ended segregation with the Civil Rights Act. The next year they passed the Immigration Reform Act that did away with quotas and opened the gates to immigrants from all nations regardless of religion or color. During the debates on this fair-minded law, many congressmen finally expressed dismay that our country had been so racist and unwelcoming in previous decades.

In the years since World War II there have been several very distinct waves of immigrants who have come into the country. The most notable waves include:

- "DP's" (Displaced Persons) from the war, many of them Jewish survivors of the Nazi concentration camps.
- Chinese who left their country after Mao Zedong emerged victorious in the civil war and instituted communism in China.
- Hungarians who fled their country during the failed anti-communist revolution in 1956 when Soviet tanks rumbled through Budapest terrorizing the people.
- Cubans, who entered the country mostly in Florida as they fled from Castro's communist takeover of their country.
- Vietnamese and other Southeast Asians who fled their countries after the Americans left South Vietnam and the communists took over.
- Millions of people from Mexico, Central and South America, and Caribbean Islands such as the Dominican Republic who have entered the United States, some without legal status, to find jobs and a better standard of living.
- Approximately 20,000 Syrians who have fled the civil war in their country to come here to find security. (By comparison, Germany has taken in over a million Syrians.)
- Other immigrants from Middle Eastern countries have been arriving for the usual reasons – to find economic opportunities and freedoms they did not have in their homelands. Increasing numbers of Muslims — dark-skinned men with

beards and women in hijabs — are appearing on the streets of cities and towns across the country, but often in enclaves such as Hamtramck, Michigan, the first city in the country whose city council has a majority of Muslims sitting on it.

The people of the United States have shown a compassionate and welcoming face to most of these people, especially when they have appeared to be industrious and hard-working contributors to the economy. However, the Hispanic people from south of our border have received an ugly reaction in some places where the specters of drug gangs and welfare cheats have hung in the air. And, of course, since the attacks of September 11, 2001, and other terrorist incidents, many Americans regard Muslims with suspicion, if not hatred.

What we have now, as we work our way through the twenty-first century, is a polyglot country that is still in need of defining itself. We are a wonderful mix of English, European, Native American, Hispanic, Asian, Middle Eastern, and many other cultures, and yet we haven't figured out how to treat newcomers who want to join us. Are we the welcoming people who speak through Emma Lazarus's poem on the Statue of Liberty – "Give me your tired, your poor, your huddled masses yearning to breathe free" – or are we the people of the Know Nothing Party, the Ku Klux Klan, and the Quota Acts? Both sides of our national character have shown themselves in many ways throughout our history, but it has never been more important for each of us personally to decide where we stand than it is today. Unfortunately, our current President has rooted his politics in xenophobia and, unless more generous and open-minded people respond effectively, we may record another dark chapter in our nation's history.

ANDREW JACKSON AND THE CIVIL WAR

PRESIDENT TRUMP SAID JACKSON WOULD HAVE PREVENTED THE CIVIL WAR. COULD HE BE RIGHT?

Hypothetical history is mostly a useless activity. As Professor William Freehling at the University of Michigan once said in response to the question — "Was the Civil War inevitable?" – "Of course, it was inevitable. It happened!" It is a waste of time, he said, to discuss what *might* have happened. However, since President Trump has raised the issue, it might be worth a brief analysis to consider what would have happened if Andrew Jackson had been President rather than Abraham Lincoln in 1861 when the Civil War began.

In 1832, when Jackson actually *was* President, a crisis arose that was very similar to the crisis that led to the Civil War twenty-nine years later. South Carolina, enraged at the new tariff law that had been passed, issued an "Ordinance of Nullification" declaring the law "null and void" within its borders. In other words, the state would not collect tariff import duties at the port of Charleston. President Jackson, although he was a Southerner himself and also opposed tariffs, flew into a rage. By nullifying the tariff, South Carolina was threatening the very existence of the Union. "Disunion by armed force is treason!" he exclaimed and prepared to lead a federal army into the state and hang every nullifier he could find from the nearest tree. In 1832 the country braced for civil war and Jackson began raising troops to fight it. He induced Congress to pass a "Force Bill" giving him the authority to force South Carolina to obey the tariff. "I will die for the Union!" he announced.

Fortunately, that year cooler heads prevailed. Senator Henry Clay of Kentucky proposed a more moderate tariff, one that started with high rates but gradually went lower over a ten-year period, and the South Carolinians indicated they would accept the new tax. Jackson accepted South Carolina's acquiescence. He ignored the nullifiers' nose-thumbing gesture when they nullified the Force Bill, thus signaling that they *still* felt they had a right to strike down a federal law. The people breathed a sigh of relief that war had been averted.

If President Trump had told this story to support his claim that Jackson would have made a deal to avoid civil war, his statement would have some credibility. However, he did not tell this story. So, let's go to 1861 and delve into hypothetical history just this once and try to imagine Jackson in the White House when South Carolina — yet again – announced it was seceding from the Union. First of all, this requires a great leap of imagination because the reason South Carolina left the Union in 1860 was that the new President (Lincoln) had run on a platform of excluding slavery from the western territories. Jackson, by contrast, was a Tennessee slaveholder, so it is difficult to imagine that South Carolina would have felt any need to secede if HE had been elected. But, let us carry our hypothetical analysis even further and presume that South Carolina and other southern states *had* seceded – perhaps because the newly elected Congress was full of Republicans who opposed slavery's expansion. What would Jackson have done?

In real life, there was a compromise possibility in 1861 that President Lincoln rejected. Senator John J. Crittenden of Kentucky – the man who held Henry Clay's old seat – proposed a compromise to keep the southern states in the Union. The compromise proposed a constitutional amendment guaranteeing the existence of slavery as long as any state wished to keep it, and another amendment that would draw a line – the old Missouri Compromise line of 36-30 latitude – across the continent below which slavery would be permitted. Lincoln rejected this plan mostly because it allowed slavery to go into the territories – a factor that expressly violated the very platform on which he had just been elected.

Now, let us put Jackson in the White House in place of Lincoln. He would have been enraged at South Carolina's unpatriotic impudence in attempting to leave the Union, but would he have accepted the Crittenden Compromise? Logic tells us he certainly would have. As a slaveholder and defender of slavery his whole life, he would have been just fine with slavery's extension all the way to the Pacific and to any islands in the Caribbean we might acquire in the future.

So, it is possible to imagine a compromise deal accepted by President Andrew Jackson that would have averted civil war . . . for the time being. Probably into the twentieth century the United States would have been a nation with as many as twenty states that allowed slavery and protected it with state laws. That was the deal President Jackson would have had to make in 1861 and, whether President Trump knew it or not, that was the alternative history he was extolling when he said Jackson was "very angry" about the Civil War (huh? Jackson had been dead for fifteen years!) and would have made a deal to prevent it. Would that "deal" have been a good thing? Would the "author" of *The Art of the Deal* approve of it? I hope not!

DONALD TRUMP THE POPULIST?

IT DEPENDS ON WHAT WE MEAN BY "POPULIST."

As people try to make sense of what is happening in our country these days they use many political terms in ways that are not necessarily accurate historically. One of those terms is "populist." Donald Trump is a "populist," columnists and news commentators proclaim, and at first blush, the name seems to fit. He seems to be speaking for the average Joe and Josephine. He tells us he is creating millions of good-paying jobs and that he will keep foreigners from coming into the country and stealing those jobs. What hard-working American couldn't relate to that? Clearly his message resonated with over sixty million people – mostly in the heartland – so doesn't that, by definition, make him a "populist?" Historically, no . . . not in the purest sense.

Some analysts start with Andrew Jackson. They tell us he was the first "populist" President, and they surmise that is why Trump ordered Jackson's portrait hung in the Oval Office. Jackson did, indeed, speak for the "common man" – a term that came into standard use during his presidency – and he did try to extend the right to vote to more of them by urging states to eliminate property qualifications. He also, rather recklessly, tried to guard the economic wellbeing of average Americans by destroying the National Bank that, he said, was a tool of the wealthy. But, neither Jackson nor any of the people in the Democratic Party at the time used the word "populist." It was radical enough to use terms such as "democrat" and "common man." When Jackson said he was protecting the wellbeing of the "farmers, mechanics and laborers" against the machinations of the "moneyed interests," his opponents shouted that his bank message was a "manifesto of anarchy." Proclaiming himself a "populist" would have made Jackson the originator of an entirely new –- and very radical – political term. "Old Hickory," by the way, probably would have disliked a big money man such as Donald Trump.

The actual term "populist" did not become part of the political lexicon until the late nineteenth century. The political leaders of the Jackson era had passed from the scene, but their offspring, especially in the rural areas of the country, took up the cause once again. This time they did use the word "populist" and, in 1892, organized a new political party that they called the "Populist Party." The party originated in the prairie states and its cause was primarily the plight of the farmers who were being swindled by the railroad managers and banking tycoons in the East. The Populist platform called for government ownership of the railroads, a graduated income tax, and an expansion of the currency through the "free and unlimited coinage of silver." Populist rallies featured colorful speakers such as "Pitchfork Ben" Tillman of South Carolina, and Mary Elizabeth Lease of Kansas who shouted that the country was being run by Wall Street and only for the benefit of Wall Street, and who preached that farmers should "raise less corn and more hell."

When Mary Lease, Pitchfork Ben and other Populists of the 1890s such as "Sockless Jerry" Simpson described the enemies against whom they were fighting, their characterizations would have looked like Donald Trump himself: powerful multi-millionaires who took advantage of the money system – the loans, the interest rates, the lack of government regulation – to enrich themselves and leave the average farmer and working man literally out in the cold. If Mary Lease could return to us today she would see Donald Trump and his tower as the very symbol of all that she and her Populist friends were crusading against.

Thus, it is ironic, if not outright wrong, to call President Donald J. Trump a "populist." Consider the incongruities:

His tax reform bill reduced taxes on wealthy people and the corporations. He celebrates the way he avoided paying income taxes for years because he was "smart."

The Populists wanted to create a federal, graduated income tax – which I am sure they did not want rich people to avoid paying.

His administration is reducing government regulations of business and allowing more "free enterprise."

The Populists wanted the government to *own* the railroads and to coin more money so there would be more inflation and farmers and workers would find it easier to pay back their loans.

There is, however, one area of agreement between the Populists of the 1890s and Donald Trump today: immigration. The Populist Party Platform of 1892 condemned the "present system of immigration which opens our ports to the pauper and criminal classes of the world and crowds out our wage earners." President Trump would be happy to include those exact words into his next speech on immigration. Perhaps it is on this basis that people say he is a Populist.

We each have to make our own call on whether Donald Trump is a true populist. What I hope I have done here is to clarify the background of the word. In my view, President Trump is a populist with a lower case "p." Except for his views on immigration, he is not really in sync with the Populist *Party* or even with his hero, Andrew Jackson. But he does appeal to a broad base of the people who yearn for the old days — the 1950s when the white middle class had it all the way it liked it.

THE PRESIDENT AS CHIEF LEGISLATOR

ANY PRESIDENT WHO WAITS IN THE WHITE HOUSE FOR CONGRESS TO ACT ON HIS PROPOSALS IS USUALLY A "LOSER."

A GOOD PRESIDENT WANTS TO MAKE THINGS HAPPEN AND KNOWS THERE ARE GUIDELINES FROM THE PAST TO SHOW HIM HOW TO DO IT.

So far, President Donald Trump has been a loser once and a winner once in getting his major initiatives through Congress. In the spring of 2017 he and his Republican majority in Congress failed to pass legislation to repeal the Affordable Care Act. In the fall, he managed to push through a tax reform bill that cut the corporate income tax rate from 35% to 21% and gave tax cuts of some description to nearly every individual taxpayer. As these battles over lawmaking unfolded we saw anew the centuries-old struggle between the executive and legislative branches, waged in the context of the checks and balances system. The stories of previous dramas reveal that the President has powerful cards – if he knows how to play them – and he comes out the winner so often that he could be called "the nation's chief legislator." Yet, Congress has power as well, and the President has to be careful not to overplay his hand. Four Presidents – Abraham Lincoln, Woodrow Wilson, Franklin Roosevelt and Lyndon Johnson – had major confrontations with Congress. President Trump can learn from them, but first he would want to know who were the winners and who were the losers. Two were winners and two were losers, and their identities may surprise you. More importantly, the principles involved in their victories or defeats can inform us . . . and our current President.

In 1865, President Abraham Lincoln was pushing the House of Representatives to pass the 13th Amendment to the constitution by a two-thirds vote and send it to the states for ratification. The amendment outlawed slavery across the country, completing the work done by Lincoln's Emancipation Proclamation, a document that had outlawed slavery only in the "areas still in rebellion against the Union." Lincoln worked very hard to convince congressmen — even a few Democrats — who were still on the fence, inviting them to the White House for amiable conversations. Most likely — although it cannot be proved — those conversations involved striking a few political bargains. (Appointing a congressman's friend to be postmaster in his town seems like a reasonable price to pay for a vote to end slavery in the United States.) At the last minute, when it seemed some Democrats might refuse to vote for the amendment because there were rumors that peace commissioners from the Confederacy were in town and the war could possibly be ended without abolishing slavery, Lincoln told a bit of a lie when he sent a note to the House saying, "So far as I know, there are no peace commissioners in the city, or likely to be in it." He knew very well that peace commissioners were, indeed, on the way, but he did not want to give any congressman a reason to vote "no." The 13th Amendment then passed with but two votes to spare and Abraham Lincoln became "The Great Emancipator."

In 1920, the Senate of the United States was about to make its final vote on ratification of the Treaty of Versailles. President Woodrow Wilson had gone to France at the end of "The Great War" to negotiate the treaty, and it included his brainchild, the League of Nations. Wilson was convinced that the League would serve as a world peacekeeping body that would help make the recent horrific conflict the "war to end all wars." But the Senate — particularly on the Republican side — was resistant. There were enough Republican members opposed to the treaty as it stood to block passage by the required two-thirds vote. The only way they would vote for it was if Wilson agreed to amendments proposed by Senator Henry Cabot Lodge of Massachusetts. Those amendments required among other things, congressional approval of any U.S. participation in League peacekeeping operations. In other words, if the League voted to send a military force into Palestine to step between warring factions, the U.S. Congress would have to vote to send a contingent of soldiers. Wilson stubbornly refused to agree to the Lodge Amendments, so he and his fellow League supporters lost the vote. The Treaty of Versailles was not ratified, and the United States never joined the League of Nations. Four years later Wilson died a bitter and broken man. He might have avoided that heartache, and perhaps U.S. presence in the League might have helped the world avoid a second world war, if he had only agreed to compromise.

In 1937, Franklin D. Roosevelt had just won re-election with sixty percent of the vote and every state in the Union except Maine and Vermont in his column. He thought he was invincible and that he could get Congress to pass almost anything he proposed. His Democratic Party controlled both houses of Congress and he was at the peak of his popularity. And so he decided to attack or, as he preferred to put it, *reform* the Supreme Court. Many Presidents have had a problem with the Court, but Roosevelt was particularly incensed at it because he had watched it strike down four of his major pieces of legislation, including the National Recovery Act (N.R.A.) and the Agricultural Adjustment Act (A.A.A.). FDR's view was that the Court was out of step with the times, that the old justices on the Court were from the "horse and buggy era" and didn't understand the needs of a modern economy. He introduced a "reform bill" that would allow the President to appoint a new justice for every justice who was over seventy-years-old, up to a total of six. This was to help the aged justices do their work, he claimed. But even Democrats resisted this "court reform" and called it "court packing." They did not want to practically nullify the checks and balances system by giving the President – even their own party's President – practically dictatorial powers, which he would have if he controlled the Congress *and* the Supreme Court. Roosevelt used every bit of his persuasive charm on congressmen and offered every appointment, bridge and water project it was feasible to give, but when the day for the vote on court reform came his Vice President, crusty old Texan John Nance Garner, told him, "You haven't got the votes, chief." For the first time in his four years as President, FDR lost a major vote in Congress and his aura of invincibility evaporated. After that, he would have to work a little harder for every vote on every piece of legislation he wanted passed.

In the spring of 1964, President Lyndon Johnson knew he would have to employ every one of his considerable legislative skills to secure passage of the Civil Rights Bill that President Kennedy had sent to Congress the previous year. The bill outlawed segregation and racial discrimination in hiring. It was vehemently opposed by nearly every southern representative and senator, and even a few Northerners in Congress. While he lived, John F. Kennedy had had a very hard time convincing congressmen to support the bill but, ironically, his assassination enabled Johnson to win some votes for the cause as a way to offer tribute to the fallen leader.

But still there was resistance, particularly in the House Rules Committee chaired by arch-segregationist Howard Smith. The only way to get the bill out of Smith's committee and onto the House floor for a vote was to get 218 members (a majority of the members) to sign a "discharge petition" that would send the bill to the floor without a vote in the committee. To get congressmen to add their names to the list, Johnson personally lobbied dozens of them. LBJ would give them "the treatment." He would charm, cajole, make promises, invite them to lunch at the White House, and more. If the soft approach didn't work, he would get nasty. He would threaten to cut a representative's pet projects from the federal budget or veto a bill the hapless representative had been working on for over a year. Congressmen told stories of Johnson, who was a large man, getting so close they could feel his hot breath on their faces as he hissed that they better "do what's right." After several weeks of presidential pressure, the discharge petition had the necessary 218 signatures and the Civil Rights Bill went onto the floor for a vote to pass that amounted to a victory lap. L.B.J. signed the Civil Rights Act, with Dr. Martin Luther King, Jr. looking on and receiving one of the signing pens, on July 2, 1964. Three hundred forty-five years of racial segregation were at last – at least officially – over.

What can a President take away from these four stories? Certainly, it is clear that no President who expects to accomplish anything can expect to propose bills and then wait placidly to see if Congress passes them. The great Presidents have excelled at knowing when to exert pressure and how to do it. Most have been inclined to use rewards for co-operative congressmen rather than arm-twisting, but no President aspiring to Mount Rushmore level fame can expect to avoid having to engage in some unpleasantness in the Oval Office. And then there is the ability to know when you have used all your weapons and rewards and the time has come to compromise. That is the lesson Woodrow Wilson, self-righteous – and as ill — as he was, never learned and that is why I would never put him in the top tier of our nation's leaders. He should have compromised with Henry Cabot Lodge and that is all there is to it!

Our new President tells us in his book that he knows how to make a deal. If his television show was any guide, he has shown that he knows how to dominate and threaten. But it may take some hard knocks – such as the one he experienced when his health care bill went down – to teach him one more important lesson. President Eisenhower's favorite maxim for life and leadership was: "Never make a mistake in a hurry." As much as a leader, especially a "rookie" leader, may want to show he can get the job done, he should proceed cautiously and slowly, waiting until he actually has all the information he may need in hand before he makes his move. President Trump's healthcare bill was ill-advised and thrown before Congress without enough preparation. No amount of threatening or cajoling is going to overcome a bumpy start such as that.

FDR's experience can teach us one further point. No matter how popular a President is, he cannot expect Congress to be willing to do something that will tend to aggrandize the President or give him too much power . . . even if his party controls both houses of Congress. As I write, the President is talking about a giant military parade that he wants to take place down Pennsylvania Avenue in November, 2018. I think he pictures tons of military hardware rolling along and thousands of soldiers marching past him and saluting him as he stands, nose in the air Mussolini style, on the reviewing platform. This kind of extravagance, at a time when a four trillion dollar deficit budget is before Congress for approval, will not go down well even with Republicans. Even to them it will seem that the President is only trying to show the world how powerful he is.

Donald Trump holds a job that is two hundred thirty years old and has a rich history. Forty-four men before him have sat in his chair and have exercised the powers he holds and have been stymied by the same things he is stymied by. Every evening, instead of watching television or composing tweets, he should read as much as he can about those men and try to get a grip on the principles of leadership that apply peculiarly to the office of President of the United States. I have given a sample of the major concepts in the President's legislative leadership. The experiences of previous Presidents also teach principles of military leadership and foreign policy. The Presidency has a rich history and the current President should spend as much time as possible reading up on it instead of watching re-runs of "The Apprentice."

JFK, TRUMP AND NUCLEAR BRINKMANSHIP

WHEN INCINERATION COULD BE THE RESULT, WE ALL HAVE TO BE NERVOUS.

The current world situation, particularly concerning North Korea, has me musing erratically. The global picture is so muddled I hardly know what to think. Some of my thoughts go to the early 1960s when nuclear weapons were constantly on our minds. At other times, I think of the character of the major world leaders who have control of nuclear missiles and I quake. My thinking is very muddled; I'm like that when I'm nervous. I believe I will just start writing and let my thoughts take me where they will. Please bear with me; I'm not at all sure where this will end up.

In October of 1962, President John F. Kennedy addressed the nation regarding the recently discovered Soviet missiles in Cuba. I recall sitting in the cafeteria of my college dorm as the speech was broadcast over the public address system. The large room filled with eighteen-year-olds was tense and silent, especially when Kennedy spoke this line: "It shall be the policy of this nation to regard any nuclear missile launched from Cuba against any nation in the Western Hemisphere as an attack by the Soviet Union on the United States requiring a full retaliatory response upon the Soviet Union." Of course we all left the room that night frightened beyond description, certain that a nuclear war was only days, or even hours, away.

We would have been even more frightened if we knew that one of Kennedy's top military advisors was Air Force General Curtis LeMay, the man who had directed the firebombing of Tokyo during World War II and who, later, during the Vietnam War, said of the North Vietnamese, ". . . They've got to draw in their horns and stop their aggression or we're going to bomb them back into the stone age." In October of 1962, LeMay was urging Kennedy to allow his air force to bomb the missile sites in Cuba. Fortunately, Kennedy rejected his advice, chose a blockade and diplomacy instead, and the crisis ended peacefully.

Of course, the game that was being played at that time was nuclear brinkmanship or, to put it less formally, "nuclear chicken." The Soviet Union knew that we had nuclear weapons that could annihilate their cities and kill millions of their people. President Kennedy had to make them believe that unless they backed down from their efforts to gain a strategic advantage in Cuba, we were prepared to use those bombs and destroy their country. Perhaps LeMay's presence in the National Security Council served that purpose. How effective would "nukes" be as a deterrent if the enemy didn't believe you would actually use them?

In recent years the North Korean regime has worked hard to develop a nuclear capability that will, if achieved, upset the strategic balance in East Asia and across the Pacific. Every President since Harry Truman has opposed North Korea's ambitions and has tried to get the Kims (Kim Il Sung, Kim Jong Il, and now Kim

Jong Un) to give up their nuclear research and development. The current Kim has been particularly intransigent and reckless. The need to stop the North Koreans has become increasingly urgent.

Enter President Donald Trump. At the United Nations General Assembly last year he startled the world – and even his own countrymen – when he said in his most bombastic style, "No nation on earth has an interest in seeing this band of criminals (North Korea's leaders) arm itself with nuclear weapons and missiles. The United States has great strength and patience, but if it is forced to defend itself or its allies, we will have no choice but to destroy North Korea. 'Rocket man' is on a suicide mission for himself and for his regime!"

The news media went ballistic (if you'll pardon the expression) over the President's speech. On MSNBC, Chris Matthews said that President Trump doesn't seem to realize that nuclear weapons are there only as a deterrent; they are not to be used. The problem with that logic is that unless the enemy thinks you *will* use them, they are *not* a deterrent. As I said before regarding Kennedy, what does an enemy have to be afraid of if he knows you would never dream of sending a nuke his way?

So, should we be as frightened as we were in October, 1962? There is no Curtis LeMay in the White House, but perhaps President Trump himself serves in that capacity. Richard Nixon's "mad man syndrome" might be in play: If an enemy thinks you are crazy enough to use the ultimate weapons, he will back down. The North Koreans must know that if they start something their country will be reduced to ashes. I think Kim Jong Un, as crazy as he is, will not launch a nuclear attack against us or our allies and face his own certain incineration.

I guess where I'm ending up is this: nuclear brinkmanship ended peacefully in the 1960s (Kennedy and Khrushchev), the 1970s (Nixon and Brezhnev) and the 1980s (Reagan and

Gorbachev). It could end well this time (Trump and Kim Jong Un) if the two of them, each believing that the other is fully capable of drastic action, stop engaging in nuclear road rage and stumble toward the right solution. Everyone down on your knees and pray!

Note: Shortly after I wrote this, President Trump spoke at the annual Gridiron Dinner. His monologue had some humorous – and, amazingly self-deprecating – moments. Regarding Kim Jong Un, Trump said, "I won't rule out direct talks with Kim Jong-Un. I just won't. As far as the risk of dealing with a madman is concerned, that's his problem, not mine. It's his problem." Donald Trump can do ironic humor. Who knew?

WHEN THE UNITED STATES DID NOT LEAD

AFTER WORLD WAR I THE U.S. CHOSE NOT TO BE A LEADING WORLD POWER. HOW DID THAT WORK FOR US?

It is very tempting for Americans to think we would be better off if we focused our attention on ourselves, tended to our own needs, made our own country prosperous, and told the rest of the world to boil in its own oil. Why should any American have to die in some disgusting hellhole such as Afghanistan or Iraq where the people do not want us and "victory" – whatever that looks like – is almost impossible to achieve? We can do quite fine on our own, so why don't we just cut our loses everywhere and spend all the money we would save on nice stuff for ourselves such as roads, bridges, free college tuitions, great healthcare, etc., etc.?

It is an important question, especially for a country that truly does possess almost all the resources it needs to run a success-ful economy and has an ocean on each side to insulate it from whatever might be happening elsewhere. President Trump has a tendency to think along those lines. But, before he does anything more than withdraw us from the Paris Climate Agreement and thus abrogate leadership in that important area, and before he starts pulling troops back and erecting tariff walls and other kinds of walls "to make America great again," he should consider what has happened in the not-so-distant past when we tried to isolate ourselves.

In 1920, our Senate voted down the Treaty of Versailles and the United States failed to join the League of Nations. For the next twenty years American Presidents, Republican and Democrat, conducted foreign affairs as a sideline business and they forayed into it only on special occasions. "Isolationist" would be a little too simplistic a description of American foreign policy during those two decades, but we were, at least, "standoffish." The policies of the 1920s and 30s — and the catastrophic events that evolved partly because of them – should serve as a cautionary tale for those who might like to see us follow a similar path today.

In the 1920s, we were actually a little more involved in world affairs than is commonly believed. In late 1921 President Harding and his Secretary of State, Charles Evans Hughes, hosted the Washington Naval Conference. Attended by nine nations, this was the first general disarmament conference ever held, and it produced results that seemed worthwhile at the time and that kept the peace for the next decade. The signatories pledged to maintain the "open door" in China – that is, to respect China's territorial integrity – and established a ratio of tonnage of warships to which each power would limit itself. Japan agreed to build only sixty percent of the naval power that the U.S. could build, which sounds like "advantage, U.S.," but since we have to maintain a two-ocean navy, it gave Japan a 3 to 2.5 preponderance in the Pacific. Yet, there was not an arms race in the twenties and, if the United States had continued to be at least marginally involved in the enforcement of this agreement – and, the terms of the Treaty of Versailles to which, of course, we were not a signatory – then events might have gone a different way.

Instead, we opted out and stood on the sidelines. We proposed a couple of plans under which Germany might be able to pay the exorbitant reparations bill she had been handed at Versailles, but those plans, like almost everything else the winners of the "Great War" came up with, failed miserably. We also tried to get the nations of the world to sign a pact whereby they all renounced war as an instrument of policy. Initiated by U.S. Secretary of State Frank Billings Kellogg, and the French foreign minister Aristide Briand, this "Kellogg-Briand Pact" was signed by every nation in Europe and later scorned by every nation that declared war in 1939-1940.

In the United States, the 1930s was much more an isolationist decade than the twenties had been. The "Great Depression" was just getting started in 1930, and Congress responded by passing the Hawley-Smoot tariff. This act set the highest import tax rates of any tariff bill since the "Tariff of Abominations" of 1828. In an attempt to entice American consumers to buy only American-made products and get people back to work in the factories that made them, thousands of imported goods would be taxed at 60%. The predictable result was that other countries raised their rates, world trade atrophied, and even more people in the United States and elsewhere in the world lost their jobs. The "Hawley-Smoot Tariff" is one of the famous laugh lines in the movie *Ferris Bueller's Day Off*, but it really was a very important part of the story of the Great Depression.

In 1933, when the depression had become worldwide, sixty-six nations met in London to try to find ways to foster greater economic cooperation and prevent the world from sinking even deeper into the economic mire. King George V of the U.K. set the tone for the conference when he proclaimed, "There is a new recognition of the interdependence of nations and the value of collaboration between them. Now is the opportunity to harness this new consciousness of common interests to the service of mankind." United States Secretary of State Cordell Hull pushed for trade liberalization and a ten percent across the board tariff reduction. It all seemed to be going so well. And then, the conference was torpedoed from a very unexpected direction.

On July 3rd, a message arrived from President Franklin Roosevelt of the United States. This "bombshell," as one member of the conference called it, stated flatly that the United States would not join in rate stabilization, that it would maintain the rates set by Hawley-Smoot, and that it would remain off the gold standard. Why the President, long an advocate of free trade or, at least, low tariff rates, sent such a message has long been debated. Perhaps he was spooked by the thought of Americans buying coal from Britain and putting U.S. coal miners out of work. Whatever his reasons, his message sent the meeting spinning down in a death spiral and the London Conference broke up without accomplishing its goals. The worldwide economic depression continued.

In Germany, Hitler's government put people to work building a highway system and the gigantic facility for the Olympic Games that the Reich would be hosting in 1936. The German armaments industry also stepped up production. Hitler was more than pleased that his future enemies had failed to work together to solve their common problems.

In 1935, as it was becoming evident that Germany was rearming and that Europe might be sliding toward another war, Congress responded by passing the first of what would become a series of "neutrality acts" designed to guarantee that the United

States would stay out of a new war – to guarantee we would not make the same mistakes we had made in the "Great War," a war that sucked us into a fight that caused the deaths of over fifty thousand young American men and thousands more wounded; a war that had netted us absolutely no worthwhile gains. By 1937, it was illegal for any American company to sell arms to any country that was at war, for any American to travel on any ships of countries that were at war (There would be no future *Lusitanias*) and no loans could be made to any country that was at war. In effect, if a new war started in Europe or Asia, the United States would do what a turtle does when a storm comes. We would draw into our shell and wait for the storm to pass.

In 1936, the peace of the world began to unravel. Hitler sent German troops into the Rhineland section of Germany, an act strictly forbidden by the Treaty of Versailles. In 1937, Japan invaded China and Japanese soldiers massacred thousands of people in Nanking. In 1938, Hitler demanded the Sudetenland section of Czechoslovakia, and the premiers of Britain and France allowed him to take it. The following spring he took the remainder of Czechoslovakia and the world knew war was inevitable. In September, 1939, Hitler sent his Wehrmacht into Poland, Britain and France declared war on Germany, and a new war was underway.

Even at this point the American people did not want to get involved. After Hitler's armies blitzed through Western Europe and even occupied Paris, President Roosevelt knew we would at some point have to fight to prevent a Nazi domination of the western world, but it took a year of German bombing of London and the prospect of an imminent British collapse before even a slight majority of Americans believed we should join the fight. Finally Japan, who had been advancing through China and Indochina for four years, slapped us to our senses with its devastating attack on our naval base at Pearl Harbor.

It is probably a waste of time to conjecture what might have been different if the United States had played a much more active part in all the events leading to the outbreak of the war. Yet, can there be any doubt that vigorous enforcement of the terms of the international treaties that Hitler broke with impunity would have prevented the Second World War, at least in Europe? We know from documents captured after the war that Hitler and his generals were planning to pull their troops out of the Rhineland in 1936 if the British and French showed the least sign of resistance. A retreat such as that would certainly have slowed, if not stymied, the dictator's march to war. Furthermore, can there be any doubt that the United States, with its enormous resources, industry and manpower, could have rallied the European democracies in the 1930s to confront Hitler before he built his almost invincible war machine?

Simply put, if the people of the United States, and their Presidents, had shown true leadership and rallied the democracies to stand up against the international bullies of that era, the world war of 1939 to 1945, which caused the deaths of forty million people, the destruction of trillions of dollars' worth of property, and untold misery across the globe, could have been averted. We can look back now and rue the fact that our parents and grandparents were not more proactive in keeping the peace in the 20s and 30s. We should make sure *our* grandchildren, in fifty years, are not similarly rueful that *we* failed to lead and allowed the planet to become polluted, and the "bad guys" in the world to prevail. With great power comes great responsibility.

SOURCES AND SUGGESTIONS FOR FURTHER READING

Most of the facts in this book were drawn from my general knowledge of American History, much of which I acquired from classes and seminars at the University of Michigan. I was specifically inspired by lectures on Thomas Jefferson by Professor Bradford Perkins which compelled me to think more critically about that "great man," and by conversations with Professor William Freehling in his graduate seminar on the Civil War which gave me the concept of the "Bowl of Cherries Theory of History."

Listed below are books that I consulted while writing these essays. The reader may find this list helpful if he or she wishes to pursue a topic further.

How the Scots Invented the Modern World, The True Story of How Western Europe's Poorest Nation Created Our World and Everything in It, by Arthur Herman
    This is a very convincing (especially if you are Scottish) account of Scottish contributions in the realm of thought and technology to the development of the American republic.

The Autobiography of Booker T. Washington, by Booker T. Washington

When freedom came to Booker T. at age six, he saw immediately that there would be many problems accompanying that "jubilee." Washington's approach to those problems -- "We need to prove ourselves worthy" -- and his willingness to accept the limitations placed on his race by the white leaders were, and still are, controversial. In spite of every negative thing that has been said about him, I still like and admire the man as I make clear in "Billy G., Booker T., and Me"

All on Fire; William Lloyd Garrison and the Abolition of Slavery, by Henry Mayer

This is the most thorough biography of William Lloyd Garrison ever written and it does an excellent job of making the case that this radical reformer had more of an influence on the events that led to the Civil War and emancipation than previously thought. Mayer's vivid description of the mob attacking Garrison on the streets of Boston reveals the galvanizing effect Garrison's work had on the people of the North. My descriptions of the 1835 incident in the essay "Mr. Garrison and the Respectable Mob" are drawn from this book and from *The Life of William Lloyd Garrison As Told by His Sons.*

John Adams, by David McCullough

David McCullough tells Adams's story sympathetically and it convinced me to write "John Adams Deserves Better."

1776, by David McCullough

In this fascinating book, McCullough tells the story of how Jefferson made the concepts of John Locke accessible to the people in the Declaration of Independence and how fog saved Washington's army.

Thomas Jefferson; The Art of Power by Jon Meacham

Meacham tends to become a devotee of the people he writes about and here he even writes sympathetically about Jefferson's ownership of slaves and his relationship with Sally Hemmings.

Henry Clay, The Essential American, by David and Jeanne Heidler

The Heidlers do a solid job describing the many critical compromises Henry Clay arranged in 1820, 1832 and 1850 to avoid civil war.

Andrew Jackson, His Life and Times, by H.W. Brands

Brand's book was the basis for my comparison of Donald Trump and Jackson and the essay on whether Jackson would have prevented the Civil War.

Lincoln, by David Donald

This thorough and readable biography is a great place to start for those who want to know more about the sixteenth president. Lincoln's comments on how to make a great speech are based on what Donald tells us about the Gettysburg Address and about Lincoln's relationship with his wife, Mary Todd.

The Life and Times of Hannibal Hamlin, by Charles Eugene Hamlin

Written by his son, this biography extols Hamlin's contributions to the Lincoln administration perhaps more than they deserve, but it does give the basic facts about Hamlin's life and provides enough substance for me to describe how things may have been different had Hamlin continued to be Lincoln's vice president. It seems to me that a thorough and objective biography of Hannibal Hamlin might be an interesting project for someone.

Grant, by Ron Chernow

Chernow, once again, has written a thorough and fair biography, this time about a man who has been subjected to considerable criticism, particularly about his presidency. Whether or not anyone ever writes a musical about Grant, I had fun taking the outlines of his story as told by Chernow and suggesting how that musical might be organized.

The American Miracle; Divine Providence in the Rise of the Republic,
by Michael Medved

Medved sees the hand of God in the miraculous events that saved the United States or enabled it to grow more powerful. Whether or not you see events that way, Medved's stories about Nicolas Trist's guava marmalade, General McClellan's acquisition of Lee's battle plans, the fog that saved Washington's army, and the ice that made the Louisiana Purchase possible help to make *my* case that small and seemingly insignificant events – such as eating a bowl of cherries – can change the course of history.

Reminiscences, by Douglas MacArthur

MacArthur's memoir is self-serving and pompous, to be sure, but it is especially useful in understanding the general's point of view in his feud with President Truman, and it is a fascinating account of his leadership in reconstructing Japan after the war.

American Caesar, Douglas MacArthur, 1880-1964, by William Manchester

Manchester has written the definitive biography of MacArthur and it is a good fact check on the general's account of his life. I used Manchester's book as a source for my essay on George Kenney, MacArthur's indispensable man.

Eisenhower, Soldier and Statesman, by Stephen Ambrose
Eisenhower's cautious approach to leadership gets a thorough analysis in Ambrose's book. "Never make a mistake in a hurry" should be the mantra of every great leader.

The Woman Behind the New Deal, The Life of Frances Perkins, FDR's Secretary of Labor and His Moral Conscience, by Kirstin Downey
This excellent biography about this pioneering woman formed the basis of my essay that she was truly a little known yet very consequential person in American History.

Wilson, by A. Scott Berg
Berg's sympathetic biography recounts Wilson's many travails while he was in office and it served as the basis for my essay, "Forgive me, Wilson!"

A Diplomatic History of the American People, by Thomas Bailey
This monumental work runs the full gamut of American diplomatic history but, unfortunately, ends with the Vietnam War. Nevertheless, it confirms that Nicolas Trist did, indeed, head off an "all of Mexico" movement in Congress in 1848 when he stayed in Mexico City to negotiate in spite of President Polk's order to return to Washington. It also served as a good source for the story of Woodrow Wilson's failure to get ratification of the Treaty of Versailles.

ABOUT THE AUTHOR

Robert MacDougall taught American history at the high school and college level for almost fifty years. He is the author of three previous books: *The Agitator and the Politician*, the story of the very different roads to the abolition of slavery followed by the radical abolitionist, William Lloyd Garrison and the conservative politician, Abraham Lincoln, *Leaders in Dangerous Times*, a comparison of the leadership styles of Douglas MacArthur and Dwight D. Eisenhower, men who played critical roles in two world wars and the Cold War, and most recently, *American History; It's More Than the Crap You Learned in High School*, which introduces readers to his creative approach to American History and explains how knowledge of the subject has practical value for all of us.

WA